Outdoor Site and Facility Management

Tools for Creating Memorable Places

Outdoor Site and Facility Management

Tools for Creating Memorable Places

Wynne Whyman

HUMAN KINETICS

Library of Congress Cataloging-in-Publication Data

Whyman, Wynne, 1961-
    Outdoor site and facility management : tools for creating memorable
places / Wynne Whyman.
        p. cm.
    Includes bibliographical references and index.
    ISBN-13: 978-0-7360-6845-1 (softcover)
    ISBN-10: 0-7360-6845-7 (softcover)
    1. Recreation centers--Management.   I. Title.
    GV182.W59 2008
    790.06'9--dc22

                                    2007027579

ISBN-10: 0-7360-6845-7
ISBN-13: 978-0-7360-6845-1

The Web addresses cited in this text were current as of July 5, 2007, unless otherwise noted.

Acquisitions Editor: Gayle Kassing, PhD; **Developmental Editor:** Ragen E. Sanner; **Assistant Editor:** Anne Rumery; **Copyeditor:** Patsy Fortney; **Proofreader:** Julie Marx Goodreau; **Indexer:** Betty Frizzell; **Permission Manager:** Dalene Reeder; **Graphic Designer:** Nancy Rasmus; **Graphic Artist:** Yvonne Griffith; **Cover Designer:** Bob Reuther; **Photographer (cover):** Peter Aron/Esto/IPN; **Photographer (interior):** © Human Kinetics, unless otherwise noted; **Photo Asset Manager:** Laura Fitch; **Art Manager:** Kelly Hendren; **Associate Art Manager:** Alan L. Wilborn; **Illustrator:** Accurate Art; **Printer:** Sheridan Books

Printed in the United States of America   10   9   8   7   6   5   4   3   2   1

Human Kinetics
Web site: www.HumanKinetics.com

United States: Human Kinetics
P.O. Box 5076
Champaign, IL 61825-5076
800-747-4457
e-mail: humank@hkusa.com

Canada: Human Kinetics
475 Devonshire Road Unit 100
Windsor, ON N8Y 2L5
800-465-7301 (in Canada only)
e-mail: info@hkcanada.com

Europe: Human Kinetics
107 Bradford Road
Stanningley
Leeds LS28 6AT, United Kingdom
+44 (0) 113 255 5665
e-mail: hk@hkeurope.com

Australia: Human Kinetics
57A Price Avenue
Lower Mitcham, South Australia 5062
08 8372 0999
e-mail: info@hkaustralia.com

New Zealand: Human Kinetics
Division of Sports Distributors NZ Ltd.
P.O. Box 300 226 Albany
North Shore City
Auckland
0064 9 448 1207
e-mail: info@humankinetics.co.nz

CONTENTS

Contents

PREFACE

"Wish you were here. . . ."

Scrawled on postcards since time immemorial, this phrase shows just how closely people associate memorable experiences with a place.

The photo on the postcard—a beautiful building, a majestic overlook, perhaps wildlife—only confirms the importance of surroundings. Whether setting the stage for a seminar, a camp, spiritual growth, an educational program, or a life-changing event, the place itself is an essential ingredient for making an experience memorable.

People readily acknowledge the life-changing role that programs play in creating memorable experiences. But not everyone recognizes the importance of sites and facilities. Consider the following:

1. Your site and facilities make up the "four walls" that bring together your program and your mission for the express purpose of transforming lives. Your structures do more than provide shelter from the storm. They are places for people to gather to support and enrich each other's lives. They are places to broaden horizons and create new career opportunities. Sleeping areas are more than places for campers to restlessly await "lights-out." These are living spaces and nurturing environments where participants develop interpersonal skills, broaden their knowledge, personally learn and grow, and cultivate lasting friendships.

2. Your site and facilities are your largest financial investment—your "hard assets." Those picturesque buildings and grounds have a bearing on the viability of your business and your financial success. They must be well maintained and well run to yield the expected return on your investment and, more important, to deliver value to the participants you serve.

3. Your site and facilities are "home" for your organization. Like a home, your property should provide the safe environment and positive atmosphere so necessary to a successful participant experience.

Experienced staff and volunteers know that their "property" is crucial to the success of their program. They see their site and facilities as key to delivering quality programs and accomplishing their mission.

Comprehensive, Strategic Approach

The intent of this book is to help you manage your site and facilities successfully. This requires more than a simple commitment to "keep the place up." It demands an approach to property care that is both comprehensive and strategic.

Site and facility management is not the sole responsibility of one department or one individual. One new board member alone can ask only so many questions; a piece of software is only as good as the time and personnel who work on it; a new property manager can do only so much work; running a "deferred maintenance" campaign is only temporary; and the list goes on. Managing sites and facilities is complex—it requires an integrated system composed of knowledgeable people, cross-functional processes, and organizational sponsorship.

The payoff of such an approach is substantial:

People

- An inviting, positive place where participants feel safe and secure and want to participate in what you have to offer. A pleasant atmosphere plays a key role in driving your outcomes.
- The ability to proactively manage health and safety concerns for participants, staff, and volunteers.
- The positive morale of staff and participants. With a quick visual assessment, people know that monies are well spent and that attention is given to their well-being.

Financial

- The enhanced marketability of your business by displaying to prospective customers, investors, and others a clean and efficiently run operation. This keeps you competitive in today's market.
- An efficient, cost-effective operation.
- The ability to forecast long-term needs to plan for staffing and financial resources.
- Increased use of your facilities as a result of planning and scheduling maintenance around usage—instead of having to temporarily close the facilities to complete unexpected repairs.
- Improved life expectancy for buildings and equipment resulting in sustained or increased equity in your assets.

Environmental

- An increased awareness among participants of their place within the natural systems.
- Improved ecological stewardship.
- The assurance that future participants will experience either the same natural setting that exists today or an improved setting.

Overall

- Regulatory compliance and effective management of property-related risks, especially important in today's litigious society.
- Relief from operating in crisis mode, in which solutions are hastily improvised when things go wrong. A good management system places you in "proactive mode" and gives you peace of mind.
- Cooperation rather than competition for resources among the site, facilities, and program.
- The ability to act systematically rather than haphazardly.
- The sustained, long-term viability of your operation to continue serving your mission for years to come.

Through the lens and practice of sustainability principles, your organization's consistent, intentional commitment to site and facilities is the key to your long-term future.

Purpose and Audience

Fortunately for professionals, there is an abundance of books that address the development of excellent programs. In addition, there is a plethora of commercial property management books (for military bases, universities, manufacturing plants, hotels, apartments, and others). Less plentiful, however, are resources that offer concise, up-to-date information and guidance about property management for outdoor programs and educational, religious, and nonprofit organizations. To meet the long-standing need for practical, easy-to-understand information, this book integrates the critical components of superior property management with the associated program and educational needs of the organization. If you have a site or facility role within your organization as a volunteer, administrator, on-site manager, finance committee member, property manager, board member, or student, this book is for you.

The material presented addresses the needs of a wide range of sites and facilities:

Outdoor Properties

- Resident and day camps
- Conference and retreat centers
- Outdoor learning sites and environmental education centers
- Government parks and recreation centers (e.g., state, city, national parks and monuments, national forest campgrounds)
- Educational and cultural sites (e.g., farms, living history)
- Commercial campgrounds (e.g., KOA, Good Sam)
- Dude and guest ranches

Educational and Nonprofit Properties

- Community centers, senior citizen centers
- Hostels
- Nonprofit organizations (offices and program sites)
- Religious organizations (synagogues, churches, mosques, educational facilities)
- Schools (including private, religious)

The people who take part in the programs at these organizations may be campers, guests, students, clients, visitors, learners, or members. As a result, the term *participants* is used to describe the targeted audience of the organization's mission.

Scope

This book offers a broad perspective on property management, as shown in the lighter area in figure 1. The other two areas are also essential for your property: (1) technical skills (how to replace a furnace or repair an eroded trail) and (2) site development, master planning process, and expansions (analyzing current capacity for projected growth, organizing a successful capital campaign, and so on). However, because many books, resources, consultants, classes, and workshops are available on these two topics, they are not addressed in this book.

This book covers site and facility management for all ages of properties, the newly built and those with a long history of delivering programs. The book also covers a broad

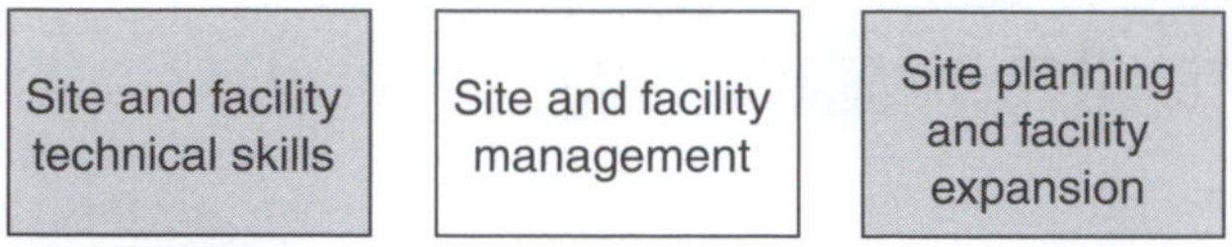

Site and facility technical skills	Site and facility management	Site planning and facility expansion

FIGURE 1 Site and Facility Knowledge Areas.

spectrum of property sizes from an urban setting with only one building to a property in a rural setting with multiple buildings on a significant acreage. Throughout the book, and included on the CD-ROM, are techniques for making site and facilities accessible to disabled participants.

Note that the material presented in this book does not substitute for the professional expertise of service providers in specialized areas such as property rights, contracting, forest management, historic preservation, hydrology, plumbing, and electrical work. Rather, it provides a good general grounding in the areas encompassed by site and facility management and offers useful recommendations for and guidance on working with these outside professionals.

The term *site* encompasses the natural resources and the land, which includes woodlands, lawns, watersheds, grounds, roads, and so on. The term *facilities* refers to buildings, structures, equipment, tents, and other physical program components used for group instruction, meeting, recreation, living, or other functional purposes. The term *property* is often used when discussing the site and facilities collectively. The person who is responsible for the overall site and facilities is called the property director. The property director role may be part of another position, such as an operations director, an administrator, or another management role. The administrator is the person responsible for managing the overall organization.

The first chapter explains that place is an integration of program and property. Also in the first chapter is the framework of the book, including a site and facility management model to give you an easy way to sort the work and put the components together. Each of the remaining chapters covers different components of the model, with relevant threads woven among the chapters.

The book provides creative strategies for managing day-to-day operations, including planning, forecasting, developing an effective organizational model, hiring staff, budgeting and financial oversight, time management, record keeping, and risk management. It covers in detail the key areas of site and facility management—from the preservation and protection of the land and watershed, to the maintenance of building infrastructure, to the role of organizational governance in developing a property management plan.

Long-Term Approach

As you seek to make the kind of memorable place where life-changing experiences can happen, you will need to establish processes and procedures enabling you to be a good steward of your property's physical assets. This book provides essential information for managing your site and facilities efficiently and cost effectively while protecting your financial investment. However, managing your property is more than simply a business function; it is essential in improving people's lives as articulated in your mission.

It is my hope that this book gives those professionals charged with the important task of managing their properties the resources they need to run and maintain their memorable places for generations to come.

ACKNOWLEDGMENTS

I want to thank the many people who generously encouraged me, supported the work, and unselfishly gave their knowledge and time, especially Joe Calovini, Cathy McGuire, Lorraine Streckfus, Kathy Trotter, Charles Wallace, and my family: Paul, Zoë, and my parents.

I am deeply grateful to Melody Snider for her unfaltering support of the book and her tireless energies.

My thanks are also due to Jim and Jo Newell, from whom I have learned so much. I want to thank the children, youth, volunteers, parents, and staff who have touched my life, as well.

Thank you to those who helped with various pieces of the book: Suzi Arnold, Sharon Betsworth, Dennis Block, Pat Boykin, Jim Cox, Nick Crews, Will Evans, Wendy Ford, Jane Johnson, Cherry Kenney, Susan Lander, John (Jack) Little, Tom Neppl, friends, colleagues, and the countless people who shared their stories.

Thanks to the local libraries whose doors are open to community members: Nazarene Bible College, Pikes Peak Library District, and Regis University. I would also like to recognize the American Camp Association for its resources.

To Human Kinetics I am grateful for bringing the book to life and letting it blossom.

Finally, I'd like to acknowledge and thank the many people working quietly in the background who magically made this book a reality with their dedication, expertise, and professionalism.

HOW TO USE THIS BOOK AND CD-ROM

This book is unique in the field. Nowhere else can you find a comprehensive, one-stop source of information, best practices, guidance, and practical tools you can begin using today.

The book's content touches all parts of the organization, from the part-time maintenance worker to the board of directors. When you put the knowledge and processes into practice systematically, it can bring lasting change at your organization. Stellar site and facilities management is essential in accomplishing your mission.

Get started now, everything's ready for you!

Who Might Use This Book?

Individuals, teams, and organizations might use this book differently:

- New site and facilities employees
  - To learn the various aspects of site and facility management
- Seasoned site and facilities employees
  - To look for different ways of doing work, as part of a continuous improvement process
  - To locate a community resource to help with a project
- Property directors
  - To conduct a new employee's orientation
  - To develop a site and facilities tactical plan, anchored to the rest of the organization's work
- Administrators
  - To write site and facilities job descriptions
  - To develop his or her knowledge of site and facility management
  - To measure site and facility progress
- Boards of directors
  - To orient new board members
  - To train members in their specific board responsibilities of site and facilities
  - To revise the administrator's job description to include site and facility responsibilities
  - To make educated, strategic decisions about the property

- Specialty areas (finance, fund development, marketing, public relations, archives, risk management)
  - To know how their area of expertise is needed in site and facilities management
  - To be able to describe in reports, grants, literature, and promotional materials how site and facilities play an important role in fulfilling the organization's mission
- Organization or cross-functional teams
  - To build a framework for the site and facilities operation as part of the organization
  - To affirm what you are already doing well
- Workshops, training, or courses
  - To use as the core curriculum

Different people have different needs, so there's no "one size fits all" for using the book. If you are new to the field, start at the beginning of the book and work your way through. Or, if you have only a short amount of time, zero in on the topic that is of most interest or an area that you are currently addressing. You may use the information at different times during your fiscal year: budgeting, training new staff members, tactical planning, hiring staff, and so on. The book and the resources are designed to be flexible.

Book Components

The book and CD-ROM are full of a variety of resources. Below are the many components you'll find in the book.

- Site and Facilities Model—Get organized! Site and facility management is less overwhelming when you can organize information into smaller topics. Furthermore, the model can help you build a mental framework of how everything fits together.
- Tools—Want practical exercises, checklists, plans, templates, and ideas? Each chapter has practical tools to immediately apply to your organization. You will be able to tell that a tool is available on the CD-ROM by the appearance of this icon 💿 in the book next to a scaled-down version of the tool. The tools cover a wide spectrum of organizations; you will need to decide which tools make sense for your organization.
- Best practices—Wondering how you're doing? At the end of each chapter you'll find a list of best practices that serve as indicators of successful management. Self-assess your organization for a specific topic or all topics by using tool 1.1 in chapter 1.
- Sample job descriptions—Ready to modify a job description? There are lots of ideas in the book for the administrator's job description, and in the appendix are five job descriptions to assist you. The job descriptions are also on the CD-ROM for your convenience.
- Glossary—Need to know what a term means? At the end of the book, there is a glossary that defines common site- and facility-related terms. Also, the first time a word is discussed in the text, it is **bolded.**
- References—A listing of all of the sources used within the book.

CD-ROM Components

Hundreds of electronic resources, available at your fingertips!

- Sample job descriptions—Need a job description? Simply copy the one on the CD-ROM, make revisions, run it by your legal counsel, and you're set to go.

- Resources—Need more information about a topic, but don't want to fall into the black hole of a Web search? Look at the topics according to chapter and subject titles within the list. Or use your regular search function to search by key word(s) within the program. These detailed resource listings provide ideas for further reading and point you to professional assistance available in specialized areas of property management. Many of the resources have Web sites, so simply copy and paste the URL into your Web browser.

- Tools—Ready to use a tool at your facility? Copy the tool from the CD-ROM, modify it, and you're ready to go. These forms and templates are designed to give you a "hands-on" workbook for virtually all aspects of your site and facilities. In some cases, a filled-in version accompanies the blank tool so that you can see an example of how you can utilize the tool.

You can easily customize all the tools in this book for your organization. First follow the directions at the back of the book to move the blank templates from the CD-ROM to your computer. Then customize the tools by adding your organization's name at the top of the tools, rearranging information, deleting what does not apply, and adding information specific to your operation.

After you have customized the tools, below are some suggestions on how to record information and implement these tools. You may use a combination of all three techniques or just one. You will need to decide what's best for your organization, depending on your organization's needs, time, and staff skills.

- Print the tools and handwrite your organization's information in the tools. You might want to store the sheets in a manila file system or in a 3-ring notebook.

- Use the electronic version in Microsoft® Word and type your organization's information directly into the tool. Print the report only when you need to (for meetings, backup copies, or working with the information).

- Copy the tool into Microsoft® Excel or another spreadsheet application. This technique can be helpful for the following tasks:
  - Manipulating of numeric data, such as financial information.
  - Making multiple worksheets (tabs) within one file. For example, you can make one equipment file but have one piece of equipment inventory on each worksheet.
  - Creating pie charts and bar graphs.

Organizing Electronic Files on Your Computer

To keep your electronic files organized on your computer's hard drive or network drive, here are some suggestions:

- Make electronic folders for various topics or types of information: photographs, electronic documents (such as a downloaded equipment manual from the web), equipment inventory, financial plans, and so on.

- Create subfolders within your main folders to further organize.

- Rename each file. "P7160001.JPG" does not tell you much. "20070825Office building-north view.jpg" is very descriptive. This renaming will help you to easily find your information later. By putting the date at the front of the file, you can sort chronologically. This date system is helpful when you scan in a photo—it tells you in the file name when the picture was taken, rather than when the scan was performed.

For all cases, remember to regularly back up all electronic files!

Tool Summary

Tools can be completed by a variety of people. It may be one person or a small committee. They may be completed by an internal staff person, a hired consultant, or a volunteer.

Number	Title	Description	When to use
1.1	Best Practices Self-Rating Tool	Use this tool to evaluate how your organization stacks up to the best practices suggested by the book.	• When you need to baseline your organization. • When you have implemented changes and need to reassess; usually 1-3 years later.
2.1	Site and Facility Information to Share With Participants	Use this tool to examine how site and facilities information is progressively conveyed to participants prior to their arrival.	• When you need to evaluate your participant information. • Whenever information or procedures change—so you see how the change might affect other areas.
2.2	Historical Time Line of Site and Facility Events	Use this tool to record significant events that have had an impact on your organization's site and facilities.	• When revising the risk management plan. • When you want to make a participant timeline. • When orienting new staff members (property and nonproperty).
2.3	Sample Participant Time Line	Use this tool as an outline to create a Web-based or physical timeline.	• When you are updating your participant timeline. • When you are teaching history to participants.
3.1	Maintenance Requests, Suggestions, and Kudos	Use this tool for participants to make suggestions and requests to the staff.	• Whenever participants are on the property. Put this tool in easily accessible locations.
3.2	Site and Facility Staffing Needs	Use this tool to determine the staffing levels needed, based on your programming, property, and organizational structure.	• Whenever conditions change that affect staffing. • When the staff workload increases or decreases.
3.3	Specialized Skills Inventory	Use this tool to determine the specialized skills needed, based on the projects you are doing.	• When doing a new type of project and you need to determine staffing. • When writing a job description and you need a list of specific skill requirements.
3.4	Clarifying Your Expectations of Staff	Use this tool to analyze whether staff expectations and legal requirements are covered in policies, procedures, and handbooks.	• When you need to evaluate your staffing procedures and policies. • When you are revising policies, procedures, and handbooks. • When you are giving a new employee orientation.
3.5	Annual Volunteer Project Summary	Use this tool to describe the key aspects of volunteer projects.	• When you are advertising for volunteers, simply publish this list. Usually 1-2 times each year.

Number	Title	Description	When to use
3.6	Volunteer Interest Survey	Use this tool to match project needs with volunteer skills and interests.	• When new volunteers are recruited. Ask them to complete this survey. • When existing volunteers develop new skills. Ask them to update their information every 2-4 years.
3.7	Volunteer Feedback	Use this tool to solicit volunteer feedback for each volunteer project.	• When you are doing a volunteer project. Ask volunteers to complete before leaving.
4.1	Property Record Catalog	Use this tool to make a summary of all your site and facility records.	• When the property director is on vacation and substitute staff need to find records. • When a staff member is leaving. Make sure the catalog is updated. • When orienting a new property staff member. • When making backups of property records.
5.1	Walk-Through: Grounds	Use this tool to assess the condition of and projects to be done with your grounds.	• When budgets need to be developed, when conditions change, or after a specified weather season. Usually 1-2 times a year.
5.2	Walk-Through: Utilities	Use this tool to assess the condition of and projects to be done with your utilities.	• When budgets need to be developed, when conditions change, or after a specific weather season. Usually 1-2 times a year.
5.3	Replacement and Maintenance Schedule: Site	Use this tool to plan future site expenditures.	• When budgets need to be developed or revised. • When developing long-range plans. • When creating fund development plans.
6.1	Natural Resources: Comprehensive Inventory	Use this tool to record and summarize natural resources information, such as historical, regional characteristics, uniqueness, and so on.	• When events occur or conditions change. • When items need to be updated or verified. Usually every 2-5 years. • When orienting new staff members who are new to the region.
6.2	Walk-Through: Natural Resources and Land	Use this tool to assess the condition of and projects to be done with your natural resources.	• When budgets need to be developed, when conditions change, or after a specific weather season. Usually once a year.
7.1	Energy Conservation Audit	Use this checklist to develop creative ideas for saving money by conserving energy.	• When you need to baseline your energy conservation practices. • When you have implemented changes and need to reassess. Usually 6-12 months later.
7.2	Electric Meter Readings	Use this tool to record monthly utility expenses to analyze trends.	• When budgets need to be developed or revised. • When you need to correlate usage with energy conservation initiatives (tool 7.1).

(continued)

Number	Title	Description	When to use
7.3	Maintenance Work Analysis	Use this tool to categorize the maintenance tasks that occupy a staff person's time.	• When you need to baseline the type of maintenance work you are doing. • When you have implemented changes and need to reassess. Usually 3-6 months later. • When you need to analyze where a staff member's time is being spent. • When you need to reevaluate your staffing levels.
7.4	Master To-Do List	Use this tool to track all work and its status.	• When developing staff schedules. • When budgets need to be developed or revised. • When developing long-range plans.
7.5	Inventory and Maintenance Log: Equipment	Use this tool to record information about the purchase, equipment features, and maintenance performed.	• When a staff member needs to know the maintenance history of the equipment. • When budgets need to be developed or revised. • When you update your property portfolio or insurance records. • When developing staff schedules.
7.6	Inventory and Maintenance Log: Building	Use this tool to record information about the building construction, major components, and maintenance performed.	• When a staff member needs to know the maintenance history of the building. • When budgets need to be developed or revised. • When you update your property portfolio or insurance records. • When developing staff schedules.
7.7	Equipment Preventive Maintenance Schedule	Use this tool to develop a schedule for equipment preventive maintenance.	• When developing staff schedules. • When budgets need to be developed or revised.
7.8	Replacement Schedule: Facility and Equipment	Use this tool to keep track of the age and replacement of your equipment.	• When budgets need to be developed or revised. • When developing long-range plans. • When creating fund development plans.
7.9	Walk-Through: Facilities	Use this tool to assess the condition of and projects to be done with your facilities.	• When budgets need to be developed, when conditions change, or after a specific weather season. Usually 1-2 times a year.
7.10	Contractor Bid Comparison	Use this tool to evaluate which contractor to use.	• When you will be outsourcing a major project and will be receiving bids.
8.1	Where Does Your Time Go?	Use this tool to determine where time is spent by a staff member.	• When you want to analyze where changes could be made. • When job descriptions need to be revised.
8.2	Work Priorities for Site and Facilities	Use this tool to create a standard priority system for the entire organization.	• When decisions need to be made about which project will be done first. • When you need to explain the rationale behind a decision.

Number	Title	Description	When to use
8.3	Gantt Chart	Use this tool to list the tasks of a project, develop a schedule, and give a visual timeline.	• When you have a large project or a project that extends over a length of time.
8.4	Stages of Site and Facility Management	Use this tool to assess the stage of development of each aspect of site and facilities management.	• When you need to determine your priorities in your strategic planning. • When you have implemented changes and need to reassess. Usually 1-3 years later.
8.5	Annual Priorities for Site and Facilities	Use this tool to determine the tactical objectives for the year in each area, after you have completed tool 8.4.	• When you are developing your tactical plan. Updated annually.
8.6	Understanding Your Time Cycles	Use this tool to record key time periods to do various projects.	• When you have a new staff member and need to orient him or her to your operation. • When you are planning your yearly schedule.
9.1	Pie Chart of Annual Operating Expenditures	Use this tool to analyze how the property is a piece of the organization.	• When analyzing site and facility expenses. • When developing a long-term financial plan.
9.2	Condition of Facilities Using FCI	Use this tool to objectively calculate the condition of each building.	• When summarizing the condition of all buildings for prioritization, statement of need, or informing others. • When developing a long-term financial plan. • When prioritizing which buildings will be worked on first.
9.3	Chart of Accounts	Use this tool to analyze if your chart of accounts is sufficient.	• When revising your chart of accounts. • When you need more accounts for data analysis.
9.4	Utility Budget	Use this tool to analyze your utility budgets.	• When the operating budget needs to be developed or revised.
9.5	Capital Budget	Use this tool to keep track of all your assets and their useful life projection.	• When the capital budget needs to be developed or revised. • When creating fund development plans.
9.6	Capital Replacement Fund Considerations	Use this tool to discuss and then agree upon how the long-term needs of the property will be funded.	• When the board is doing strategic planning. • When developing the operating and capital budgets. • When assessing the financial goals of the organization. • When writing fund development plans—the target goals can be included.

(continued)

Number	Title	Description	When to use
9.7	Site and Facility Financial Plan Outline	Use this tool to develop a comprehensive financial plan.	• When the board is doing strategic planning. • When you are assessing progress on your site and facilities. • When you need to recalibrate. Usually every 3-5 years.
9.8	Tips for Saving Money	Use this tool to see where you might save money for your site and facilities.	• When your organization is reevaluating and looking for additional ways to save money.
10.1	Record Retention Worksheet	Use this tool to create a record retention schedule.	• When you need a guide to solicit expert advice for developing a records retention schedule. • When you need to set standards for your operation.
10.2	Archiving at a Glance	Use this chart to guide proper storage of archived property management records.	• When you are setting up or re-evaluating your records storage location and processes.
11.1	Brainstorming Site and Facility Risks	Use this tool to revise the site and facilities component of the organization's risk management plan.	• When revising your overall organizational risk management plan, you can include these site and facilities elements.
11.2	Risk Management Checklist for Site and Facilities	Use this tool to verify you have these specific site and facility areas covered in your organization's risk management plan.	• When revising your overall organizational risk management plan. • When updating your site and facilities procedures and policies.
11.3	Workplace Safety Operating Procedures	Use this tool to verify you have these points covered in your procedures.	• When revising staff safety procedures.
11.4	Evacuation of Building (On-Site Emergencies)	Use this tool to develop your on-site evacuation procedures.	• When revising on-site evacuation procedures.
11.5	Evacuation of Site	Use this tool to develop your off-site evacuation procedures.	• When revising off-site evacuation procedures.

PLACE

Integrating Program and Property

Birchwood Camp, Chugiak Alaska.

Most organizations strive to be memorable places. They have specific settings, facilities, and programs to accomplish their mission. What makes a lasting impact is the successful integration of program and property. Place is not just a site and facilities. Neither is it just a program. A memorable place is a seamless expression of an integrated organizational mission.

"Where were you last week, anyway?" a girl asks her friend.

"At camp."

At camp. These two quietly spoken words conjure up the image of a memorable place, a garden of growth and development where lives are changed forever. Think back to any life-changing moment you have experienced. What comes to mind? Probably the place where it happened. Perhaps you visualize an archery range at a sports camp 30 years ago, when you—a gawky kid who was one of the last kids chosen to play on sports teams at school—picked up a bow for the first time. With individualized coaching from the activity counselor and a positive environment to learn new things, you scored a bull's-eye after practicing. You learned for the first time, "I can do this!"

Today, if someone mentions the words *sports camp,* a flood of memories may come to mind. You may instantly visualize the archery range, or you may be filled with the positive emotions from the day you scored your bull's-eye. Perhaps you remember the smell of the fresh summer air and the biting flies. It was the place associated with learning the skill of archery, the place where kids your age did lots of fun activities, the place where you gained confidence.

Place

Place is more than just an X on the ground where something happens. The concept has a spiritual dimension. Place exercises a deep-seated, even primal hold on us. It is the familiar ground around which the most cherished associations are collected, those things that occupy abiding places in people's hearts, minds, and being.

Sharing life.
© Corbis

Perhaps nowhere is the significance of place more evident than at an organization dedicated to personal development and enrichment. At such a place participants experience the joy of growth through structured programs and supportive communities. People learn skills, find inspiration, open new doors, and make new friends. They withdraw from the demands and pressures of everyday life to reflect, study, and grow.

This chapter explores the essential components of a memorable place: program and **property.** *Program* is the broad term for all the activities, including educational, spiritual, religious, recreational, and developmental. Programs encompass what participants think, experience, and do while they are with you. The property is the physical location where the program takes place. It might be in buildings, outside on a grassy field, or in the woods.

Conceptual Framework: ITS

Participating in an educational, personal growth, or religious experience means removing ourselves from the busy, distracting world to a setting that promotes self-development and enrichment. As participants step into these settings, they become set apart from their daily tasks and surroundings. They find themselves detached—physically and emotionally—from consuming and stressful daily pressures. Indeed, a key benefit of a residential center is the refuge it offers. It gives guests a way to unplug from their routines, to find the space, balance, and social interaction needed for growth and development.

William Duncan, vice president and chief academic officer of Aurora University, created a theory to explain why a camp or center creates an effective environment for personal growth (Duncan, 1982, 1991). His theory of the isolated temporary system, or ITS, was later expanded and adapted for teaching by Charles Wallace, former president of United Camps, Conferences, and Retreats (UCCR) (Wallace, 1994, 2004). The ITS concept suggests that the apartness of the camp or center setting is what enhances the learning environment. Learning is supported when participants are immersed in an isolated temporary system, a refuge from the world.

The benefits of the ITS for participants include the following:

- Less distraction, ability to better focus on one predominate learning task
- Holistic learning environment
- Close working relationship between the teacher and student (or counselor and camper)
- Intimate setting that promotes communication, trust, and a spirit of engagement among a community of participants
- Dramatically increased retention of learning

A residential camp, conference center, or retreat center can function as an ideal ITS environment when it does the following:

- Ensures that staff members understand the desired outcomes and are trained to tap the power of the isolated temporary system to deliver desired outcomes
- Provides physical space and equipment specifically tailored to enhance the experience

KEY COMPONENTS FOR AN EFFECTIVE ITS

- Location requiring travel to the camp or center
- Temporary residence at the camp or center
- Freedom from physical needs (food and housing provided by others or prepared by participants as part of the program)
- Sense of being "at home"
- Freedom from external time structures
- Freedom from roles (e.g., dress, social status, economic status)
- Natural beauty (helpful but not essential)

Adapted, by permission, from C. Wallace, 2004, "Isolated temporary system (ITS) theory," International Association of Conference Center Administrators (IACCA).

A NOTE ABOUT CONNECTIVITY

ITS, now a 25-year-old theory, was developed in a world much less "connected" than it is today. Many program participants now arrive at residential camps and centers with the technology that keeps them connected to virtually all aspects of their everyday world. In this world that accepts connectivity as essential, will ITS remain a viable educational model? The "temporary system" portion of ITS may continue to be effective, but the "isolated" portion will probably require modification. Creative planners will likely find ways to include connectivity in emerging models.

Adapted, by permission, from C. Wallace, 2004, "Isolated temporary system (ITS) theory," International Association of Conference Center Administrators (IACCA).

Integrating Program and Property

The spiritual properties of place, the power of the isolated temporary system to enhance learning—these concepts underscore the importance of **site** and **facilities** to a successful program. Revered and educational properties aside, though, the program still happens in a very physical place—buildings, courtyards, grass lawns, basketball courts, swimming pools, and, if a nonurban location, woodlands, ponds, and trails.

The tension between program and property always exists because, for professionals, the core mission is clearly rooted in human development. When it comes to painting and grounds upkeep, people know these are necessary, but they tend to ask themselves, "Are these things really as important as what I do for my participants?" The answer is yes, because only a fully integrated, cooperative working relationship between program and property will allow an organization to fully realize its mission.

Think of program and property as part of a dynamic system rather than as opposite ends of a spectrum, each vying for resources and attention. As with all dynamic systems, you can expect a constant ebb and flow between the parts. Program and property should continually inform and shape one another, as shown in figure 1.1. Their interdependent processes rely on each continually adjusting and adapting to support the mission and its goals.

A few examples will help to illustrate the interrelatedness between program and property for different organizations. Frequently, some of the best programs come out of the property on which they are situated. Do you have a majestic view that activities are built around? This is an example of the site influencing the program. The influence can also flow the other way. Can the choice of aesthetically pleasing, comfortable furniture placed in strategic locations contribute to small-group discussions? Here, the program outcomes determine the type of facility furnishings.

Without question, participants come and use the property, and you provide services. However, property management is more than just providing services or support. What's more important is creating the strong relationship between the program and the property. The property is a *part* of the programming. Pine and Gilmore (1999) described the events that go beyond providing service as experiences that engage people in a personal way. These experiences involve participants in an unfolding story. For example, you are immersed in an experience at Disneyland, rather than just taking an amusement park ride.

What type of experience are you creating with your property that actively engages participants? Renewal away from a hectic world? Enriching education? Experiencing a step back in time (living history)? A western experience (dude ranch)? Immersion in nature? In all of these examples, the property is an essential part of the experience.

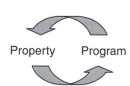

FIGURE 1.1 Program and property influence and support each other.

Programming coupled with a majestic view can be inspirational and life changing. This shows how the site can influence the programming.

© Craig Wolinsky/Aurora Photos

Selecting the right furniture for your programming is one way your program and property can work together.

Photo courtesy of Heartland Presbyterian Center, Parkville, MO.

Setting Priorities for Program and Property

Consider this simple equation:

Good facilities = an improved ability to offer good programs.

Make sense? Of course. But achieving a constant balance is often easier said than done. The missing variable is people. **Administrators** and staff need to agree about what constitutes good facilities and good programs—and then put their concepts into practice.

Setting priorities for site and facilities versus program needs is difficult, especially these days, when many organizations are experiencing significant external pressures. With limited dollars available, and a seemingly infinite number of things to spend them on, most organizations face difficult decisions when attempting to balance goals, needs, and available funding.

Some of the most common problems center on deciding what things need to be done now. For instance, should monies in the budget be used to replace a furnace on its last legs or replace the piano that is always out of tune? People may even realize that a Band-Aid approach to site and facility management can be far more expensive in the long run than a comprehensive, systematic plan of upkeep. But can they afford to spend more money now to save more money in the long run?

The everyday realities of limited funding and having to juggle varying or even conflicting priorities, perspectives, and values can create special challenges. As tempers flare, the situation may appear to boil down to the question, Which is more important—program or property? But this is the wrong question! Both are critical. Instead, your aim should be to bring both pieces together. This takes work to seek out a solution built on mutual respect and appreciation of the roles of all concerned.

The one thing everyone will likely agree on is that the organization is a community. The concept of a community is helpful for combining the various interests into a whole. A community includes many parts: the people involved (administrators, staff, and participants), the place (physical location, site, **grounds,** and buildings), and the overall enclosure (mission, activities, and overarching philosophy). For the community to remain healthy and vital, these parts must have a commitment to working on common goals.

For all these reasons, a strong connection between your program and property must be the cornerstone of your effort to integrate property management into the organizational structure. The elements must be integrated into a seamless whole in order to enjoy all the benefits.

CREATING ALIGNMENT

You and your fellow staff members work hard to create and maintain your memorable place, but competing priorities sometimes lead to people working in isolation and not having a dialogue. To work toward alignment within the group, consider the following:

- Mission and purpose
- Impact on participants
- Impact on other areas of work
- Needs and priorities of all who use the facilities
- Financial implications of possible solutions
- Varying viewpoints
- Long-term implications and risks

An understanding of the interrelationship of property and program creates the supportive team relationship that ensures good decision making and a smooth operation.

Making a visual interpretation of the camp's motto can bring it to life for camper artists and others around them.

Photo courtesy of G. Graham, Camp Ton-A-Wandah CIT project.

Integrating Power of a Mission Statement

We've all heard them—those folks who consider mission statements so much mealy-mouthed word spinning and window dressing. However, **mission statements** bring real value to an organization. They provide a framework for understanding an organization's work and for developing strategies and tactics. This is as true for a small organization as it is for any Fortune 500 business.

A mission statement articulates the overall purpose of your operation. It describes why your organization exists and what participant needs your program will meet. A mission statement defines who you are, which touches and shapes all aspects of your business.

A good mission statement can be a great help to your site and facility management operation. It can do the following:

- Be the governing principle that shapes how you use your site and facilities
- Describe how you integrate program and property
- Define where property management fits into an operation's overall functional structure
- Create a sense of place

OPERATING UNDER A PARENT ORGANIZATION'S MISSION STATEMENT

Sometimes an organization is involved in many related, but diverse, areas. The mission statement of a parent organization may be too broad to define a specific area's purpose adequately. If this is your situation, you may want to develop a secondary mission statement, or "purpose statement." This can clearly define the mission of your area while aligning it with the broader organizational mission.

Lasting memories are created when there is a sense of place—an integration of the activities and their surroundings.

© Corbis

Mission Statement Guidelines

Your mission statement should recognize the dynamic interrelationship between programming and the property. While mission statements address the program-related elements of an operation, they can also provide a focus for a property management approach. Your mission statement can strengthen the vital link between your program and property, enabling your organization to create a memorable place for your participants.

To realize its potential value, a mission statement must be balanced—it must tie together all organizational elements. A good mission statement integrates various operational elements, including property management, into a single agenda of action. This gives a common footing to all the elements.

If your organization's mission cannot be accomplished without a specific type of property, then your mission statement should signal the role of the property in meeting the organizational goals. Let's look at some examples. The following mission statement successfully identifies property as a critical component of the desired outcomes:

Swift River Conference Center provides guests with personal growth experiences in comfortable surroundings, while underscoring our value of respecting and caring for the earth.

What makes this a strong and effective mission statement? First, it specifically states that the mission pertains to a conference center. It acknowledges the role of property (comfortable surroundings) in delivering enriching personal growth experiences. Finally, it underscores the organization's commitment to safeguarding the environment by "respecting and caring for the earth."

Contrast this with another mission statement:

Through well-designed, fun educational opportunities, children at Swift River make new friends, respect others as individuals, and improve their physical fitness.

This statement lacks specificity on several key points. It neglects to describe Swift River as a camp, after-school program, or school. It does not tie the site and facilities into the overall mission of the operation, nor does it show what is unique about Swift River. It also fails to define the important role of site and facilities in realizing the program goals.

As these examples show, the wording of a mission statement helps to forge the important link between program and property.

As you develop or revise your mission statement, you will need a clear understanding of your organization's philosophy regarding the natural resources, if your property has natural resources to consider. For example, you'll need to know whether the natural

The dance facility must be large enough to accommodate large groups and have an atmosphere conducive to creating community.

resources of the site will be used simply for recreational purposes, whether site **steward-ship** is incorporated into the program, or whether the site is intended to reinforce lessons learned in the program. These specifics will be essential to good property management, helping you to make decisions about wildlife **habitat,** decor, land management, and the atmosphere you want to create.

Integrating Site and Facility Language

If your current mission statement poorly integrates program and property, consider introducing language that relates site and facilities to program outcomes. Such integrating language will benefit your operation in many ways, from helping to secure property-related funding to unifying the vision of your operation among staff. Table 1.1 shows some examples of language that could integrate site and facilities into your mission statement.

A word of caution: If all this talk of mission statements has you straining at the leash to go and change the document that has guided your organization for many years, don't be in such a rush. Your mission statement is fundamental to the structure of your organization. Before you start rewriting it, consider its importance and the legal implications of any changes. Revising your mission statement deserves time and careful thought. It can also be hard work. You may wish to retain an experienced facilitator who has the skills to assemble the right group of people needed to complete the process.

In the meantime, you and appropriate staff, board members, and key volunteers may want to add comprehensive site and facility language to other documents that support your mission statement, such as a statement of values, purpose, or philosophy. The intent is to articulate the role of your site and facilities in your organization's guiding statements.

QUESTIONS TO ASK OF YOUR MISSION STATEMENT

Does your organization's mission statement reflect a solid understanding of the role of site and facilities in the overall operation? Put it to the test. Your mission statement, and the values it represents, should provide enough information for you to develop answers to many of these site and facility questions:

- What color theme will you select for your indoor paint colors?
- Will your landscaping be trimmed lawns or native vegetation?
- Will you use concrete, asphalt, or chips for your walkways?
- Will the organization play an active role in local community watershed management?
- How will program facilities need to be maintained—proactively or only when they need it?
- Will furnishings be casual or formal?
- What decor supports the atmosphere you are trying to create?
- How much outdoor lighting will be used?
- Does the current physical location support the mission?
- How you will manage your land and your forest?
- Will a conservation easement be considered?

Table 1.1   Examples of Strengthening the Mission Statement

Mission statement language	How could the organization use this language?
Safe place for children to play and grow.	To provide facilities that are safe, are equipped with play areas, and have space for learning at the drop-in center.
The center provides and maintains top-level facilities for our guests to grow and learn.	To make decisions knowing that both the property and program deserve attention and financial resources. To allocate resources (people and money) so that facilities are maintained at a top-level condition.
An environment for personal development.	To make purchasing decisions about the type of décor, furniture, and landscaping that are in congruence with the programming.
The camp is an outdoor learning center.	To develop programs, materials, and themes tied to the natural site. To maintain the site to ensure there are opportunities for learning. To strengthen a wetland preservation grant proposal by describing the intent of the "outdoor learning center."

Girls can join in the cooking with a size-appropriate countertop. The colors in the tile, wall, and paint are bright and inviting to kids. These activities in a well-kept facility fulfill the mission of the organization.

Photo courtesy of Girl Scouts Camp Silverbrook, West Bend, WI. Wynne Whyman photographer.

PHRASING YOU CAN USE

Here are some phrases you can use to integrate program and property in a mission statement. Notice how several of these phrases link site and facilities to program goals.

SITE USE

- Safely learn and enjoy adventurous outdoor activities
- Provide a place for families to gather

FACILITIES

- Preserve our cultural facilities
- Provide a safe environment that promotes learning
- Provide and maintain state-of-the-art facilities
- Offer facilities that complement the natural environment
- Provide residential camping facilities for people with physical limitations
- Provide welcoming facilities

STEWARDSHIP AND CONSERVATION

- Model ecological responsibility
- Protect an undeveloped area for scientific research
- Use the serenity of the outdoors to instill . . .
- Respect and care for God's creation

The lesson here is to do everything you can to ensure that your mission statement underscores the role your property plays in the success of your program. But exercise care—have a rich conversation during your **strategic planning** process to determine the role of site and facilities within your specific organization. If your group determines that the property is *not* instrumental in delivering the program, then don't force site and facility language into a mission statement. Second, if your organization's intent is to protect a piece of property, programming verbiage in the mission statement needs to be carefully crafted.

The benefits of giving property an appropriate presence in your mission statement will soon become apparent: By articulating the role your property plays in achieving mission-driven program goals, you will be able to strengthen both program and property initiatives, open the door to funding opportunities for site and facilities, and know the role of the land in your operation as you participate in community natural resources projects. Perhaps most important, the mission statement will help your staff see and understand the dynamic flow between program and property that helps to define the strategic plan and the subsequent operational steps.

Putting It All Together

With all the topics covered in this book, it may seem that your list of property management activities is endless and daunting. The context for clustering and organizing the myriad tasks is shown in figure 1.2.

The outer oval represents the most important elements—the mission and values statements that surround and guide all site and facility work. Caring, capable people are at the heart of the system, as shown in the center oval. Between the inner and outer circles are the six areas where staff and volunteers will focus the majority of their work.

The model may seem to isolate your site and facility operation from the rest of the organization, but this is not its intent. Throughout this book, an integrated approach to site and facilities is emphasized to ensure a smooth operation. Furthermore you must integrate site and facilities with other areas of the organization and the surrounding community.

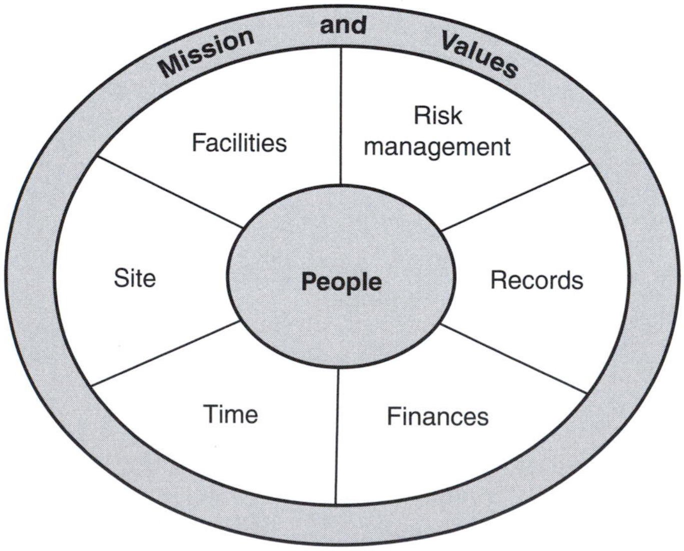

To be successful, property management must be integrated with all aspects of your organization. Your property staff can work with the programming staff to choose appropriate colors and furniture specific for your site. Working together, the program and property staff can create exciting, site-specific environmental activities that address current issues. They can work with the fund development staff to write compelling grant proposals to fund

FIGURE 1.2 Site and facilities model. A way to frame the aspects of site and facility management.

Developed by Wynne Whyman, 2004.

facility improvements. They can work with the local community to protect the watershed. There is power in integration, and participants will benefit from these efforts.

A Sustainable Organization

You now have your mission statement. The rest of the book gives you techniques, tools, and processes for different areas of the organization to develop and implement. All organizations have areas that are not as effective as they could be. When you work on improving these areas also remember that you have already done good work in your organization, or it wouldn't be in existence today.

Keep in mind that change usually takes a long time; site and facility work is ongoing. To measure how much work you and your organization have done, you need to benchmark where you are today by doing self-assessments, and then redoing them to see your progress. The CD-ROM at the back of the book provides tools for addressing various elements of site and facility management. You can do an overall evaluation of how your organization stacks up on the best practices in this book by completing tool 1.1.

However, property management is more than the sum of its individual parts. All of the areas covered in this book need to work together as a seamless whole.

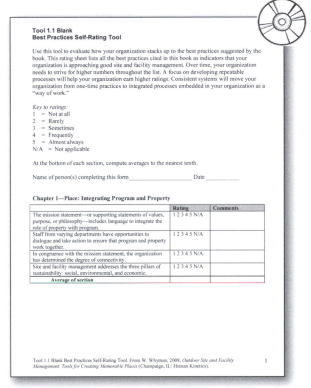

TOOL 1.1 Best Practices Self-Rating Tool.

When program and property elements work together, you can say, "Our organization is prepared to provide the best experience" and "We genuinely care about you and want you to return to experience more."

Organizations focus on the social aspects of their mission—the life-changing impact of the program on the participant—and the site and facilities are integral to this mission. Property management must also strike a balance among social, environmental, and economic factors. Thoughtful, skillful management of site and facilities does the following:

- Provides participants with a memorable place to grow and learn
- Ensures that your natural resources can remain pivotal to accomplishing your mission
- Integrates the financial needs of the site and facilities with the rest of the organization's needs for the long-term viability of the operation

These three pillars of **sustainability**—social, environmental, and financial—help you protect what you have today for tomorrow's generations.

BEST PRACTICES

✓ The mission statement—or supporting statements of values, purpose, or philosophy—includes language to integrate the role of program with property.

✓ Staff from varying departments have opportunities to dialogue and take action to ensure that program and property work together.

✓ In congruence with the mission statement, the organization has determined the degree of connectivity.

✓ Site and facility management addresses the three pillars of sustainability: social, environmental, and economic.

PARTICIPANTS

A Welcoming Invitation

Photo courtesy of Meredith Stewart.

At the end of a program or event, you hope that your participants leave your property with positive, memorable experiences. Much happens while they are with you, and their experiences are enriched by excellent programming, responsive staff, and well-maintained facilities. But equally important is paying attention to participants' well-being before they come and extending a warm hand of hospitality when they arrive. You'll want participants to be knowledgeable about what to expect, to feel comfortable, and to be mentally and physically ready for the positive experiences that await them.

After you have been working with your property for a while, things become commonplace, if not routine. So take a fresh perspective. You will want the lens of a first-timer who is not even familiar with the state where the property is located. You can even have fun "playing dumb" to question all assumptions, voicing your needs and describing a newcomer's expectations. Through this first-timer lens, you can look at participants' initial experiences to see whether the property is integrated with programming to create a memorable place that beckons them to come.

Mission and Participants' Needs

When an organization brings its tightly integrated mission statement to life, the mission radiates through the organization. People work hard and take pride in what they do, which contributes toward a positive impression of the operation. The work they do is visible to participants, including a trimmed lawn, a polished floor, furniture that is well matched to the program, and a nonleaking roof. Participants form immediate impressions from their visual assessments and their experiences on the property.

When all the elements of the site and facilities work together, in partnership with the programming, participants receive the best experiences possible. Parents can see that the school is attended to and ready for their children to learn. People walking through a cultural site sense that they are about to learn and be inspired. Children who attend a camp see exciting activities awaiting them and their friends—and parents notice a safe environment.

People come to your site with expressed and unexpressed wishes. Maslow's hierarchy of needs (1943) offers a way to think about people's wishes. Maslow stated that physical needs, such as for food and shelter, must first be attended to before other, higher needs can be met (see figure 2.1). From the perspective of site and facilities, people must have their physical needs met and feel safe before the programming can make a full impact.

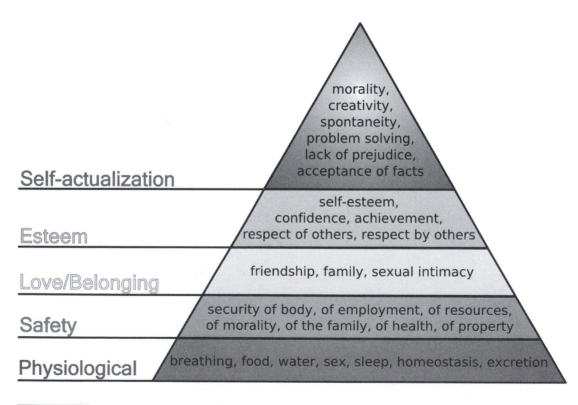

Self-actualization: morality, creativity, spontaneity, problem solving, lack of prejudice, acceptance of facts

Esteem: self-esteem, confidence, achievement, respect of others, respect by others

Love/Belonging: friendship, family, sexual intimacy

Safety: security of body, of employment, of resources, of morality, of the family, of health, of property

Physiological: breathing, food, water, sex, sleep, homeostasis, excretion

FIGURE 2.1 Maslow's hierarchy of needs.

Safety tasks and needs are described throughout this book. When you address your risks, you focus on protecting the organization while also attending to the health and safety needs of participants. You do **walk-throughs** to assess the state of the building to protect your assets, but also to provide a safe building. You keep records to have the data to make informed decisions, but also to have the knowledge to be financially prepared to cover future projects. To have life-changing experiences, participants must first be psychologically and physically safe.

Positive Anticipation

Doing the work is only half of the story, however. Many participants may not recognize the work that you have done in preparation for their arrival. You need to tell them what you have done and how it benefits them. For example, "Come see our beautiful new floor and experience the warm new color our volunteers painted our walls a few weeks ago. It is a great place for groups to hear speakers."

Newcomers, guests, parents, outside rental groups, and others who have never visited your property might not know what to expect. People need to be prepared for new experiences, which helps them to feel at ease. You need to give them a mental picture. Participants need to know what to wear to be physically comfortable, how to find the property, and perhaps even the quality of the cell phone reception. People want to feel welcomed and safe and to know that their needs will be met.

Participants who are staying overnight will need to know what to expect when they arrive at the facilities. If the sleeping facilities are located at an outdoor property, participants

Making it easy for newcomers, with directional signage and a welcoming message.
Courtesy Ragen E. Sanner.

need to know about the site and what it will be like living with nature given that many of them may be coming from an urban environment. The information you provide can help them anticipate a positive stay, rather than a stay marked with anxiety and uneasiness.

Shaping Expectations

When you walk past the building, look out for what appear to be fallen logs on the ground. They could be alligators.

Huh? For participants who live in Florida, this statement is just a reminder, but for those new to the state or unfamiliar with the area, this comment could raise a few questions: What if I accidentally get too close? What is too close? Should I make noise or keep quiet? What times of the day are they more likely to be on shore? and, perhaps most important, Who can answer my questions about alligators?

A participant could be shocked and even frightened to hear the warning about alligators during an orientation session. What if a few paragraphs describing the alligators on your property were included in their mailed materials or on the Web site? Then the reminder could be presented as reassurance: "Remember what you read about the alligators before you came? While you're here, we'll show you what we are doing to help protect their habitat and how you can do your part. Oh, and your timing is good—there's an alligator right over there on the shore of the lake. Just give him a wide space and you'll be fine. You can also learn more about alligators at our kiosk."

To begin shaping your participants' expectations, you should share information at first contact. With each additional contact, you can progressively give the appropriate information. Your goal is to successively build on the previous information so that it is nonrepetitive and the amount of information is not overwhelming. This progression continues through participants' arrival on your property and during their stay. Choose the channels that are appropriate for your organization.

- *Promotional materials.* Introduce key points about site and facilities in printed brochures, in DVDs, and on your Web site. If your organization intentionally keeps a low profile with the general public, be sensitive to the type of information you include.

- *Welcoming or confirmation packets.* Inserts give you the opportunity to provide more detailed information on what to expect.

- *Orientations or tours.* Orientation sessions and tours are a good way for participants to see what they have read about. They allow you to reinforce key points and expand on the previously received materials.

- *On-site information.* Put information in the meeting areas, in on-site welcome packets, at check-in points, and in sleeping areas. Make informational signs and maps as described in this book.

Well-informed, well-prepared participants will have fewer concerns and less stress. This is a first step toward that positive, memorable experience you want your participants to have. Some of the information that will make participants feel comfortable and safe is identified in tool 2.1. To the right of each statement, in the appropriate columns, make notes about the information you want to convey. Whenever possible, use photographs with the text to show what you are describing.

You have some of the best knowledge about what makes your property special. Share what you know with participants. If you've created a cozy atmosphere in the common area with small, round tables that encourage people to sit and visit, tell them. You'll be helping to shape a positive vision of what to expect when they arrive.

It's fine to even brag a bit about your hard work. Let participants know that they will be staying in well-maintained facilities. Express that, behind the scenes, you and your staff will work to ensure their safety and comfort by updating facilities with fresh paint or new furniture, or plowing snowy roads and sidewalks prior to their arrival. Many participants will find comfort in statements such as, "We take pride in our well-maintained facilities to ensure a quality experience."

When preparing information about site and facilities, be as descriptive and as inviting as you can be. Rather than "After the meeting, you are welcome to join us in the McKnight room," say "After the meeting, you are welcome to join us in the McKnight room, which is located next to dining area." Instead of "You'll be staying at the lodge," say, "You'll be staying at Evergreen Lodge, which has a majestic view of the sunrise." Avoid using internal terms that outsiders will not understand—statements such as "Use the back entrance." Unless the back entrance is associated with a well-marked feature or there is good signage, it may be impossible for a new person to find it.

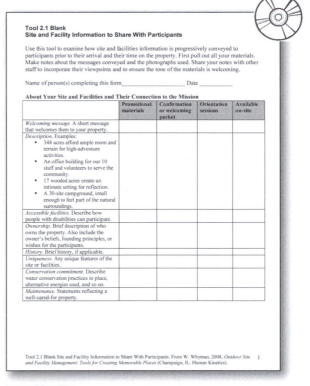

TOOL 2.1 Site and Facility Information to Share With Participants.

Include professional-looking pictures in promotional and confirmation materials. All pictures should show a welcoming, clean appearance and generate excitement in the participant.

Photo courtesy of Gary Forster, YMCA of the USA.

Giving comprehensive, integrated information to participants takes teamwork with the program, property, guest services, administration, marketing, and office staff. Each specialty has a unique viewpoint to contribute. Be sure to share your draft version of tool 2.1 with the rest of your staff and ask for their perspectives. Together, look at all property-related communications participants receive, using tool 2.1 as a basis to evaluate the effectiveness and positive tone of each one. After this discussion, all staff will be well informed and able to explain and interpret the site and facility information with participants.

Opportunities to Educate

Your decor, artwork, and signs can be opportunities to educate participants about the landscape, history of your property, and, if applicable, your natural setting. Here are some ideas:

- Create a master site and facility time line using tool 2.2. This is a good way to see your property at a glance; it identifies key milestones and shows their proximity to other events.

- Have participants make a time line to hang in a prominent place in a common area. Give completed copies of tool 2.2 to participants to use in completing tool 2.3. Tool 2.3 can be given to participants to be completed as

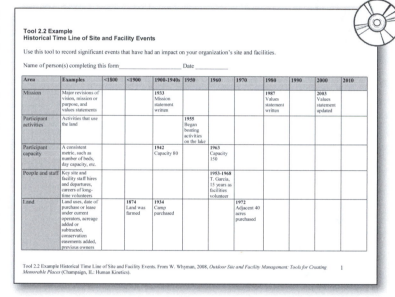

Tool 2.2 Example
Historical Time Line of Site and Facility Events

Use this tool to record significant events that have had an impact on your organization's site and facilities.

Name of person(s) completing this form_____ Date _____

Area	Examples	<1800	<1900	1900-1940s	1950	1960	1970	1980	1990	2000	2010
Mission	Major revisions of vision, mission or purpose, and values statements			1933 Mission statement written				1987 Values statement written		2003 Values statement updated	
Participant activities	Activities that use the land				1955 Began boating activities on the lake						
Participant capacity	A consistent metric, such as number of beds, day capacity, etc.			1942 Capacity 80		1963 Capacity 150					
People and staff	Key site and facility staff hires and departures, careers of long-time volunteers					1953-1968 T. Garcia, 15 years as facilities volunteer					
Land	Land uses, date of purchase or lease under current operators, acreage added or subtracted, conservation easements added, previous owners		1874 Land was farmed	1934 Camp purchased			1972 Adjacent 40 acres purchased				

Tool 2.2 Example Historical Time Line of Site and Facility Events. From W. Whyman, 2008, *Outdoor Site and Facility Management: Tools for Creating Memorable Places* (Champaign, IL: Human Kinetics). 1

TOOL 2.2 Historical Time Line of Site and Facility Events.

an individual activity or you can ask the group to make a large timeline to display on the wall of a building. Give participants a 2- × 50-foot roll of durable butcher paper on which to mark and illustrate key events on the time line, such as building remodels, significant decisions about the property, and different ways the property is used for programming. If you are in a natural setting, participants may include mining operations, environmental changes, habitat improvements, and cultural activities. An example of a participant time line is shown in tool 2.3.

- Duplicate a historic picture of a prominent building and hang it next to a recent picture. In a short paragraph underneath the photographs describe how and why the building has changed and the story about the people and their passion that helped to make it possible.

- Duplicate a historic picture of the site—perhaps before the property was purchased. In a short paragraph you can tell about the history of the area.

- Have previous participants write their stories of how your "place" (property) was inspirational in their lives.

- Include a map and description of the property's location within the local watershed. Urban and rural properties are each part of a watershed.

Time lines are a great way for long-time participants to tell newcomers about the organization and its important milestones. They can be done in a variety of formats and styles and posted on a wall—as well as on the Web.

Photo courtesy of YMCA Camp Chingachgook, Lake George, NY. Wynne Whyman photographer.

- For visually impaired participants, create a large tactile map of the property to hang on the wall (see the CD-ROM for resources).
- Describe what you have done to make your building "green" and energy efficient and how participants can help.
- Create signage with a positive educational focus. Instead of "Don't waste water," say, "Save water." Instead of "Don't feed wildlife," say, "Keep wildlife wild."
- For unique or possibly dangerous animals, such as alligators or badgers, paint footprints on the walls or sidewalks. Create an easy-to-read sheet that describes the animal's lifecycle, including its habitat, the number of square miles of its range, and how to act if one is seen. Hang environmental posters describing why the population is growing or falling; whether it is an endangered, threatened, or protected species; and other pertinent points.
- Create a short statement or list of your sustainability practices.

Tool 2.3 Blank
Sample Participant Time Line

Use this tool as an outline to create a Web-based or physical timeline.

For organization history, use the historical site and facility information captured in tool 2.2.
For the regional and world history, add cultural milestones from an almanac or encyclopedia, or the Internet. This history places the organization's events in historical context.

Name of person(s) completing this form_____ Date_____

Regional, world history												
	1900–1904	1905–1909	1910–1914	1915–1919	1920–1924	1925–1929	1930–1934	1935–1939	1940–1944	1945–1949	1950–1954	1955–1959
Organization history												

Tool 2.3 Blank Sample Participant Time Line. From W. Whyman, 2008, *Outdoor Site and Facility Management: Tools for Creating Memorable Places* (Champaign, IL: Human Kinetics).   1

TOOL 2.3   Sample Participant Time Line.

21

These ideas, plus others of your own, can create opportunities to educate participants about your site and facilities. In addition to teaching, they become part of the decor and help to create your unique atmosphere. This decor can be a conversation starter for newcomers. Rather than talking just about the weather, they can talk about your organization. These readily accessible items can also be woven into programming to serve as catalysts for alumni events, environmental education, and teaching about sustainability practices.

Positive Attitudes Toward Site and Facilities

The participant, volunteer, and staff beliefs about the property are central to an organization's success. The property needs to be a valued treasure that serves and changes lives. Ask yourself and your staff: Do you see your site and facilities as an opportunity to create the best place possible for your mission—or as a burdensome overhead necessity? How people answer this question reflects the beliefs they hold and the values that pervade the organization.

One's underlying belief is reflected in one's work. For example, is your work to find the best method to wisely spend the budgeted money to fulfill your organization's mission and meet the needs of participants, or is it simply to cut as many corners as possible? In both instances, the bottom line is decreased, but the attitudes and mental energies are radically different. The overall attitude of the organization determines the level of motivation of staff and volunteers in their daily work. That attitude is the foundation on which all decisions are made, and it reverberates all the way to the participants.

If site and facilities are not valued by individuals or within the organization's culture, you will need to address these issues. Changing people's attitudes or an organization's culture can be difficult, but it can be done through compassionate, skilled **leadership** and solid **management**. Striving for what is best for the organization is what matters in the long run.

Your memorable place.
© Eyewire/Photodisc/Getty Images

Creating Your Memorable Place

When your staff and volunteers appreciate and value all that the site and facilities bring to your participants, this attitude permeates all of their work. From their first contact, participants know that you care and have taken the time to ensure that they are physically and psychologically prepared. They sense that you are eagerly anticipating their coming. Act I of participants' experiences is not their arrival; Act I starts with that first interaction with you whether on the Web or through a brochure or a phone call. Do everything you can to inform and educate with realistic expectations, sharing the vast opportunities you have at your property.

BEST PRACTICES

- ✓ Information about the site and facilities is conveyed to participants in a variety of ways prior to their stay.
- ✓ Participants are educated about the site and facilities while they are on-site.
- ✓ The attitude toward the site and facilities is positive throughout the organization.

PEOPLE

Your Greatest Asset

© IPNstock

Your people are the strong foundation on which to build your property management strategy. As your greatest asset, people bring to your operation the insight, knowledge, and skills essential to running a quality property. People do far more than teach the programs, cook the meals, and maintain the grounds. They are key drivers of your results and outcomes. They translate your mission into action.

Does that crack in the foundation of the new building mean anything? How much time will there be between groups to clean the floors? Looks like that roof is leaking again. I wonder if it'll last another season.

Look inside the head of a property director, and chances are you'll find thoughts such as the preceding. It makes perfect sense for buildings, roads, and infrastructure to be uppermost in the mind of someone charged with the upkeep of site and facilities. But there is something even more important than wood, plumbing, steel, grass, or trees to successful operations. It's the asset that everyone in your organization, whether involved in programming, **governance,** or any other area, would probably identify as most important. It's your people—your staff, administrators, and volunteers.

Most organizations develop detailed policies and procedures covering their human assets. Your manuals probably include policies on recruiting, hiring, training, scheduling, supervising, managing, and evaluating. These will be invaluable to you. But some issues, though just as important, are less universally addressed in written policies. The following discussion will help you think about these issues throughout the organization.

Working Together—Creating Memories

An integrated approach to property management means uniting your staff around shared operational responsibilities. Your people bring the benefit of many perspectives to the management of your property. If two heads are better than one, then imagine the power of engaging your entire staff in the property management process. No longer is maintenance just the job of those folks on the lawn mowers. Instead, it's everyone's job in ways that range from small to significant. Everyone contributes, whether to the general upkeep of a property or to other facets of an operation such as program or health and safety.

This is not to suggest that everyone on staff should be out swinging a hammer or wielding a wrench. Actual hands-on work should remain the responsibility of your maintenance crew or a hired **contractor.** But you can build awareness that site and facility issues touch everyone, from the board member who helps secure a grant to the participant who hears "We all care about the property so we all pick up after ourselves" on his first day.

BRING YOUR STAFF INTO THE PROCESS

Facilitate a discussion to generate ideas on how various areas can support one another.

- Use a flipchart to list the various job areas, including programming activities, food service, site and facilities, and so on.

- Have your staff split into mixed small groups with the assignment to brainstorm ways they can partner with one another.

- Using a consensus process with the staff, pick one project from the brainstorming list. Further develop the project and implement it.

- Follow up at staff meetings by asking for specific examples of how areas are partnering with each other on the project.

- Create a sense of shared responsibility to strengthen the support system for all functions. Encourage integrated thinking!

A Pivotal Role: The Administrator

At the core of successful site and facility management is the administrator. The administrator of an organization needs to create and support opportunities to strengthen the property management program.

Common wisdom says that the administrator makes better decisions when the site and facility management staff are part of a collaborative management team than when they are not. In practice, though, what sounds like a makes-sense approach can be difficult to pull off, especially when things get busy. We've all heard it: "There's no time. I'll just make the decision myself." Yet, busy or not, administrators should involve the site and facility staff in the executive decision-making process at critical stages. Staff members bring valuable perspectives from firsthand experience. As the people who will actually do the work, they may have the best grasp of what is needed, possible, and financially feasible. Involving them is also an excellent way of gaining buy-in, a key ingredient to the smooth implementation of any decision or plan.

Executive decisions based on sketchy facts can grow into all-consuming problems. As one respondent to a field survey succinctly put it, "A five-minute discussion in a meeting can take five months to complete in the field." Talking with the staff who will implement a project serves as a reality check on what the budget will really support and what personnel can realistically accomplish.

An example illustrates the value of having all the staff involved in site and facility decisions. Let's say a retreat center faces serious budget cutbacks from the parent organization. To see where cuts can be made, the administrator asks the property director to prioritize projects that have been identified for completion. With this prioritized list in hand, the administrator does a walk-through to look at the operation firsthand.

By getting out, looking around, and asking questions of the staff, the administrator gets the information needed to make informed, constructive decisions. This improves her ability to work effectively with other unit managers and to sell them on maintenance or property-related projects, if needed. An informed administrator can explain the situation from a personal perspective. She can remind the budget committee that last year the roof was only patched, not replaced, and that it was then damaged by a severe storm. This informed approach bolsters the property director's recommendations and supports budget requests.

Organizations that incorporate integrative, collaborative language in an administrator's job description demonstrate a commitment to good property management. Following are some examples:

- Protects site and facility assets for the long term
- Promotes integration of program and property work

Thoughtful decisions by the administrator are needed for property management.

- Keeps the board informed of site and facility plans, progress, and concerns
- Implements the board's strategic decisions concerning site and facilities by partnering with the property director to develop **tactical plans**
- Decides the best staffing structure based on input from site management
- Oversees the hiring and supervision of the site and facility staff
- Oversees sound fiscal management of the property
- Promotes stewardship of the environment
- Ensures that the organization's **risk management** plan includes site and facilities
- Oversees regulatory compliance
- Oversees a safe environment for the participants, volunteers, and staff

These statements describe the broad responsibilities and authority the administrator has for the property. Success starts at the top of the organization, so craft well-written job descriptions.

The administrator who takes his site and facility responsibilities seriously is invaluable for the long-term viability of the property. He is the final decision maker for approving prioritized projects, sets the tone for the perceived importance of work, interfaces with the broader community for possible grants, is in a position to create a practical organizational chart, and champions integrating the property with the program. Having the responsibilities spelled out helps set the expectations for the work.

Creating a Unified Team

Whenever the functions of an organization are divided among people with specific expertise, staff tend to focus only on the needs of their specific areas. Even the most dedicated worker can fall prey to those deep, dark functional holes that divide staff members and create separate territories.

"Collaboration" should be the motto of anyone who supervises people. To work together effectively, staff need to see the big picture of the organization. Working independently can prevent program staff from seeing what's happening on the property management front, and it can keep property directors from understanding the impact of site and facility functions on program.

Creating the time for staff discussions is one way to help build bridges between departments.

© PhotoDisc

WHAT CAN AN ADMINISTRATOR DO?

Here are some of the ways an administrator can guide staff and set expectations for site and facilities:

- Encourage your staff to share a sense of property stewardship. Champion the philosophy that everyone is responsible for taking care of the site and facilities. Tell your staff, "We make every effort for a clean and safe property for our guests." Think proactively, and encourage your staff to do the same.

- Clearly communicate your maintenance approach to bring your staff into alignment with your goals. Define clearly the expectations and belief systems that are to govern their work. If quality and timeliness are most important, tell them so.

- Establish property management as an equal partner with all other operational areas. Take every opportunity to stress the essential role of property management in enabling your organization to achieve its mission.

- Supervise and support your property management staff, but don't micromanage. Give your staff the latitude they need to use their skills to their fullest and to initiate novel solutions to problems.

- Keep a pulse on site and facility work and issues by touring the property with the property director or site manager on a regular basis. Coordinate one of your walkthroughs with your budget cycle so that major building and repair expenses can be integrated into the next year's budget.

- Allocate time during the annual planning process for staff to coordinate the functions of site and facility maintenance, fund development, and programming activities.

- Ask everyone to report their concerns, suggestions, and ideas promptly. A sample maintenance request and suggestion form is provided in tool 3.1 later in this chapter.

The responsibility for collaboration should not rest solely on the shoulders of the organization's administrator. Everyone on staff must commit to working as a team. A successful administrator knows that bringing about effective collaboration among staff requires an integrated approach to property management.

People as Your Eyes and Ears

Your people are an important source of information about what needs to happen in the site and facility arena. Acting as your eyes and ears, everyone using or working on your property can bring diverse and valuable perspectives to the property management process.

For example, a staff member stops you to say that the toilet in the restroom is leaking. This information proves valuable—you're able to repair the seal promptly, thus avoiding possible flooding. The staff member's heads-up saves your operation time and money.

Maintaining this kind of relationship with vigilant staff members can help you learn about and address site- and facility-related needs throughout your organization. It also lays the groundwork for a we-all-help-each-other culture.

Maintenance Requests and Suggestions

Administrators must give staff the opportunity to provide input into aspects of site and facilities. Because your staff act as your eyes and ears, they might have specific knowledge and suggestions that might help to make your facilities and program a better experience for participants. However, don't stop with the staff. The voices of volunteers and participants also need to be heard. Verbal suggestions from everyone are always welcomed, but having a written form is better. It also helps to remember items when they are written down. Maintenance request and suggestion forms offer an excellent way to collect suggestions and input from staff, volunteers, and participants. You can use a form similar to the one shown in tool 3.1.

Put the forms where they are easily accessible. It may be in the office, in a central lobby, in a common activity area, as part of a participant orientation packet, or for conference centers, in individual bedrooms. You may consider asking similar questions on an evaluation form or checkout sheet as well.

Follow a simple routine to make sure this information is collected and receives a prompt response.

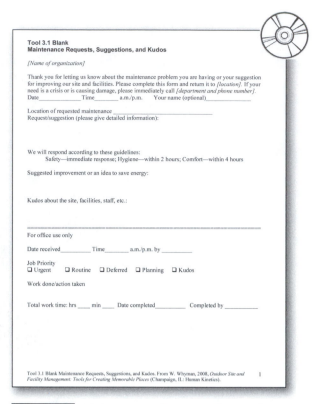

TOOL 3.1 Maintenance Requests, Suggestions, and Kudos.

- Establish one or two centrally located places to deposit the completed forms.

- Identify one person to collect the forms on a regular schedule.

- Have this person log each request or suggestion and disseminate it to the appropriate manager for action. Information may need to go to the property director, the guest services manager, or in a few cases, directly to the administrator. At predetermined times, a staff person should summarize the log and how items were addressed for the administrator. This standard procedure gives the administrator a way to keep a hand on the pulse of the activities.

Make it a priority to follow up on suggestions and respond to questions. It never hurts to publicize some suggestions in newsletters or on Web sites: for example, "Thanks to an anonymous suggestion, we now have . . . ." People quickly lose interest if they believe their comments are going unread or being ignored.

Staffing for Success

Finding the right people to run an organization is a little like assembling a jigsaw puzzle. No matter where the pieces fall and how they are put together, the objective is to build a complete picture. Whether your people consist of paid staff, volunteers, or service providers under contract, your property management team must reflect the right capacity and mix of skills to meet your operational needs.

The first step in determining the staff you need is to look at your entire operation and ask yourself these questions:

- What duties must be covered by the site and facility staff?
- Where can you expect help from participants or volunteers?

Preparing for participants' fun in the snow.

Photo courtesy of Girl Scouts of Frontier Council-Camp Foxtail. Emily Smith photographer.

- What work must you keep in-house, and what work can you outsource?
- How will you balance staffing needs with budget realities?

To help you determine the number and type of staff you need based on the work to be done, use tool 3.2. Describing the work will clarify the scope of the site and facility responsibilities. It will help you determine whether you need a part-time custodian, a full-time maintenance staff person, an occasional caretaker, or a full-time person who lives on-site. The information you generate will help you describe all the tasks and thus the scope of all the property staff and volunteer work.

Remember that staffing is not a one-time event, but an ongoing, fluid process that responds as your needs change. After using tool 3.2 to set a baseline, regularly review and update the chart to keep current with your staffing needs.

Once you have completed this tool, you have the scope of the work that needs to be done. Taking this information, you can divide the work into job descriptions. There are no magic formulas to determine what will work for every organization, because the type of work, buildings, grounds, volume of participants, and organizational structure vary greatly. You will need to rely on your historical data, the information in tool 3.2, and your expertise. To align with your strategic plan, consider the following in regard to the areas of the chart in tool 3.2.

Location

How remote is the site from the town or main office? Is it easy for site and facility staff to travel to and from the site? Describe the types and conditions of the roads that staff need to travel during all seasons (freeway, highway, rural road, or unpaved). What is the distance from emergency services, such as fire, police or sheriff, ambulance, and other basic services?

Site description

How large is the site? Include the number of **acres**, types of roads, trails, forests, and infrastructure systems (septic, well).

Grounds maintenance and landscaping

**Tool 3.2 Blank
Site and Facility Staffing Needs**

Use this tool to determine the staffing levels needed, based on your programming, property, and organizational structure.

Name of person(s) completing this form_____ Date _____

Property type _____

Areas to consider	Description	Impact on site and facility staff	Type(s) of person(s) needed, skill sets
Participant and outside group rental volume			
Participant scheduling and contracting of outside user groups			
Participants—program amenities			
Participants—amount of cleaning at the end of their stay			
Participants—extent of services			
People—maintenance staff structure			
Staffing ratios—similar organizations and industry averages			
Organizational structure			
Volunteers—quantity of projects			
Land and location			
Grounds			

Tool 3.2 Blank Site and Facility Staffing Needs. From W. Whyman, 2008, *Outdoor Site and Facility Management: Tools for Creating Memorable Places* (Champaign, IL.: Human Kinetics).

TOOL 3.2 Site and Facility Staffing Needs.

How much of the land is professionally landscaped? Is the philosophy to use native vegetation, perennials, or annuals? Is there a sprinkler system, or is there enough rainfall so that no watering is required for the lawn? Is the lawn just mowed? Are fertilizers used and soils tests performed?

Natural resources

The number of acres, the organization's natural resources philosophy, the involvement in the community, and the current condition will determine the natural resources work required for the site.

Facilities description

Include the number of buildings, garages, sheds, tents, dorms, and shelters; the types of buildings, such as school buildings or an office building with a conference room; and the total number of square feet to maintain.

Program amenities

What program amenities require maintenance, such as gyms, all-purpose activity areas, swimming pools, basketball courts, climbing walls, waterfronts, and mountain bikes?

Organizational structure

What organizational issues affect the management of the site and facilities, such as the philosophy of the organization, its organizational structure, and its mission? Does the property director devote 100 percent of her time to the property, or must she balance additional responsibilities? What types of staffing and volunteer structures have worked or not worked in the past? If there is a parent organization, such as a religious organization or an agency, does the property staff share space with the main office or other properties? What are the defining boundaries? You might consider any issues that would need to be resolved surrounding autonomy, workload, and role clarity.

Risk management

What risk management responsibilities (see chapter 11) will the site and facility staff have? Include anything that will be outsourced and overseen by property staff members.

Staffing ratios

What type of and how many staff are similar organizations using? Talk with your neighbors and learn about their staffing patterns. Check with your association, industry, or field for norms, as well as the included CD-ROM.

Participant and outside group rental volume

Is the participant volume consistent or varying? Describe the number of participants at different times of the year: weekends, summer or winter, and so forth. How many outside groups are using a portion of the site or facilities? Are the people using different parts of the building, or are they using the land differently? For example, is one conference room being used more often than the others?

Extent of services

What is the extent of staff services? Do they just check people in and out? Provide a key? Perform full custodial and cleaning services? Are they on call 24 hours while participants are on the site?

Scheduling and contracting of outside user groups

Who answers questions, provides information, maintains certificates of insurance, signs contracts, and interprets what activities can and cannot be done on the site and in the facilities?

Maintenance

Who handles **work requests** and maintenance? A maintenance assistant? A fully skilled site manager? How are work requests submitted and responded to? Will property emergencies be handled on-site or by a call to the office?

Participant help

How much work do you expect participants to do? For example, some participants may be willing to take out the trash and sweep in exchange for a less expensive rental package.

Volunteer help

What volunteers are available to assist with the site and facilities? What are their skill sets, what **licenses** do they hold, and what is their availability?

Security

Is the organization concerned about issues such as vandalism and trespassing? What security responsibilities might site and facility personnel have?

Site and Facility Job Descriptions

Job descriptions are just that—descriptions of roles and responsibilities—but they can be much more. Job descriptions offer the chance for management to tailor jobs in a way that promotes a cross-functional approach to all elements of an operation, including property management. They can also clarify the purpose of a job and provide a detailed vision of the expected results.

Many excellent resources are available to help you write job descriptions that are effective, useful, and legally sound. In many situations, the language and format of your job descriptions will be predetermined by the format and language your organization uses. It is strongly recommended that you have all job descriptions reviewed by legal counsel or by a human resources expert. Sample job descriptions for site and facility positions are available in the appendix of this book and on the CD-ROM.

When You Need Specialized Skills

Depending on your property's infrastructure and local regulatory requirements, some tasks and work situations may require the specialized skills of a licensed practitioner. Tool 3.3 shows a blank and sample completed specialized skills inventory. Use this inventory to determine what type of staff you need to hire and which functions should be outsourced. The information from the inventory can be used to create job descriptions and staffing structures. Completing this inventory will also help you budget appropriately for outsourced services.

Licenses and certifications vary a great deal from region to region, so you will need to become familiar with your local requirements. In many areas, licenses or certifications require fees, references, proof of experience, examinations, and bonding or proof of liability insurance. Check with your local authorities to create a list of the types of work requiring licensed professionals.

Tool 3.3 Blank
Specialized Skills Inventory

Use this tool to determine the specialized skills needed, based on the projects you are doing.

Name of person(s) completing this form_____ Date _____

Type of work	Type of person to do work	Required license?*		Who does the work?			Comments
		Yes	No	Outsourced	Staff	Volunteer or gift in kind	

*License or certification is often required; verify with local authorities.
C= Certified

Tool 3.3 Blank Specialized Skills Inventory. From W. Whyman, 2008, *Outdoor Site and Facility Management: Tools for Creating Memorable Places* (Champaign, IL: Human Kinetics).   1

TOOL 3.3   Specialized Skills Inventory.

For instance, if you need staff and volunteers to drive your minibuses, you'll need to consider the type of driving expected and the duties of the driver to determine any specialized skills needed. How many vehicles does the property have? How often will they

Having staff with specialized skills makes it possible to get the work done efficiently and safely.
Photo courtesy of Camp Hickory Hill.

be used? Would a regular driver's license be sufficient, or is a commercial driver's license required? You may need special licenses or training for staff responsible for driving ATVs (all terrain vehicles) or other special vehicles.

How often do you need a plumber? If rarely, then you may want to outsource. If plumbing problems are more frequent, but the organization wants to transfer the risk of the plumbing work rather than manage the risk itself, then outsourcing is again the appropriate solution. In both cases, the work is outsourced but for different reasons.

Special Considerations for Maintenance Staff

Clarifying boundaries, expectations, and job responsibilities is key for maintenance staff employees' success on the job, as well as for creating a memorable place. These issues should be clearly addressed not just in job descriptions but also in employment agreements, employee handbooks, and personnel policies. All of these should be reviewed by your tax accountant, legal adviser, or human resources expert.

To help you intentionally assess some of the most common issues for maintenance staff, complete tool 3.4, Clarifying Your Expectations of Staff. This tool will help you see how thoroughly you've addressed these issues verbally and in your documents. The following sections address the areas you should consider as you complete the tool.

Licenses held and renewed

The organization needs to define clearly whether the organization or the individual pays for licenses required for the job. One philosophy says that the organization should pay, because it is a job expectation. The other philosophy says that holding a license is a condition of employment—the employee should have the skills to do the job, and if he left the position, he would carry the license with him. Both methods work, but you need to be consistent across all staff positions, consider the norms of the field, and understand your legal responsibilities.

Hours worked

Each organization has its own peaks and valleys in terms of the usage of the buildings and site. Nonprofits may have staff working in the day and volunteer groups using the building at night. Other organizations may have high volumes during the evenings and weekends and rent the facilities to outside groups during the regular workweek. Outdoor facilities may have their peaks during the summer and on weekends during the school year. Determining the schedule that is needed for custodial, maintenance, and property staff is key. Once determined, this schedule needs to be clearly communicated during the hiring process and then consistently applied.

In addition, backup plans and coverage should be determined for special requests, sick leave, and vacation coverage. Describe who has the responsibility of finding staff or volunteers for backup coverage, maintaining an on-call list, communicating the needs with as much advance notice as possible, contacting

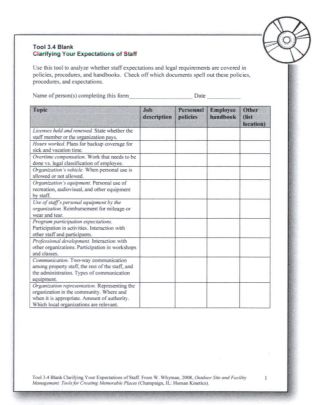

TOOL 3.4 Clarifying Your Expectations of Staff.

WHAT ABOUT EMPLOYEE BENEFITS?

Consider carefully the benefits package you offer to property management staff. Camps and conference and retreat centers nationally are offering a wide range of benefits. Many applicants will weigh the attractiveness of the benefits package along with the allure of the salary or of the camp or center itself. The benefits package for site and facility staff must align with the benefits offered to other staff.

In its benchmark survey of 456 camps, the American Camping Association (2003a) found that 63 percent of the respondents had a full-time maintenance director position. When asked what benefits they provided for that position, they reported the following:

- 87 percent paid vacation
- 81 percent health and dental insurance
- 74 percent retirement contribution
- 56 percent disability insurance
- 56 percent housing* or stipend
- 55 percent life insurance
- 50 percent utilities
- 50 percent meals
- 32 percent transportation or stipend
- 30 percent professional memberships

*Check with your tax consultant on this issue. Housing may not be considered an employee benefit if it is for the convenience of the employer.

Note that the survey asked about a general full-time "maintenance director" position. Because there are some fine nuances within this job categorization, the survey may have elicited answers about other full-time staff including property director, site manager, and so on. See the appendix for definitions of various job positions.

Adapted from *Camp Benchmarks,* American Camping Association by permission, 2003.

backup employees, and then supervising their work. Having clarity on how things work and prior **planning** helps you avoid stressful situations.

Overtime compensation

Custodial, maintenance, and property work can work like clockwork some weeks. However, because property management occurs 24 hours a day, unexpected incidents and projects must be attended to immediately—whether it is during the day or night. Outdoor properties usually require extra maintenance and property work during the summer.

Employees classified as nonexempt (i.e., paid hourly wages) need to be compensated with overtime wages in accordance with state and federal regulations. For salaried (exempt) employees, you might have a **policy** that requires them to take time off in the next payroll period immediately following the payroll period in which they worked overtime. Salaried employees working at outdoor properties may be given extra time off in the fall, after the busy summer season. Carefully work through fair and legal compensation, consulting with the experts in the field.

Personal use of the organization's vehicle

Generally, the organization's vehicle should be used only for organizational business. However, sometimes an organization may grant permission to use the vehicle in special circumstances. Other organizations may allow personal usage as a benefit. Still others may need a staff person to be on call and have the vehicle parked at his off-site house. You need to determine whether or when the organization's vehicle can be used for personal reasons. Whatever your decision, you then need to work with your insurance agent to understand the organization's vehicle policy coverage.

Personal use of the organization's equipment

The organization will probably own recreation or audiovisual equipment. If staff are allowed to use the equipment during off-hours, you will need to make sure it is returned and ready for participant use. In addition, you should determine whether participant rules apply to the staff. For example, if you have a swimming pool, must staff never swim alone? The use of personal equipment can be a benefit, yet you want staff to be safe and have equipment available for regular participant usage.

Use of personal equipment

Because of its size, the nature of its work, or its financial condition, the organization may not own a maintenance vehicle. If a vehicle is required to do the work, such as hauling materials to and from the project site, are personnel expected to use their own vehicles? If the organization does not own the power tools needed to complete a project, are staff expected to use their own power tools? Because use causes wear and tear, how will staff be compensated? For vehicles, the IRS mileage reimbursement may be used. For personal tools, perhaps a preagreed biyearly amount will be paid, so staff don't feel taken advantage of and the organization recognizes the full cost of maintenance. To protect the organization, you may have the condition that only properly working, safe tools and equipment will be used. As an alternative, you may decide to rent tools and equipment for larger projects. Whether tools and equipment are owned by the organization, privately owned, or rented, your goal is to have the right tools and equipment in safe, working order.

Program participation

You will need to determine whether your maintenance and property staff will do their work behind the scenes, be visible with that work, or interact with participants. The interaction of staff with the participants can build the credibility of your organization and make participants aware of the hard work that is done for them. How much time can the custodian join in program activities, such as discussion groups or basketball games? Can site personnel eat meals served by the organization? Are they expected to participate in specific activities? Are they expected to interact with other staff, participants, or guests? If so, how often and when? You want to protect the staff's precious time to make sure the work is done, while still allowing them to interact with participants.

Professional development

Participation in workshops, conferences, and formal classes keeps staff current on industry best practices and in touch with the professional community. Are staff encouraged and supported financially to attend? Are staff encouraged to interact regularly with other organizations to share best practices and ideas? Continuous improvement of your property requires staff to be updating their skills and learning new ways of doing projects. Organizational support in the form of time and reimbursement sends a clear message of its importance.

Communication

When things get busy, it is easy for the property function to minimally interact with the other departments. Two-way communication needs to happen between the departments. Updates and awareness of issues must be communicated from the property department to other parts of the organization. By the same token, needs, requests, news, and scheduling information must be communicated to the property staff. In addition, staff need to know when they need to be a site and facility representative on a committee.

Communication between the property director and his supervisor is important. How often do face-to-face meetings or telephone conversations occur? Are written monthly or quarterly summary reports required? When will the supervisor do walk-throughs to see and understand the issues firsthand?

What types of communication equipment are necessary and will work at the site? Two-way radios with the proper range work well with staff who are continuously mobile. Cell phones are also common for locations with cell phone coverage.

If the main office is separate from the work site, how often does the staff person need to go to the office? How will the site staff be kept informed of the organization's activities? It takes intentionality to keep remote staff connected and informed.

Representing the organization in the community

The organization needs to be connected to the local community—involved in the appropriate issues, visible, and aware of local events. Some activities may be monitored and attended by nonproperty staff. For topics relating to the site and facilities, it may be appropriate for the property staff to be involved. On-site staff may be involved in natural resources topics, as well as maintaining good relationships with government agencies, surrounding property owners, and key local organizations. Although staff members should be encouraged to represent the organization, they need to know which types of long-term decisions need organizational approval, rather than individual approval. Examples include controversial issues such as new development, natural resources management techniques, and authorization to sign contracts.

Where and when is it appropriate for property staff to act as representatives of the organization in the community? What are the local organizations that are important to have a good working relationship with? What property issues require administrative or board approval?

On-site staff considerations

Staff who live on the site have additional considerations. They need a clear separation between work and personal time or space. Frequently they are on call during off-hours. For example, if a waterline breaks in the middle of the night, staff may be expected to respond during their downtime. If not handled well, these issues can quickly cause on-site staff burnout, an air of entitlement since they are doing extra work that is not required of other staff, or even unexpected legal situations regarding overtime.

Housing provided by the organization

Because of the nature of the work, the work hours, or the need for security, a staff person may be needed to live on the property in the role of caretaker, site manager, property director, or administrator. In addition, religious leaders may be provided housing on-site or at a separate property location. Whatever the case, when housing is owned by the organization, certain issues need to be addressed.

First, not all housing can be considered a benefit for tax purposes. Sometimes housing is provided for the "convenience of the employer." Another issue is determining when religious organizations are exempt from paying property taxes on housing provided by the organization. A few resources are located on the CD-ROM, but make sure you seek tax and legal counsel to interpret these issues and others for your state.

Commonly, the organization pays for the utilities if housing is provided; staff members pay for renter's insurance to protect their personal possessions and contents. The housing may be partially furnished, fully furnished, or not furnished at all. Sometimes a damage deposit is required. Pets and smoking may or may not be allowed. A procedure that is fair to the employer and employee should stipulate the circumstances under which supervisors can enter the house unescorted. You will also want to be clear about when other staff can visit staff members at their houses, to be respectful of the separation of work and nonwork space.

Both the organization and the staff member should be clear about the responsibilities associated with housing to avoid any misunderstanding and to follow any legal requirements.

Livestock and farm animals

If the acreage is sufficient in size and if zoning allows, on-site staff may wish to have personal animals. Animals should not be a disruption to the activities of the property; they should be healthy and not interfere with wildlife. Under what conditions can dogs, horses, chickens, or other personal animals be kept on the property? Are they in separate facilities? Are documented health immunizations required? Will they be penned separately from the organization's animals?

A Treasured Resource: Volunteers

Volunteers are a cherished resource for any organization. Volunteers may already be involved in your organization, in parent groups in schools, alumni groups, and service project groups. In addition, some people are looking for ways to improve the local community, service clubs are looking for worthwhile projects, high school students need community service hours for graduation, corporations want to sponsor community days, Girl Scouts want to do Gold projects, Boy Scouts want to do Eagle projects, people in national service organizations are looking for volunteer opportunities, and people need to perform community service hours required by the courts. Each of these groups of volunteers represents people with unique experiences, expectations, and needs. As a result, you may work differently with each group as you manage your site and facility projects.

Most volunteers are motivated by a true desire to make a difference. Volunteers can be your ace in the hole, enabling projects to be completed that might otherwise languish

Do you have projects that are appropriate for a variety of volunteers?

because of lack of funds or labor. Be aware of the following volunteer trends when selecting and designing volunteer projects:

- Volunteer time is limited, and sometimes decreasing. According to an Independent Sector report, *Giving and Volunteering in the United States* (2001), 44 percent of the adult population volunteered 3.6 hours per week, a total that may be divided among many organizations. In the 2004 Canadian study, *National Survey of Giving, Volunteering and Participating*, 45 percent of the population volunteered an average of 3.2 hours per week. (Mandatory community service is included in these estimates.)

- People who volunteer often want shorter-term or one-time activities rather than long-term commitments.

- Regulations are specifying the types and boundaries of some volunteer work.

- Through the use of technology, volunteers across the country can do volunteer work at home.

There is some new vocabulary to reflect these changes such as *episodic volunteers* for short-term volunteers and *virtual volunteers* for volunteers who work at a distance. When soliciting volunteers, use language that speaks to their needs. In addition to describing the work, describe how the work will be done, such as, "work with a team to tear down the old drywall" or, "learn new skills from our team captain extraordinaire." You'll also want to describe the impact the work will have on the participants, such as "taking down the old fence will clear the way for the next crew to install a playground fence that will be safer for the children."

Keep in mind that people volunteer for many reasons. It is not just about the work getting done; people are looking to feel a sense of accomplishment, do something much needed for participants, learn a new skill, or meet people with similar values. Organizations benefiting from the work of volunteers must give something back to those volunteers, while keeping an eye on the mission of the organization. Invite volunteers to join in the activities by enthusiastically expressing your appreciation and showing them how they can connect.

When people think of site and facility volunteers, they commonly think of physical projects: painting, cleaning, electrical work, and so on. However, an effective volunteer program for site and facilities can include work such as cooking a meal for the work crew, being a photographer, or conducting research on the Internet at home. Others may wish to contribute gifts in kind or send a check. Other volunteers are interested in planning, organizing, or governance committee work. Consider all forms of volunteering in your planning. Clearly define the volunteer opportunities available and outline the time requirements for each.

To keep your volunteers feeling valued, strive to place them in jobs that best use their talents. A useful method is to briefly describe the projects that need to be done and allow volunteers to sign on for specific projects. This helps establish a clear understanding between the organization and the volunteer. When you use a chart similar to tool 3.5, potential volunteers have a clear

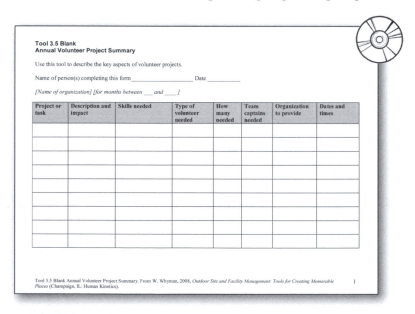

TOOL 3.5 Annual Volunteer Project Summary.

understanding of their commitment, the value and importance of the project, and the expectations of the project.

Volunteers come to organizations in a variety of ways. Some call, e-mail, or send a resume when they move to town. Others you may actively recruit because of the skills you know they have. A general organizational interest survey is helpful if you have many volunteers to keep track of. The types of site and facility questions you can include are shown in tool 3.6. You may also decide to combine the interest survey with a volunteer application to include a photograph release and background check.

The interest survey can help you determine the depth and breadth of a volunteer's skills. After discussions with the volunteer for clarification, you are ready to verify any specialized skills by verifying photocopies of licenses and certifications, performing reference checks, or having a tryout period with an initial project.

When you collect volunteer information, it is essential to have a process in place for accessing and using the data. For example, if you need plumbing help, you need to be able to easily use your list or database to find volunteers with plumbing licenses without looking at every paper form. Being organized gives you a short list from which to choose.

Volunteers should be successful, and their projects should be worthwhile to the organization. The last thing you want is for a staff member to have to redo a volunteer project because it was not done well. This is frustrating for volunteers and staff alike. Thus, select, design, and supervise projects so all can be successful.

A high-quality volunteer program can add depth, value, support, and financial savings to the organization. However, a successful volunteer program doesn't just happen. It takes hard work by the volunteer coordinator, volunteers, and staff. The program is not just about getting the work done successfully; it is also about focusing on the volunteers themselves. The organization needs to care for the volunteers, use their strengths, respect their time, and provide a fantastic experience—all while keeping the needs of the organization in mind.

The tasks for organizing a volunteer program can be grouped into five parts as described in the Working Effectively With Volunteers sidebar. Addressing the five points of the star in figure 3.1 creates star volunteers and star projects.

Tool 3.6 Blank
Volunteer Interest Survey

[Name of organization]
[Welcoming message, how this form will be used to match skills and interests with the organization's needs]

Name _____ Today's date _____
Address _____
City _____ State _____ Zip _____
Home phone _____ Work phone _____ Cell phone _____
E-mail address _____

Availability
General dates and times available _____
____ Occasional one-time projects
____ Ongoing project. I can volunteer about ____ hours per month.

Interests
I am interested in the following volunteer opportunities (check all that apply):
____ General projects
     ____ Gardening
     ____ General maintenance
     ____ Noxious weed inventory
     ____ Painting
     ____ Trail maintenance
     ____ Other. Please list area(s) of interest _____

____ On-site ranger
     ____ Substitute for during busy times or cover during vacation.
     ____ On-call for peak seasons to be another pair of hands
     ____ Other. Please list area(s) of interest _____

____ Nonphysical work
     ____ Checking in people during the volunteer event
     ____ Computer data entry
     ____ Computer database design
     ____ Cook or food preparer, lunch
     ____ First aid or EMT
     ____ Photographer
     ____ Planning committee member
     ____ Writer for newsletter articles
     ____ Other. Please list area(s) of interest _____

Tool 3.6 Blank Volunteer Interest Survey. From W. Whyman, 2008, *Outdoor Site and Facility Management: Tools for Creating Memorable Places* (Champaign, IL: Human Kinetics).   1

TOOL 3.6   Volunteer Interest Survey.

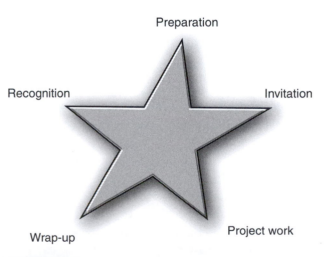

FIGURE 3.1   Volunteer star: Steps for successful volunteer projects.

WORKING EFFECTIVELY WITH VOLUNTEERS

There are five points for managing your volunteer program (see figure 3.1.) to make it stellar.

PREPARATION

- Develop and implement a clear risk management plan for volunteer work. (See chapter 11 for risk management concerns in working with volunteers.)
- Investigate and clarify regulations and codes pertinent to the projects.
- Develop an annual volunteer project chart that includes the details of timing, specific skills required, and number of people needed (see tool 3.5). Include direct project work (skilled and general work) and indirect work (first aid, photography, cooking, publicity, article writing, database work, virtual research). Where possible, schedule tasks around the volunteer's schedule, provide flexibility, and offer options. Include appropriate projects for youth and older adults. Can a nonskilled crew prepare the materials for the skilled labor a week prior?
- Develop an annual wish list of gift-in-kind needs, including supplies and materials for work projects.
- Prepare written materials, such as job descriptions, a photography release, agreements (expected hours, milestones, benchmarks, and project begin and end dates), applications, and a volunteer handbook (with policies and procedures).
- Do you need a volunteer planning committee?

INVITATION

- Coordinate with the publicity person to highlight volunteer opportunities and their beneficial impact on participants. Publish in newsletters and on the Web, send e-mails, and post on strategically located bulletin boards.
- Collect volunteer applications. Input information in a volunteer database.
- Use screening techniques: Check licensing, verify work experience, gather references. Verify skills using an external source when appropriate.
- Match volunteers' work styles and philosophies to the organization's mission, needs, and strategic plan.
- Confirm project information to volunteers, including dates and times, meal(s), materials to bring, and clothing.
- Sign written agreements as appropriate.
- Hold an orientation and give general information about the organization: its mission, policies, and procedures; the impact of the volunteer program; and benefits. This may be done at the start of the project work.

PROJECT WORK

- Don't waste a volunteer's time. Be completely organized when volunteers arrive to work. Have tools and supplies assembled and prepared as appropriate.
- In case of emergency, have communication equipment, a first aid box, and an emergency vehicle ready.
- Conduct a training specific to the project, including expectations, the availability of first aid, project hazards, and skill training.
- Plan for volunteers to be supervised by skilled people who focus on the safety of volunteers and the quality of work. Choose team leaders who have the required lead-

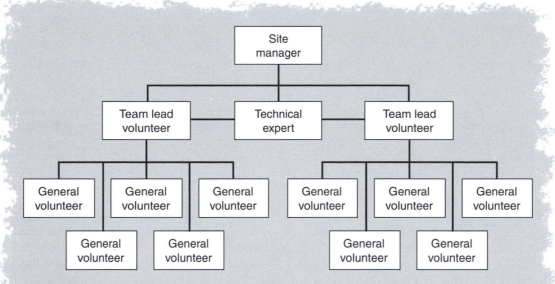

FIGURE 3.2 Volunteer organization chart. For larger projects, using an organization chart can help to organize the volunteers into smaller groups, with a preassigned team leader for each group. This organization chart illustrates a possible worker matrix, including paid and volunteer supervisory staff and volunteer workers.

ership skills, and provide leader orientation for those leading large groups or projects. Designate a "technical expert" to assist as necessary. For instance, a team leader who is a professional painter may act as the technical expert on preparing aged wood siding for repainting. Figure 3.2 illustrates a possible supervisory structure using paid or volunteer supervisory staff with volunteer workers on a short-term project.

WRAP-UP

- Clean up, gather tools, collect trash, and protect work that isn't quite finished.

- Gather volunteer feedback about their experiences using a project evaluation such as shown in tool 3.7. Provide a way for volunteers to turn in the evaluation anonymously to make sure you get the "real scoop." Be sure to address any complaints immediately. The compiled information can be used in newsletter articles, as an evaluation tool, and as data for planning other events. Comments given under the "what

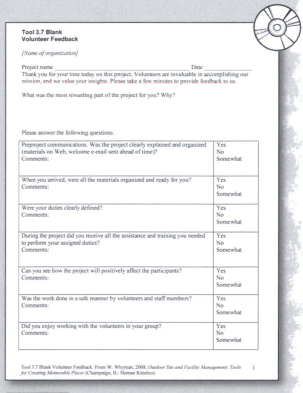

TOOL 3.7 Volunteer Feedback.

continued

continued

was the most rewarding" section make great additions to the publicity for your next volunteer opportunity.

- Evaluate volunteers, as applicable.
- Keep records, including the number of volunteers, the total hours worked, and any incidents that occurred. Summarize volunteer evaluations and project evaluations. Use the results to improve the next project and strengthen your volunteer initiatives.

RECOGNITION

- Express appreciation to each volunteer. Volunteers should feel good about the contributions they've made.
- Publicize the work that the volunteers have done in newsletters and on the Web.
- Plan for volunteer recognition awards or events.
- Hang signs or plaques on the project highlighting volunteer work.

Volunteer Boards

The last group of people needed for the site and facilities is the volunteer board. Usually the board provides oversight; sets the course for the site, facilities, and program (through a strategic plan); fulfills legal requirements and fiduciary responsibilities; and ensures that activities are in alignment with the mission. The board's role is to balance the vision of the organization with budget realities and implementation constraints. They think strategically, anticipate the future, and steer the organization in the intended direction using the resources available. This contrasts with the role of staff, who focus on **operations,** develop tactics for achieving specific aims, and manage day-to-day activities.

Volunteer board members play a key role in your site and facility management plan by doing the following:

- Ensuring program quality for future participants by protecting the organization's investment in **real property** and maintaining a healthy financial position
- Looking at whether the present site and facilities align with the organization's mission and whether things are on track today to reach the envisioned future
- Providing a fresh pair of eyes, using their strategic perspective

The board should be given a bird's-eye view of the finances and work. A list of questions the board can discuss are found in the Does Your Board Have the Right Information? sidebar.

A smoothly running volunteer program can be a good source of candidates for the board of directors and board committees. Although the nominating committee will have established criteria and will be looking to have a balanced board, it can be helpful to have one or two people on the board who also have some property skills along with their governance skills. The specific skills will depend on the needs of the organization.

As with other volunteers, volunteer board members donate their time, expertise, and money and have a deep desire to contribute to the success of the organization's mission.

DOES YOUR BOARD
HAVE THE RIGHT INFORMATION?

Materials prepared for the board should provide snapshots of the "big picture" rather than focus on details. The board needs a bird's-eye view of the property's operations, not minute details. They will be most effective when supplied with monitoring tools that provide the information at the appropriate level.

The dashboard of your car gives you key indicators of your car's performance and warning indicators: speed, fuel remaining, average miles per gallon, total miles driven, service needed, and so on. One way to give a summary to the board is to develop a **dashboard** that shows the key indicators of successful property management at a glance. The one- or two-page dashboard should give the full picture of property management: the successes, key indicators, progress, concerns, and warning signs.

The board's dashboard should be written clearly and concisely using graphs, colors, gauges, and a few financial numbers. These indicators can be pulled from your strategic plan and techniques in this book. Examples may include a **Facility Condition Index (FCI)** summary, a property financial summary, a graph showing the number of property volunteers over the past five years, a red, yellow, or green indicator showing whether a major project is on target, and a metric to show the long-term progress of an environmental project.

To make sure your monitoring tools provide the appropriate level of detail to support board decision making, ask yourself how you can address the following questions and involve your administrator or board liaison in developing the best format in which to present the data.

MAINTENANCE

- What did maintenance cost this year compared with last year? Why is it going up or down? What percentage of the total budget is spent on maintenance?
- Is there a current preventive maintenance plan for the site and facilities?
- Is there a 5- or 10-year replacement schedule for equipment?
- What are the implications from regulatory agencies' inspection summaries?

FUND-RAISING

- Does the gift-in-kind acceptance policy cover all aspects of the organization, including donations of physical assets and services to the site and facilities?
- Do certain site and facility issues need concentrated fund-raising?

LONG-TERM VIABILITY

- Does the organization's insurance policy adequately cover the assets and manage the risks?
- Are financial reserves adequate to cover insurance deductibles for loss of a building, damage from vandalism, or damage from a natural disaster?
- What plans are in place to ensure that all projects are funded, including long-term repairs and major improvements (e.g., raising fees, securing loans, or seeking grants)?
- Does the **capital budget** take at least a five-year view rather than a one-year view?
- Is a board dashboard regularly updated to monitor the important aspects of site and facility management?
- Does the property director's work extend beyond day-to-day operations to include the long-term future of the site and facilities?

Boards need time to work together to develop their overall strategy, which includes the property. If the board is not familiar with the property, you might invite them to have one of their sessions at the property.

Photo courtesy of Jon O'Brian YMCA Onyahsa.

Your People = Your Success

People are a key focus for any organization wishing to strengthen its property management program. Whether staff, administrators, volunteers, or board members, people can bring the insight, knowledge, and skills needed to manage all aspects of your operation effectively.

To make the best use of these all-important assets in managing your property, you should review carefully what work needs to be done, create a structure that supports this work, and use staff and volunteers effectively. An organization that honors and respects its human assets reaps a great reward; their commitment and dedication help carry out the organization's mission successfully.

BEST PRACTICES: STAFF

✓ The administrator's job description includes site and facility responsibilities.

✓ Site and facility staffing matches the needs of the organization.

✓ The needs and expectations of staff who live in housing owned by the organization have been articulated (see tool 3.4).

✓ Property job descriptions include appropriate responsibilities for both the day-to-day operation and the long-term future of the site and facilities.

BEST PRACTICES: VOLUNTEERS

✓ A volunteer project chart is distributed annually (see tool 3.5).

✓ An annual wish list of gift-in-kind needs is developed and distributed.

✓ A system of processes and written procedures exists for all aspects of the volunteer program.

BEST PRACTICES: VOLUNTEER BOARDS

✓ The board regularly reviews the site and facility operational plan to ensure alignment with the strategic plan.

✓ The board reviews the site and facilities' monitoring data to determine long-term viability and alignment with the organization's mission.

✓ The board has a plan to address long-term capital needs, including maintenance, rehabilitation, and replacement of aging facilities.

LAND

Surveying Your Options

Photo courtesy of Home Place Ranch.

Lasting memories are created on your land. The options available for your staff and participants are based upon the size of the land, its location, the rights, and how much your organization has chosen to develop the land. To manage the land, you need to know the property rights that you and others own, call upon external expertise, and utilize mapping as a management technique.

Whether you have a parcel of land in the city or 52 acres in a nondeveloped area, you still have many property rights. Ownership of a property comprises a "bundle of rights," which includes the surface of the land, as well as areas above and below the ground. Included are the rights to enter, use, lease, sell, or give away the real property. Also included is the right not to do any of these things. You need to work with your organization to make long-lasting, thoughtful decisions about the land.

This chapter on land encompasses the legal ownership and associated rights. It is the first of three parts of the site. The next two chapters cover the other parts of the site: grounds and natural resources. The grounds consist of lawns, landscaping, fences, parking lots, roads, signage, and walkways, while the natural resources include woodlands, ponds, wildlife, prairies, and so on.

Nature of Property Ownership

When property is purchased, inherited, or transferred, many rights are spelled out in a property title. Your property title provides a legal description of the land. It includes the number of acres and a boundary description presented in **"metes and bounds"** or in "township and range" land measures based on the **Federal Township and Range System (FTRS).** For more details on these legal descriptors, see the glossary.

Frequently, owners are unaware that they have specific rights not covered under the title but covered in other documents, such as **air rights**, water rights, and **mineral rights** (see figure 4.1). All of these rights govern *real property*, items that may be bought and sold and have a value of their own. For example, in metropolitan areas some historical buildings, condos, and churches have sold their air rights. In exchange for limiting the size of their buildings, organizations receive money, and neighboring structures and high-rises can expand.

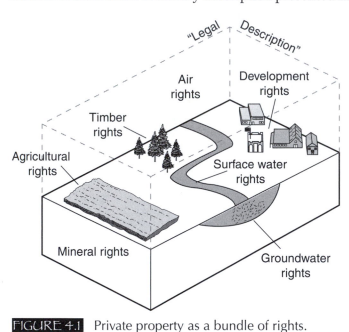

FIGURE 4.1 Private property as a bundle of rights.

Adapted, by permission, from I. Vogeler, 2006, "Private property as a bundle of rights," Geography course 270, Land Use Issues and Problems, University of Wisconsin-East Claire.

EASEMENTS AND RIGHTS OF WAY

An **easement** gives others the right to use the property. Utility companies use strips of the land to construct and maintain underground and overhead services. As a property owner, you need to keep easements clear of obstructions, such as structures and other improvements.

A **right of way** gives the right to pass through the land. Rights of way may be granted for cattle grazing; pedestrian access to an adjacent, remote property; or emergency vehicles to drive through the property to reach another property.

Various government bodies and agencies also define the limits of property ownership. They may have land use controls that apply to private property or to organizations based in federal- or state-protected forests, wildlife areas, or parks.

Rights to Water and Mineral Resources

There is no doubt that water figures prominently in your operation. The water you use may come from wells drilled into **groundwater** below or it may be diverted from a stream or lake. The water may be stored in a reservoir or other water storage facility on or off the property.

The use of water resources is governed by state law, and almost all states consider water to be a public resource. Private rights to use this public resource are often called water rights. These water rights do not give the user or landowner ownership of the resource but merely the privilege of using the water in accordance with the applicable water right.

The state laws surrounding the rights to use water are classified in two broad categories:

- **Appropriative rights** (generally western states). The rights to divert a state's public water and apply it to a beneficial use. Water rights are administered in accordance with a temporal—"first in time, first in right"—priority system based on established priority dates. In other words, if there is a shortage of supply, junior (more recent) uses are shut down until available supply is sufficient to supply remaining senior right holders.

- **Riparian rights** (generally midwestern and eastern states). The rights to use water flowing on, through, or along the borders of the land and sometimes groundwater underneath the land. The quantity of water that can be used is subject to a "reasonable use" standard. This means that you are allowed to use only your "fair share" so that downstream users also may have their "fair share." Riparian rights are usually determined in litigation.

Some western states (such as California) have a combination of both types of rights. Related water rights terms are described in the glossary. Water rights laws are administered by individual states.

To effectively manage your water rights, you must determine the following:

1. The system of water law followed by your state (riparian, appropriative, or a combination).

2. The historic water rights documents you have for your property. Once these are found, you'll need to store them carefully.

   - In appropriative states, one can often find references to such rights in legal documents (e.g., **deeds** to property). However, these documents often have only simple references to water rights without detail as to their extent. It is, therefore, usually necessary to contact the appropriate state agencies to obtain the details of any prior water rights that may have come with title to the property.

   - In most riparian jurisdictions, riparian rights to the use of **surface water** are not referenced in prior legal documents (such as deeds) and are also not on record with a state or local agency. In many cases the only available public records are court files on litigation between specific users.

   - Groundwater use requires a permit from a state or local agency in almost all states (riparian, appropriative, or a combination), although many smaller groundwater uses (below a certain number of gallons per minute) are often exempted from permitting processes. If permits are not found with title transfer documents, they can be obtained by contacting the appropriate state or local agencies.

3. Monitor the legislative activities and the legal cases in your area. By becoming familiar with the issues, you can proactively determine what may need further investigation or when you might need to consult with an expert. You'll find this information by talking with community members, subscribing to newsletters, and interacting with experts.

4. If your state requires periodic water use reports, these requirements should be carefully followed and a good record-keeping system maintained for this purpose.

5. If it is determined that your existing or historical rights or uses are insufficient or need to be modified, you should ascertain your state's requirements for filing for such changes and proceed accordingly.

Mineral rights can be just as complex as water rights. Just because your organization owns the land does not mean that it owns the rights to gas, oil, gold, or silver buried below the surface. To determine who owns the mineral rights to your land, visit the state natural resources agency, locate information on the Web, or contact your county seat.

If your organization owns the mineral rights, mining **minerals** may be another source of income for your organization. Mineral rights can be valuable commodities. Of course, a mining operation on the property may not be compatible with your mission and program. This is all the more reason to know the status of your property's mineral rights, be aware of mining activity in your surrounding community, and have a current natural resources management philosophy for your organization.

If your organization's water rights or mineral rights are uncertain, you may want to hire a real estate, water rights, natural resources, energy law, or other specialized attorney to assist you with the necessary research.

To manage your land, you need to know the geological land formations, mineral rights ownership, and the minerals that are found on your property. Once safety assessments are completed, you might offer related programs such as caving, geological excursions, and learning about historical mining.

© Corbis

Conservation Easements

Another land use issue to investigate or manage is **conservation easements**. Conservation easements serve many purposes. Some seek to restore native wetlands or other habitats. Others simply hold the land in trust and limit development. These easement programs can be initiated at the federal, state, or local level.

Many organizations enter into conservation easement agreements because they value the open space and want to curb development. Others view the restrictions or legal requirements of conservation easements as undesirable government control over their property.

Sometimes conservation easements carry benefits such as matching funds, reduced property taxes, or other financial incentives. For instance, the protected forest program in Indiana provides a significant tax deduction, and the landowner receives expert advice on managing the forest.

Work with your land trust and conservation experts to determine whether a conservation easement makes sense for your operation. Remember that such agreements are legally binding and must be entered into with care and purpose. If your site has an easement, use proper record keeping for fulfilling legal requirements.

To help you sort out and summarize these rights and ownership issues, fill in the first several sections in tool 4.1 to describe the documents you might want to store, their locations, and other pertinent information. The tool includes a column for giving a **confidence rating.** This refers to the degree of confidence you have in the quality or accuracy of the data. For instance, a 1983 map by a long-time volunteer may be more accurate than a 2006 map drawn by a new staff person. Just because a map is more recent does not make it more accurate.

**Tool 4.1 Blank
Property Record Catalog**

Use this tool to make a summary of all your site and facility records. Store the completed form in a visible location to provide easy access for all staff.

Key to formats:
Paper = Blueprints, hand drawn maps, photocopies
Scan = Graphical image of the document
Digital = CAD files, GIS, word-processed documents

Key to confidence ratings:
1 = No confidence (replace or keep for historical purposes only)
2 = Some confidence (usable)
3 = High confidence (preferred)

Name of person(s) completing this form_____
Date or revision dates_____

Legal Documents

	Date created	Description or details	Date last modified	Paper	Scan	Digital	Storage location	Backup copy location	Confidence rating
Property ownership: title or lease. Include (1) any rights included (water, mineral) and (2) any restrictions									
Sublease, other ownerships									
Conservation easement									
Covenants									
Registered historical buildings, archeological or cultural sites									
Rights of way—animal, people, emergency, other									
Surveyor—improvements									
Surveyor—boundaries									
Well permits, spring permits									
Wetland designation									
Wildlife sanctuaries									

Tool 4.1 Blank Property Record Catalog. From W. Whyman, 2008, *Outdoor Site and Facility Management: Tools for Creating Memorable Places* (Champaign, IL.: Human Kinetics).

TOOL 4.1 Property Record Catalog.

Mapping Your Site

Although of obvious importance, the legal documents of the property such as the title and easements are not as easy to understand as a graphic representation. Thus, maps are critical for good property management. They provide a variety of ways to look at property issues and help you identify potential hazards. You can use them to identify buried utility service lines, trails, and access for emergency personnel. They are also a mechanism for comparing changes over time. The uses are endless.

To begin, you'll need to gather the existing maps of the site and property that your organization has in its files. These might be historical maps, legal parcel maps, utility maps, and hand-drawn maps of an underground sprinkler system. Gather anything you can find. Next, search externally for additional maps. Any number of federal, state, and local agencies may already have created their own maps that include your property. Contact these sources and others listed in the Where to Find Existing Maps sidebar, because their maps may contain different types of information that provide different perspectives on your site.

Although you should carefully keep copies of different agencies' maps and your surveys, a greater value comes when you compile their information into one or more comprehensive maps that let you see relationships among the different components. After you have one good **base map,** you can make copies and add information to create a variety of maps showing different ways to look at your property. The number of maps you may need depends on the size of your property and the historical and current circumstances.

Although you can make maps by hand, two main types of software can help to combine several maps into one:

- **CAD (computer-aided design)**
- **GIS (geographic information system)**

These programs allow you to create a separate layer for each component, feature, or utility. Then you can turn the layers on or off to print different paper maps to use in the field, to give to contractors, to hand out to participants, or to display for planning meetings. Each layer is customizable, so you can make a system that meets your organization's needs. You may put the utilities on one layer or each utility in a separate layer. Specialized training is required to create and revise maps with CAD or GIS. You may take classes to become proficient yourself, employ students from a college or university, or hire a skilled mapmaker.

GIS software goes beyond CAD to provide the information behind your maps in database form. An example highlights the difference between CAD and GIS. Suppose CAD lets you click on a waterline to learn about its visual aspects: where it is located, the length of the line, and maybe the depth. Click on the same waterline with a GIS and you learn who installed it and when, the diameter of the line, the basic installation information, the materials used, and other information you want to keep track of.

WHERE TO FIND EXISTING MAPS

- Adjacent landowners
- Nearby city, town, or village whose jurisdiction governs the rules and regulations of your properties (you may need to contact the offices of planning, zoning, or engineering)
- Conservation or ecological research studies
- County seat
- Digital maps or **aerial photographs** available on the Web (see the CD-ROM)
- Existing architectural maps, master plans, and CAD files
- Natural resources offices, such as the Forest Service, Bureau of Reclamation, or Bureau of Land Management
- Insurance agents
- Local utility companies
- Local historical society
- Nearby parks and preserves (country, regional, or state)
- Publicly available maps at gas stations, libraries, bookstores, and sports and outdoor recreation stores
- United States Geological Survey (USGS)

A GIS is intelligent. For example, it can visually show which buildings are affected if a main waterline goes down. It can help you decide where to locate a new program area, factoring in such specific parameters as "not in drainage area, but within 500 feet of a fire hydrant, and without destroying specific vegetation." Best of all, GIS data are sharable. If your operation is near an existing GIS project, you may be able to use some of their existing data.

For an outdoor property, a GIS could focus on the natural resources and the human elements, as shown in figure 4.2. Many cities are using GIS for the management of their utilities, land parcels, tax assessments, and so on. These data are sometimes accessible either online or by special request.

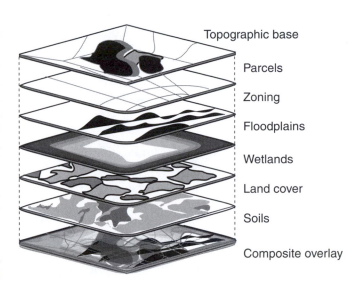

Topographic base

Parcels

Zoning

Floodplains

Wetlands

Land cover

Soils

Composite overlay

FIGURE 4.2 Each layer in a GIS is customizable to meet your needs. In addition, with GIS you can store the **metadata** in an underlying database.

Alternative Views for Maps

Here are some ideas for alternative views for maps to get you started.

- *Historical parcel map.* Shows the historical parcels of the land that now houses your operation. Frequently, privately owned lands are made up of several parcels accumulated at different times. Each parcel may have different real property rights associated with it. This is critical information for your property records and for managing the property. Use your **abstract of title** to describe the historical parcels. See the Where to Find Existing Maps sidebar for ideas on finding old maps.

    Your map should show unusual circumstances, such as the organization owning the land but another party owning certain buildings. Also show whether any restrictions are attached to a specific parcel, such as a maximum square footage for buildings constructed on the site, **covenants,** or areas of restricted use. Add to the map any historic or culturally significant sites that you need to protect, manage, or maintain.

- *Utilities map.* You need to know how utilities run through your property. In the software, put one utility on each layer. Then you can see one utility at a time, or you can see them collectively. On a paper map, if at all possible, put all types of utilities on the same map. This allows you to know the approximate location of one utility when working on another. Because many utilities are buried, it is critical to indicate as much information on the map as possible or to attach sheets with additional information. Whenever you dig to repair or install a new utility line, take photographs with prominent landmarks to document the location and type of utility buried. If the map becomes too cluttered, especially where there are a lot of buildings intersecting with utility lines, you may want to enlarge specific sections.

- *Urban utility map.* You might hand draw a map, take a digital photograph when the utility provider marks the location of buried lines, get a copy of the GIS map of your parcel, or make a photocopy of the utility easements map that came with the legal land title.

- *Adjacent property owner map.* This map is important to identify potential areas of concern such as encroachment, security risk areas, and nearby activities. You may be able to leverage your good relationships with adjacent property owners by partnering on projects that will benefit both parties such as site maintenance, habitat preservation, or boundary fencing.

- *Legal access map.* This should identify all areas where other parties have legal access to your property, such as easements and rights of way.

- *Historic activities map.* Even property rights that are no longer used may have a significant bearing on property management. Your map should answer such questions as, Was there timber harvesting? Coal mining? Silver mining? Exploratory gas drilling? Exactly where did these activities take place? Do any mining shafts or airshafts remain underneath your property? What is their location, and how are they protected? Did prior agricultural activities on the land leave overgrazed portions or the potential for toxic runoff? Historical records can help identify what rights have been used over the life of the property. What happened historically may let you know which rights have changed ownership and may have a future impact on the organization. They may also alert you to potential hazards that must be managed.

- *User map.* Show the buildings, trails, program areas, ecological areas, and historical or cultural sites. Creating this important wayfinding instrument for your participants is discussed in this chapter. Two examples are shown in figures 4.3 and 4.4.

- *Participant evacuation map.*
  - *Routes.* Includes all routes into and out of the property.
  - *Emergency routes.* Shows primary and secondary evacuation routes for each area of the property to the central gathering location.
  - *Hazards.* Marks high-risk areas or hazards (low-lying areas prone to flash floods, cliffs, flammable fuels, and so on).
  - *Common activity areas.* Marks living areas, program areas, kitchen or dining areas, and most important, the designated group meeting site(s) in case of emergency.
  - *Safety areas.* Marks the areas of temporary safety or shelter, such as reinforced buildings, basements, or buried culverts throughout the program areas.

FIELD TESTING YOUR GUEST MAP

Maps are an invaluable part of the wayfinding system. Take a copy of the map you usually give to participants and ask a few people who are new to the property for their comments:

- Is the map interesting or fun? Does it invite you to try to find the various places?
- Are roads clearly differentiated from trails?
- Can you tell where you are now?
- Where are the environmental components (compost, recycle, wetlands)?
- How far is it from where you are now to [a specific destination]?

This input can help you improve your guest map. Be sure to incorporate their advice and thoughts as appropriate.

You'll need to know the historical and culturally significant activities on your property. This 1816 cabin was part of one of Maryland's earliest free black communities, located at the Hallowood Retreat and Conference Center near Comus, Maryland.

Photo courtesy of Gary L. Pritchett.

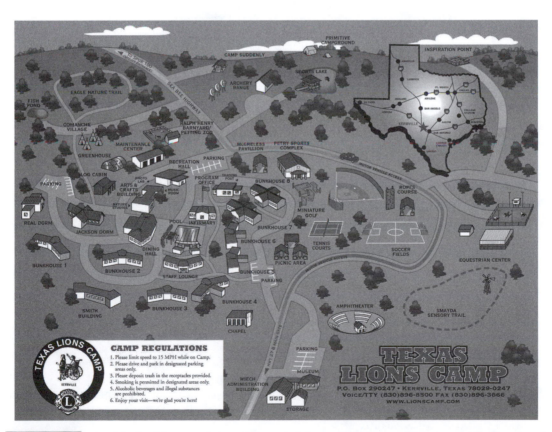

FIGURE 4.3 In this inviting participant map, bright contrasting colors are used, the map is not cluttered, and the buildings assume their real, three-dimensional shape rather than a simple two-dimensional square.

Courtesy of Texas Lions Camp–Kerrville, TX. Designer: The Clockwork Group–San Antonio, TX. Catalog #TLC02001.

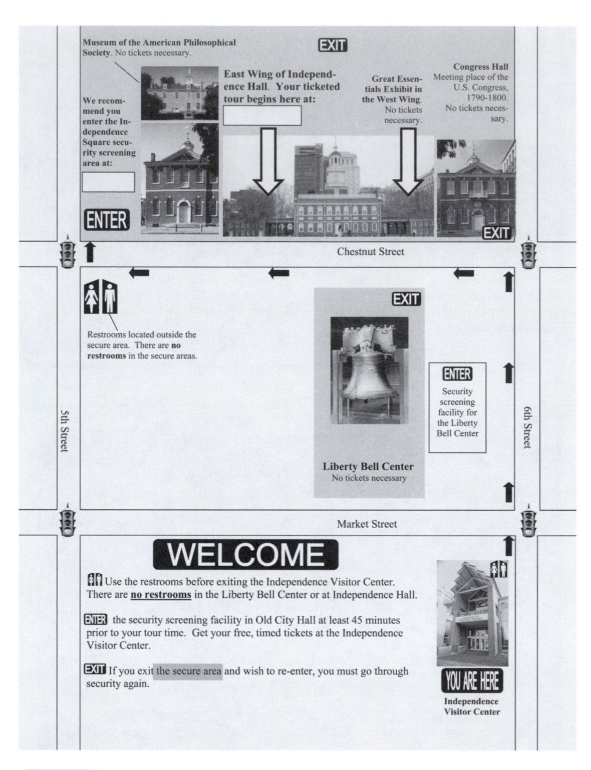

FIGURE 4.4 Using digital photographs, you can make an inexpensive but effective participant map that is easy to update. Here's an example of the National Park Service's map for visitors.

Renee Albertoli, Independence National Historical Park.

WHAT TO INCLUDE ON A UTILITIES MAP

- Communications (telephone, Internet access, cable television)
  - Location of communication lines and pedestals, whether buried or overhead, where the organization's responsibility begins (and the service provider's ends), types of cable, how deep the lines are buried
- Electrical
  - Primary and secondary shutoff points, whether the electrical lines are buried or overhead, how deep the lines are buried, where the organization's responsibility begins (and the service provider's ends), electric poles, meters
  - Backup generators (number, capacity, location)
- Fuel (propane, natural gas, heating oil, diesel, gasoline)
  - Location of tanks, whether above or below ground, capacity, primary and secondary shutoff points, how deep the fuel pipes are buried, where the organization's responsibility begins (and the service provider's ends)
- Sewer, septic
  - How deep the sewer pipes are buried, location of septic tank and leach field, access points
- Storm drainage (street drainage)
  - Location of drainage pipes, how deep the pipes are buried, disposal system
- Water system (drinking, irrigation, fire protection)
  - Storage tanks' location and capacity, required volume for emergency use, how deep the waterlines are buried, water treatment system location, shutoff valves, well locations (operating and abandoned), **spring** locations, access points, vents, control locations, meter locations

Surveyors

An essential part of your map collection is the **surveys** done by licensed surveyors. A licensed land surveyor uses precise field measurements along with interpreting deeds, maps, and other records to determine the legal locations of property lines, improvements, and so on. Clear, well-defined surveys can indicate the extent of any easements, encroachments, and unknown setbacks. They are especially useful in planning for site development and projects that are near the property lines.

You should obtain the services of a surveyor under the following circumstances:

- A boundary location is unknown or unclear.
- Property will be bought or sold.
- Improvements will be made (buildings, fences, excavation).
- Easements and rights of way need to be established.
- Timber is cut near a property boundary line.

Future Options

Managing your land is a heavy responsibility. Your land contributes significantly to fulfilling your mission and accomplishing your program goals. The decisions you make today about the land are significant, as they affect both the short- and long-term use by the participants. Thus, continue to be well-informed, stay current about property issues in your community, communicate appropriate information to your participants, update the board regularly, and involve experts.

BEST PRACTICES: PROPERTY OWNERSHIP

✓ All legal documents, including deeds, water rights, mineral rights, and so on, are kept safely.

✓ The owner names are current in the legal documents.

✓ The historical context of the local area and region (original deed, prior mining, forest clear-cutting, archeological and cultural areas) are considered in the management of the site.

✓ Water rights, mineral rights, other rights, and conservation easements are monitored, and necessary work is completed.

✓ The board or governing body is promptly informed of any issues.

✓ The organization stays abreast of regional and state regulatory activities pertaining to the land.

BEST PRACTICES: MAPS

✓ Updated maps show the names and boundaries of surrounding neighbors, easements, rights of way, and any concerns.

✓ A utilities map is maintained and updated as repairs and services are conducted.

✓ A user map is inviting and easy to use.

GROUNDS

Creating Your Setting

The grounds need to create a positive first impression from the moment when your participants arrive. Grassy areas, walkways, roads, landscaping, fences, and a host of other areas help to define your sense of place. While your participants will enjoy seeing your landscaping, many of them will also experience your grounds when they sit on a bench and talk, play on a grassy sports field, or take their dog for a walk. Underneath, invisible to the participant's eyes, is the maze of underground utility lines and pipes that serve their needs. All areas need to be well maintained for safety and creating your setting.

To make this happen, there are two broad pieces for grounds: a) the overall philosophy that describes the setting you want to create and b) using the philosophy in your day-to-day work. Based on the philosophy, you can select materials and equipment, make decisions about the type of work that needs to be done (sidewalks, wayfinding, lawns, and so on), and determine your schedule, which often revolves around the participants' needs. For example, crews will be out prior to the participants' arrival to remove snow and ice, lawn mowing will be done at a low usage time, and reinforcing a fence post will be completed only when the area is not used. However some projects are critical, such as repairing a waterline break. At that point, crews will need to secure the area for the safety of the participants. This chapter covers the many components of grounds.

Crafting Your Overall Grounds Philosophy

Every organization, regardless of the size of its property, needs to determine its philosophy about the setting it wants to create. In congruence with the mission statement, the philosophy statement guides all decisions about materials purchased and frequency of work. Will there be a mowed lawn, or will the area use rocks or wood chips? Will the flowerbeds contain perennials or annuals? Will some of the more native grasses be mowed less frequently? What types of fertilizer and **pesticides** will be used—if any at all? Will the fences be chain-link or cedar? Will walkways be asphalt or cement?

The philosophy statement needs to be one or two paragraphs in length and available to all staff members. If you have a special focus, you may want to publicly share it with all who visit your property. For example, if you have an office building in the desert, your philosophy may include a statement about your commitment to using native vegetation that has low-water needs.

Wayfinding: Beyond Signage and Maps

Feeling comfortable in a new environment is the start of a participant's memorable experience. Consistent clues for easy access to and movement throughout your property help to create for participants a positive sense of place. Navigation through a site is usually managed through a combination of signs, building layouts, landmarks, arrival points, trails, walkways, landscaping, roads, maps, lighting, and accessible staff (Aust, 2001; Muhlhausen, 2000). Together these components create your wayfinding system. To develop your system, consult with a site planner or **landscape architect,** and refer to the CD-ROM.

Organizations can easily focus on the signage component. Good signage establishes a welcoming atmosphere that helps participants feel more at ease immediately. Keep all signs focused on new visitors. What's the first sign a new person sees when she arrives on the site? Can she easily determine where she should go? Will she feel welcomed? Make a map that shows where your signs are located and the intent of each. Does each sign have a unique purpose?

As shown in the Right Sign, Right Place sidebar, signs can have a variety of purposes, but all need to be coordinated. You'll want to create a family of signs with a consistent style and color that complement your overall theme, style of buildings, and overall mission. Some operations show their logo at the bottom of key signs.

Whether you make your own signs or have a commercial business make them, you'll want to choose materials that have a long **life expectancy**. Consider materials that can survive temperature extremes, require minimal maintenance, are less susceptible to vandalism damage, and tolerate the ultraviolet rays from the sun. To extend the life of your signs, include them in your preventive maintenance schedule.

A well-conceived entrance sign welcomes people to your organization. This example shows a noncluttered sign that has the camp name and organization's logo, incorporates pleasant landscaping, and includes an inspirational quote.

Photo courtesy of Camp Classen YMCA.

RIGHT SIGN, RIGHT PLACE

Signs can fulfill a variety of purposes. Here are some of your options when considering appropriate signage:

- *Directional.* Inform people of the direction they need to take, both outdoors and indoors. Examples: road sign, "to the visitor parking lot"; sign at a fork in the trail, "mountain summit 1.3 miles" (with an arrow); trail markers along the trail to confirm hikers are on the right trail; sign telling visitors where they first need to go upon arrival, "office" (with an arrow). Some of these signs have a critical need to be seen at night, so you will need to provide lighting, add a simple reflector, or have them made of reflective material.
- *Destination.* Tell people they've arrived. Examples: building names, designated handicapped parking place, trail destinations, places of interest, room numbers.
- *Interpretive.* Describe or educate. Examples: plant species identifier, background on a historical building, plaque acknowledging the funders, photo or drawing of a vista that describes the view from a specific vantage point.
- *Inspirational.* Short text that inspires and motivates. Example: motto, scripture, poem, quotation.
- *Safety.* Inform people of potential hazardous conditions. Examples: "icy road," speed limit signs, "staff must be present."
- *Trailhead.* Use a combination of the preceding elements, including the following:
  - Map, with an arrow: "you are here."
  - Types of use (wheelchairs, ATV, pedestrian, horse)
  - Trail name
  - Types of trail markers to be found on the trail
  - Length (miles and/or kilometers)
  - Difficulty

The Art of Lawns and Landscaping

Landscaping makes you look good. The care given to landscaping quickly shows participants whether you are prepared for them and are willing to fulfill the mission. Their initial impression will last; thus, your organization should have a consistent maintenance program in place.

The first thing you will need to decide is whether the work will be done by your staff, outside contractor(s), or a combination of the two. Organizations with small properties may decide to contract all lawn care and landscaping out because there is not enough work for a staff person or they do not want to own and maintain the equipment. Some organizations decide to have staff mow the grass, but they don't want to learn pest cycles, manage the chemical treatments schedule, or take responsibility for identifying **hazardous trees;** thus, they outsource these jobs.

Your overall philosophy will come in handy when you are deciding what work you will do yourself and what work you will contract out. It sets the stage for you to clearly determine the types of services you need, the level of service you expect, the latitude of your artistic expression, litter removal, and the scheduled rotations of services. You will need to determine and communicate acceptable hours for services to be performed. You don't want lawn mower noise and equipment clutter during an important event! Also, you need to include checks on your systems as well. For example, if your lawn sprinkler system is scheduled to water at 11 p.m. when no one is around, how will you know if one of the sprinkler heads was damaged and is now a geyser? The list of expectations becomes your measurement of how the company or individuals are doing their jobs.

If you decide to outsource all or part of your lawn care and landscaping, do not just hire the cheapest contractor; equally important is how the work will be done. You'll want to have regular meetings with the supervisor of the contracted firm to oversee the work, troubleshoot any problem areas, and praise good work. The relationship between you and the outside contractor needs to be built on trust, with both parties listening and open to talking about all issues. You want someone who will take pride in her work and will take the initiative to take care of problems before she is told to do so. If there is an outsourced work crew, your job is to oversee and work with their supervisor—not to supervise.

Well-maintained landscaping creates a pleasant entrance to greet your participants.

Photo courtesy of Parks Canada Discovery Centre.

Transportation Infrastructure: A Means to Move People

People arrive, join in outdoor activities on your grounds, and then leave. Sounds simple, huh? It isn't always. You need to ensure that all areas are passable and well-maintained. Some of your challenges are standing water, **erosion,** and ice. Ensuring the safety of the participants using your grounds and avoiding user conflicts are at the top of the list of concerns.

Maintaining Parking Lots and Roads

Although participants see your landscaping, they feel your parking lot and roads. A smooth, well-maintained parking lot goes unnoticed. But a pothole when they first turn into your property? That quickly changes their perspective on your whole operation.

To give participants the best possible experience when they venture onto your property, follow these general principles:

- Look at all your roads and parking lots as a whole. What is the flow of traffic? Where does the plowed snow go? Determine and sign different types of roads: general access, maintenance roads, and so on. Do uses of the roads conflict, for example, between delivery trucks and participants? Address what you can with your existing roads, and if necessary, hire a site planner.

- Determine the specific types of parking lots and roads you need based on the region and use. Should they be asphalt, dirt, or crushed gravel?

- Manage drainage to ensure that water leaves the parking lot and roads as quickly as possible before it damages the surface and the roadbed.

- Manage runoff when it leaves the parking lot and roads.

- What type of lighting is needed? Consider the mood you are creating. How much lighting is needed in the parking lot for participants' visibility in arriving and department? How much security lighting is needed?

- Consider accessibility for staff or participants with physical challenges.

- Use only skilled personnel or contractors. Decide whether you will do the work in-house, contract the work out, or work out a partnership with a neighboring property.

- Apply your landscaping philosophy. For new construction, replant vegetation along the edges to prevent erosion and maintain attractiveness.

- Know the detailed configuration of your roads, such as the approximate slope of each road and the slope of the crown.

- Be aware of the problem areas. For example, some parts may be in the shade and thus more susceptible to ice.

- Prepare a maintenance schedule. This should include the following:
  - General maintenance, such as regraveling, regrading, resurfacing, and dust control. For example, asphalt seal coating improves the appearance and stops the water from entering the cracks, which prevents future problems.
  - Cleaning culverts of debris that could interfere with their draining function.
  - Trimming overhanging tree branches and vegetation.

People who have been involved at your operation, as well as adjacent neighbors, will have suggestions about what needs to be done on the roads with regard to the surfaces, erosion, and nearby vegetation. Your written maintenance record and knowledge of the region, climate, and type of operation can help you establish a rhythm for the work.

Select driveway lighting fixtures that contribute to the ambience you are creating.
Photo courtesy of Isabella Freedman Jewish Retreat Center.

Roads and parking lots that are well maintained present a positive appearance. Furthermore, they prevent future problems, which can degrade participants' experience and cost you additional dollars.

Sidewalks: Safety, Function, and Style

Sidewalks or walkways on your site are an integral part of your program. Participants can use the walkways for solitude, exploration, learning, and physical activity. Walkways also allow participants to move between buildings and program areas. Thus, maintaining the walkways is another important management area.

Here are some principles to consider in managing your walkways:

- What is the philosophy for the walkways on your property?
- Which walkways need lighting? What style of lighting?
- Will the walkways be edged with rocks, tree branches, low fences, or nothing at all?
- Will weed control measures be undertaken?
- Will walkways be accessible for people in wheelchairs?
- How often are they swept?
- How will your walkways be regularly maintained for snow removal and ice control?
- How often will you examine the walkways for deterioration and erosion concerns to take care of small problems before they become larger ones?

As well as being functional, walkways can be pleasant places for people to stroll and visit. They also help protect the **ecosystem** and landscaping by designating the specific foot traffic location.

Trails, Footpaths, and Pathways: Portals to Destinations

The trail led to a lovely clearing in the woods. . . .
We spent hours by the lake, just talking.

Sometimes you do not want to have a developed cement walkway. Instead, you want a simple footpath to bring people to an area, to use less costly materials, or to create a specific setting. If you have trails that lead to program areas or recreation trails, you'll need to maintain them as well.

- For dirt trails, are trail materials and erosion control materials natural or created? For example, water bars can be made from tire treads, railroad ties, lumber, or rocks. Decide on your philosophy as well as the long-term maintenance needed for these materials.
- List and categorize all your trails.
  - Do you have both activity trails and trails to buildings?
  - Do you have destinations to special features on your land, such as a cultural area or an overlook?
  - Is there a trail progression that matches the varying participant needs?
  - Are some trails available for wheelchairs?
  - Are use conflicts clearly defined? For example, if pedestrians and horses are on the same trails, who has the right of way?
- Develop a trail maintenance schedule that includes the following:
  - Vegetation trimming
  - Trash removal
  - Erosion control
  - Drainage maintenance
  - Evaluation of exposed tree roots from trail overuse
- How can you involve participants or volunteers in trail maintenance, such as picking up litter, spreading chips on the trail, or trimming overhanging branches?

The CD-ROM includes technical trail-building resources as well as techniques for building accessible trails.

Fences: Defining Areas of Use

Fences serve many purposes. They can help to define the boundary of the property, guide foot traffic, contain animals for a farm program, protect a natural area from foot traffic, add security, or act as a temporary barrier to keep people away from a hazardous construction site.

The style of your fences supports the atmosphere you are creating in your special place. A split log fence along the main entry road creates a welcoming impression. A chain-link fence could create an impression of security and limited access to visitors. In contrast, a chain-link fence around the swimming pool chemical system ensures participant safety. A chain-link fence can also be used simply to contain children's soccer balls from going into the street. You need to balance attractiveness with purpose, functionality, cost, and maintenance upkeep.

Because fences are a financial investment, take time to plan. Before beginning construction of a new or replacement fence, think carefully through the purpose of the fence, where it will be located, and the life expectancy of the materials. If you are replacing a boundary fence, you may need to hire a surveyor to determine the legal property line. Sometimes the existing fence can deviate several feet from the property line, and a survey can save money and minimize headaches in the future.

Walk-Throughs and Inspections: Taking a Fresh Perspective

Regular property work involves maintenance requests, weekly work schedules, and long-term replacement schedules. However, you'll need to step back every once in a while and look at the broader picture by taking a few walk-throughs of both your site and your facilities. These walk-throughs will give you opportunities to perform visual inspections, examine work done previously, confirm the need for scheduled work, check safety conditions, uncover additional work to be done, and discover unknown participant wear. They may also highlight an already observed deterioration made worse by hail, wind, heat, or cold.

How often should you check things? Your state's regulations and accreditation standards and guidelines provide a starting point. Use your risk management plan (see chapter 11) and your general knowledge of the site and facilities, the participant volume, and the severity of the weather in your region to determine your walk-through schedule. For example, you may conduct a walk-through twice a year—once after the rainy season and once after the hot summer—to note the impact of severe weather conditions. It would also be a good idea to take a look *during* a rainstorm to see how effectively water moves throughout the property. You may have an outside expert come out just once a year. You'll need to determine the timing and scheduling of the various walk-throughs listed in this book based on your unique property.

For a large property, the property director may be a general licensed contractor and would be qualified to perform the walk-through inspection. For a smaller property, the majority of the walk-through inspections might need to be completed by an outside expert. This is because the staff person responsible for maintenance may be hired only to perform light maintenance and custodial work and may not have the skill set needed for inspections.

The following are important considerations for all walk-throughs:

- Select carefully the person or people for each of the walk-throughs in this book; make decisions based on their assessment skills and expertise. Before engaging an outside inspector, be sure to check her background, certifications, insurance coverage, skills, and knowledge of your type of operation.

- Take note of areas where a professional may be needed or required for a part of the walk-through. A licensed inspector would be used when regulations require one, when the walk-through person is not qualified for a particular inspection, or when called for by the risk management plan. Often this professional will provide his own form; the items listed in the checklist are simply a reminder that the task needs to be completed. Examples of experts you may call include a **forester** and an electrical inspector.

- Although an on-site person may have the skills to conduct the walk-through, it can be helpful to ask an external person to conduct a walk-through to get a fresh perspective. In addition, an external person can be seen as having more authority, which helps to support a case for a project within the organization.

- Determine whether it is appropriate for the administrator to accompany the inspector during a walk-through. Her firsthand observations can be helpful for future discussions and planning sessions. You may decide, however, that it is more useful to have the administrator review the walk-through and inspection summary reports with the site personnel at a later date.

- Have the property director accompany the external inspector on the site tour to see the needs through his eyes and gather as much information as possible. Ask questions, but do not direct or try to influence him. You want to ensure his objectivity. Listen and learn from a fresh perspective, but also discuss any areas of concern. When he completes his written inspection report, you will know which areas need immediate corrective action and which areas you can incorporate into your work plan.

- Prepare a written report of your walk-though. This is important from a risk management perspective and because you need to document accurately the work needing to be done.

Remember, your staff and participants can be your unofficial inspectors on a daily basis. By training them to be observant and making it easy to submit written maintenance requests, you are never the only set of eyes looking at the conditions.

Scheduling Your Grounds Walk-Through

The previous section described the importance of walk-throughs, their value, and who should conduct them. For your property, decide the best person(s) to perform the grounds walk-through. To get a bird's-eye view of the elements in this grounds section, use tool 5.1. It includes a common set of items to examine, which is easy to modify to meet your needs.

The Network of Your Utilities

When properties are in urban environments, the utilities are often maintained by other enterprises and not your organization. Your responsibility is to know the approximate location of the service lines for the utilities, the shutoff locations, where your responsibility begins for maintenance, and any utility easements. You will need to be aware of maintenance notifications, such as changing out a gas meter. By keeping a list of all service providers handy, you can immediately call if you have any problems.

Unlike city properties, many rural properties are responsible for the majority of the utility infrastructure. They must provide for participant comfort and safety in the event of an interruption of utility services. The maintenance staff or contract workers will need to make repairs promptly, use important safety techniques such as **lockout/tagout** systems, schedule preventive maintenance, and conserve energy by installing energy-efficient devices.

As with any asset, your utilities should have a comprehensive preventive maintenance plan. But, for the most part, electrical lines, propane lines, and waterlines need just occasional **corrective maintenance**. When a problem develops, use your utility map to locate the

Tool 5.1 Blank Walk-Through: Grounds

Use this tool to assess the condition of and projects to be done with your grounds.

Note: Some of the items listed may need to be conducted by an external inspector; they are included on this list as a reminder. These external inspectors will usually provide their own written assessment forms.

Rate each listed area 1 = Poor, 2 = Good, or 3 = Very good. Note needed repairs, preventive maintenance, or improvements and upgrades. The time frame refers to how soon action needs to be taken.

Name of person making inspection_____ Date_____
Number of times each year this walk-through should be completed _____
The ideal month(s) to complete this walk-through _____

Fences

	N/A	Current condition	Project(s) to be done	Time frame
Boundary corner monuments				
Corners				
Fence lines—property boundary				
Fence lines—other (animals, traffic flow)				
Gates				
Posts				
Signage				

Lawns and Landscaping

	N/A	Current condition	Project(s) to be done	Time frame
Flowerbeds				
Gardens				
Lawns				
Shrubs				
Sprinkler system				
Trees				
Water features (garden ponds, fountains)				

Tool 5.1 Blank Walk-Through: Grounds. From W. Whyman, 2008, *Outdoor Site and Facility Management: Tools for Creating Memorable Places* (Champaign, IL.: Human Kinetics). Adapted from: Boy Scouts of America. 1975. *Camp Property Management.* Girl Scouts of the U.S.A. 1998. *Property Management in Girl Scouting.* Sharpe, G., C. Odegaard, and W. Sharpe. 1994. *A Comprehensive Introduction to Park Management.*

TOOL 5.1 Walk-Through: Grounds.

area to repair. Good maintenance records will help you see where repeated breakage might indicate a more serious problem. For example, if a particular waterline breaks frequently, you might want to replace a longer segment around the cluster of breaking points.

One area of special concern with utilities is participant safety. Utility service areas should not be accessible to participants. This includes water treatment areas, water heater controls, water well controls, and some heating and cooling thermostats.

Utility inspections are commonly conducted by qualified external personnel, such as electricians and heating fuel technicians. Utility inspections are usually conducted yearly, but the frequency for your property will depend on the regulations in your area and your risk management plan. Use tool 5.2 to guide your walk-through for utilities.

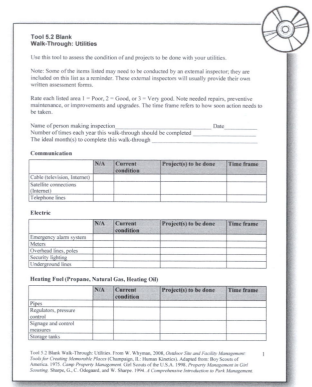

Tool 5.2 Blank
Walk-Through: Utilities

Use this tool to assess the condition of and projects to be done with your utilities.

Note: Some of the items listed may need to be conducted by an external inspector; they are included on this list as a reminder. These external inspectors will usually provide their own written assessment forms.

Rate each listed area 1 = Poor, 2 = Good, or 3 = Very good. Note needed repairs, preventive maintenance, or improvements and upgrades. The time frame refers to how soon action needs to be taken.

Name of person making inspection_____ Date_____
Number of times each year this walk-through should be completed _____
The ideal month(s) to complete this walk-through _____

Communication

	N/A	Current condition	Project(s) to be done	Time frame
Cable (television, Internet)				
Satellite connections (Internet)				
Telephone lines				

Electric

	N/A	Current condition	Project(s) to be done	Time frame
Emergency alarm system				
Meters				
Overhead lines, poles				
Security lighting				
Underground lines				

Heating Fuel (Propane, Natural Gas, Heating Oil)

	N/A	Current condition	Project(s) to be done	Time frame
Pipes				
Regulators, pressure control				
Signage and control measures				
Storage tanks				

Tool 5.2 Blank Walk-Through: Utilities. From W. Whyman, 2008, *Outdoor Site and Facility Management: Tools for Creating Memorable Places* (Champaign, IL: Human Kinetics). Adapted from: Boy Scouts of America. 1975. *Camp Property Management.* Girl Scouts of the U.S.A. 1998. *Property Management in Girl Scouting.* Sharpe, G., C. Odegaard, and W. Sharpe. 1994. *A Comprehensive Introduction to Park Management.*

TOOL 5.2 Walk-Through: Utilities.

Utilities need to complement your overall atmosphere. This water storage tank has been painted brown to blend in with the surroundings. Other techniques are to plant bushes around the tank, build a partition wall near the utility service area, or even have fun by painting them to look like people, dogs, or other animals.

Junipero Serra County Park. Wynne Whyman photographer.

Scheduling Site Maintenance

The materials used for fences, roads, sidewalks, and so forth all have a life expectancy. You can make a long-range replacement schedule based on your projections. To organize your information, make a spreadsheet as shown in tool 5.3. You can include time lines for both replacements and larger maintenance projects. Further details about preventive maintenance and replacement schedules are provided in chapter 7 (facilities).

Tool 5.3 Blank
Replacement and Maintenance Schedule: Site

Use this tool to plan future site expenditures. For each asset, record the year installed, and then use published life expectancies to estimate when it will need to be replaced. Place an R in the replacement year to give a visual representation of how replacements will fall across years. For each item, list the yearly preventive and regular maintenance projects, and place an X in the corresponding year you are planning on doing the work. You can also record completed projects (put dates underneath the Xs). See tool 9.5 to translate this into a schedule of expenses.

Name of person(s) completing this form_____ Date or revision dates_____

Asset	Purchase year	Useful life	Replacement year	Maintenance frequency	'08	'09	'10	'11	'12	'13	'14	'15	'16	'17	'18	'19	'20	'21	'22	>'22
Utilities																				
Roads and parking lots																				

Tool 5.3 Blank Replacement and Maintenance Schedule: Site. From W. Whyman, 2008, *Outdoor Site and Facility Management: Tools for Creating Memorable Places* (Champaign, IL: Human Kinetics). Adapted from Boy Scouts 1975; ACA 1981, 2004; Girl Scouts 1980, 1998; Park Management.   1

TOOL 5.3   Replacement and Maintenance Schedule: Site.

USEFUL LIFE FOR GROUNDS

Knowing the useful life of your assets is critical for long-term financial planning and work scheduling. Following are approximate life expectancies for the most common items; life expectancies depend on the quality of material, climate, proper installation for the locale, preparation, traffic patterns and participant volume, sun exposure, and preventive maintenance.

ROADS

Asphalt: 20 years, *if* designed and constructed for heavy loads from trucks and machinery.

SIDEWALKS, WALKWAYS, AND TRAILS

- Concrete: 30-40 years
- Asphalt: 5 years, depending on design, construction, and amount of heavy traffic loads to compact the surface

FENCES

- Barbed-wire: 30 years
- Chain-link: 20-25 years
- Vinyl: Lifetime
- Wood, cedar (picket, dog ear, etc.): 20-25 years. Posts will usually rot if not well treated with a wood preservative.

continued

continued

UTILITIES

- Waterline, steel: 25-30 years, but depends on soil (some soils are very corrosive)
- Septic or sewer line, clay tile: 50+ years; PVC: forever, unless, with either one, roots get in the joints
- Septic tank: 20-30+ years
- Drain field: 10-15 years
- Gas line: depends on soil (some soils are very corrosive)
- Propane tank: 10 years

Impressions That Last

Having well-maintained grounds and an invisible, but well-maintained, utility infrastructure shows you care. Selecting and supervising quality staff and outside companies help you to consistently create the setting you want. Consistency is the key to success in grounds. Consistent safety measures for staff and participants. Preventive and replacement schedules that are consistently updated and used. Last, an updated grounds philosophy statement that is consistent with the mission and the changing perception in the local community. Grounds do matter.

BEST PRACTICES

✓ There is a current articulated grounds management philosophy that is consistent with the mission and values statements.

✓ A wayfinding system is implemented.

✓ A consistent signage system is used.

✓ A schedule for landscaping and lawn maintenance is implemented.

✓ Preventive maintenance is done for roads, parking lots, utilities, fences, signs, and walkways.

✓ A walk-through of the grounds is conducted regularly.

✓ A written procedure is available for handling dangerous chemicals, including a disposal plan to control accidental runoff.

✓ Utilities are inspected regularly.

6

NATURAL RESOURCES

Inspiration, Education, and Stewardship

Spruce Lake Wilderness Camp, the youth camping and expeditions program of Spruce Lake Retreat.

People find natural beauty inspirational. You're probably providing experiences and educational opportunities to people from urban areas who have never experienced a natural setting. Whether you have 17 acres or several hundred acres, you probably consider the outdoor experience a critical part of your programs.

In a memorable place people remember the effect of a beautiful setting on their mood and activities. If the overall area is well managed, they may not notice a few dying trees or an eroding shoreline. But because of your responsibility for the property, sometimes these will be the only things you notice! Thus, stewardship of your site's natural resources is a key piece of your job. You may be involved with forest management, **noxious weed** eradication, the impact of animals and insects, and more. You'll want to use every tool and opportunity to inform yourself, your organization, and your participants about good stewardship practices.

Natural resources management means supporting the natural ecological systems of the broader region surrounding your locale. With a comprehensive strategy to protect the ecological diversity, participant needs, and renewal of your natural resources, you'll be integrating the biological, social, and economic factors into your work. **Natural systems** are complex, so you'll need to learn as much about them as possible.

Whereas grounds management is focused on the needs of participants, natural resources management is focused on the health of the ecosystem while balancing the human interface. Grounds management may involve a weekly mowing schedule. In contrast, with natural resources management, the tools are more complex, site specific, and extend over many years—sometimes longer than a person's lifetime. You'll also need to work with specialized experts in many areas.

Starting With an Ecological Framework

Several federal agencies are concerned with the management of the nation's natural resources. The Ecological Society of America (Christensen, et al., 1996) defined a framework for interagency cooperation using eight principles of ecological management. These may help you organize your own small-scale ecological goals as part of your natural resources management strategy.

According to the Ecological Society of America (ESA) (Christensen, et al., 1996), "Ecosystem management is driven by explicit goals; executed by policies, protocols, and practices; and adapted by monitoring and research based on our best understanding of the ecological interactions and processes necessary to sustain ecosystem composition, structure, and function." The eight principles noted by the ESA:

1. *Sustainability.* Ecosystem management does not focus primarily on "deliverables," but rather regards intergenerational sustainability as a precondition.
2. *Goals.* Ecosystem management establishes measurable goals that specify future processes and outcomes necessary for sustainability.
3. *Sound ecological models and understanding.* Ecosystem management relies on research performed at all levels of ecological organization.
4. *Complexity and connectedness.* Ecosystem management recognizes that biological diversity and structural complexity strengthen ecosystems against disturbance and supply the genetic resources necessary to adapt to long-term change.
5. *Dynamic character of ecosystems.* Recognizing that change and evolution are inherent in ecosystem sustainability, ecosystem management avoids attempts to "freeze" ecosystems in a particular state or configuration.
6. *Context and scale.* Ecosystem processes operate over a wide range of spatial and temporal scales, and their behavior at any given location is greatly affected by surrounding systems. Thus, there is no single appropriate scale or time frame for management.
7. *Humans as ecosystem components.* Ecosystem management values the active role of humans in achieving sustainable management goals.

8. *Adaptability and accountability.* Ecosystem management acknowledges that current knowledge and paradigms of ecosystem function are provisional, incomplete, and subject to change. Management approaches must be viewed as hypotheses to be tested by research and monitoring programs.

Christensen, N.L., et al. 1996. "The Scientific Basis for Ecosystem Management." The Report of the Ecological Society of America Committee on the Scientific Basis for Ecosystem Management. Ecological Applications.

Crafting Your Natural Resources Management Philosophy

Before you begin to manage your natural resources, you will need to write a few paragraphs that describe your approach or philosophy toward natural resources management. To begin, state the number of acres owned, how the quantity and type of area (woodlands, prairie, and so on) are important, and what you hope to accomplish with the participants with the natural resources—which all tie back to your mission. The number of acres an outdoor property owns varies, and for camps and conference centers, it is noteworthy. According to the Christian Camp and Conference Association's 2005 Industry Survey, member properties averaged 242 acres, with the median being 122 acres. In its camp benchmarks survey, the American Camping Association (2003b) tallied that properties averaged 260 acres, with the median being 200 acres.

Then you may wish to incorporate some of the principles from the previous section on ecological management. Whether principles or philosophy, you need to articulate your approach to natural resources management. Once completed, this statement will guide the decisions your organization makes and help you explain your natural resources management techniques to key stakeholders.

Writing a well-crafted natural resources philosophy gives the framework for working with your participants, stakeholders, and surrounding community.

Photo courtesy of Wynne Whyman.

For example, in the overall philosophy statement, there may be a section on forest management. Some organizations justify a forest management strategy of clear-cutting if it generates much-needed income. You may find it hard to persuade people that the cash infusion comes at the expense of the landscape. You may want to pose this question: Can we generate the same amount of cash, over time, without sacrificing the landscape?

BUILDING CONSENSUS

Decisions about land use and natural resources management are better made by a group of people including board members, administrative and management staff, owners, and donors. Among the group will be many people who care passionately about the forests, lakes, meadows, and ponds that grace your property. Getting everyone to agree on a decision may be a challenge. These tips can help you work toward consensus:

- Consider using an outside facilitator. This person can help ensure that a good group process is used, build consensus, moderate discussions, manage conflict, and give everyone the opportunity to have a voice.

- Start with your mission and values statements to establish common ground. Then develop goals for the land and ecosystem based on the mission and values.

- Give the group a distinct written charge and a defined time schedule. Everyone should know the purpose of group meetings and the deadline for their deliberations.

- Develop a thoughtful, incremental process that allows time for people to gain the awareness and knowledge they need to make informed decisions.

- Involve people from both sides of controversial issues. It is better to include everyone from the beginning.

- Focus on all aspects of sustainable land use, including economic, ecological, and social factors.

Perhaps you could increase the usage of the existing facilities through different scheduling or marketing efforts. Could it generate the same amount of income during the time period between timber harvests? The discussions can be lively and ultimately point to the need for the organization's stance on this and other issues.

Staff, board members, property committee members, volunteers, community members, and other stakeholders hold varying views of land and natural resources management. Some maintain a hands-off policy, believing that people should never interfere with natural processes. Others take a conservative approach: Manage a little bit, see how it goes, then maybe manage a little more. Yet others believe in taking an aggressive approach. It should come as no surprise that educating and managing differences of opinion will be part of your task.

A collaborative, consensus-building process is needed to align all parties on a proper natural resources management strategy. Remember to use professional consultants and research to inform the crafting of your strategy. Your philosophy should be a maximum of one page in length. This makes it easy to access and insert into other documents.

Determining Priorities

Using your natural resources philosophy, and with your mission and values statements in hand, you can help your organization define the priorities for the property. Your organization might set its priorities as follows (with the highest priority listed first):

1. Protect people's lives.
2. Safeguard the facilities and other assets.
3. Maintain a healthy ecosystem to support environmental programming.

Such clearly defined priorities would provide a framework for decision making. For example, in the event of a forest fire, your staff's first priority would be to evacuate the people. Only with personal safety thus ensured would steps be taken to protect the facilities and equipment.

Taking a Natural Resources Inventory

Knowing the principles of ecological management and having defined your organization's philosophy for the site, the next step is to take a detailed inventory of your site, using tool 6.1. The tool lets you systematically record information about historical activities on the land, average precipitation and temperatures, the ecosystem, **hydrology,** natural disaster potential, and natural resources management in surrounding areas. Because this tool is a broad umbrella for a lot of areas, you may undertake an in-depth inventory in a particular area, such as surveying the **flora** and **fauna** (see sidebar below). You may also tap into the experts involved in the resources management in your area and use their inventory forms or processes. When you are finished with your inventory, you'll be more knowledgeable about the site and also aware of some of the issues on your property and in your geographical region. You need to know what you have before you can manage it.

Tool 6.1 Blank
Natural Resources: Comprehensive Inventory

Use this tool to record and summarize natural resources information, such as historical, regional characteristics, uniqueness, etc. If information is in a separate document, state the name of the document and the location.

Name of person(s) completing this form _____
Date or revision dates _____

Land Specifications
Number of acres _____
Minimum elevation _____ ft   Location _____
Maximum elevation _____ ft   Location _____

Past or Historical Uses of the Land
Logging, mining, agricultural crops, dumps (list approximate dates and activities):

Archeological and cultural activities:

Minerals identified on property:

Precipitation and Temperature

	Jan	Feb	Mar	Apr	May	Jun	Jul	Aug	Sep	Oct	Nov	Dec
Record high temperature												
Average high temperature												
Record low temperature												
Average low temperature												
Average precipitation (inches)												
Average snowfall (inches)												

Number of sunshine days per year _____
Average last frost date (spring) _____
Average first frost date (fall) _____

Tool 6.1 Blank Natural Resources: Comprehensive Inventory. From W. Whyman, 2008, *Outdoor Site and Facility Management: Tools for Creating Memorable Places* (Champaign, IL: Human Kinetics).

TOOL 6.1   Natural Resources: Comprehensive Inventory.

SURVEYING YOUR FLORA AND FAUNA

A simple inventory of the flora and fauna on your site will help you plan ways to protect your natural setting. You should also determine what pest invasions, noxious plants, and **invasive species** may be active in your area.

If plant and animal identification is not your specialty, a **biology** or environmental science department at a nearby college or university may be invaluable. They may even have students who can help you as a class project. Or, you can start with a published list of plant and animal species in your area and note each species as you encounter it on your property. Later you can refine the list by further describing the location and approximate quantity of each species.

Additional resources may be found on the Internet or by contacting your county extension service or state department of natural resources.

A clean beach provides the place for exciting programming with boats and beach ecology.
Photo courtesy of Cabrillo Beach Youth Waterfront Sports Center. Wynne Whyman photographer.

Implementing Natural Resources Projects

Using your completed natural resources inventory (tool 6.1), your awareness of the natural resources issues in your local community, and information on the Web, you can determine the environmental concerns on your property and prioritize what to address in the short and long term. You may be able to handle some projects by yourself, whereas others may require an external expert or collaboration with several property owners. Following are some questions to help you set priorities and develop plans:

1. How can you protect and improve your immediate site?

Activities that you may want to consider:

- Can you undertake local activities that protect the regional watershed? An organization cannot develop a stand-alone watershed management plan because a watershed encompasses many properties. However, an individual property owner can maintain good practices on its part of the watershed.

- Which areas of the site host unique plant or animal species? Do some areas need to be blocked off during birthing seasons? Which areas are sensitive to overuse? Which areas are sensitive to human activity?

- What natural areas do you want to restore? Is a native prairie choked with forbs? Has runoff from neighboring fields caused a frog pond to bloom with algae?

- What habitats do you want to improve? Could the meadow be made to attract butterflies or hummingbirds? Does the lake support fish?

- Do you need a **forest management plan?** Such a plan encompasses more than just trees; it usually includes soils, climate, vegetation, and wildlife. Do your research, talk with professionals, and hire a professional forester to make or update an existing forest management plan.

2. Are you taking into account the attitudes and beliefs of stakeholders?

Many people, from staff and participants to the surrounding community, have a stake in the projects you'll be undertaking. The work needs to get done, but you may have to build some lead time into the project for outreach activities to communicate with and educate these stakeholders, along with ongoing updates once the project commences.

For example, many people think that any cutting down or harvesting of trees is unacceptable. That perception among donors or other key people can lead to misunderstandings. It is important to help them understand that, when handled properly with the help of a professional forester, techniques such as tree harvesting, controlled burns, and selective mechanical thinning can actually improve the ecological health of an area and reduce the danger to people and structures.

KEEPING YOUR WATERSHED HEALTHY

Your regional watershed is critical to your ecosystem. These tips can help you effectively manage your part of the watershed:

- Restore **riparian buffers.** Create buffers along the banks of lakes and streams using trees, bushes, and grasses. The vegetation filters polluted runoff and provides a transition between the water and human activities on the land.
- Restore your beach, stream, river, wetland, or lake to its natural state.
- Manage programming activities in shallow water, so as not to degrade vegetation.
- Maintain a vegetative cover in the watershed area. Increased stormwater runoff from development can lead to soil erosion, gulleys, and a host of water quality issues.
- Control invasive and nonnative species in waterways and watersheds.
- Keep livestock out of streams.
- Protect your wellhead area from contamination. Chemicals such as pesticides and fertilizers can enter the water supply, affecting the watershed.
- Keep your septic system well maintained, and do not dump chemicals or bacteria-killing products down the drain. A failed septic tank can pollute the watershed.
- Have a written procedure for handling dangerous chemicals, including training and a disposal plan. Problem areas to address are the kitchen (grease, oil), paint products (paint thinner, paints), cleaners (polish, bleach, oven cleaner), pesticides and **herbicides,** car products (batteries, antifreeze), and program chemicals (photography dark room, swimming pool).

GUIDELINES FOR TIMBER REMOVAL

When timber must be thinned for proper growth or removed for sale, these guidelines will help you mitigate the damage to the environment and ensure that you meet your goal of a healthy forest or a worthwhile financial return:

- Hire a consulting private or government forester to oversee the work. A forester will act in the best interests of the property and your organization, not for the timber company.
- Obtain competitive bids based on a predetermined scope.
- Seek professional advice before agreeing to allow new roads to be cut through forested areas. An engineer can advise you on the design and location of a new road.

continued

continued

A planner would look at the whole picture of the property—the relationship to the existing roads, structure, programming, and atmosphere. An ecologist can evaluate the impact on the ecologic system.

- Make sure that the soil erosion and sediment control is under the guidance of a Certified Professional in Erosion and Sediment Control (CPESC). Depending on your location and forest acreage, you may need a stormwater or erosion control plan, a perimeter silt fence or other means of preventing soil from eroding off-site, and a means to cover the soil after harvest to keep it from eroding. Other practices include a "wash basin," where the mud is washed from vehicles before they leave the site, and building a gravel road into the site (which is removed postharvest) to prevent excess soil compaction and soil "tracking" in the tires and tracks of the equipment.

- Include the following in your written agreement with the contractor:

  o Stipulations regarding the cutting of any new roads

  o A revegetation plan, which varies depending on the site conditions, location, elevation, aspect, microclimate, and your desired program or use of the site

  o Clean-up specifications, so that the forester or harvester does not leave a mess for the owner to clean up

  o Penalties for cutting unmarked trees (before the truck leaves, make sure that only marked trees were cut)

  o A system to account for every load that leaves the property

3. Are you aware of and involved in activities in the community?

What's going on in the properties around you? Local **conservation** efforts are critical to your property and may influence the timing and nature of the work you undertake. Your awareness of these efforts will minimize surprises that may affect your operation. You will want an opportunity to participate, to educate yourself or the staff, and even to build participant education into your programs if appropriate.

As with other site and facility areas, it is a good idea to take a walk-through of the natural resources, using tool 6.2. This allows you to record your observations and reminds you of projects to be done. While you are taking your natural resources walk-through, you can also look for related natural resources management projects and effects. Is a fence needed to deter people from leaving the trail and cutting unwanted trails that cause more erosion problems? Is the signage "Research area—off limits unless staff is present" effective? Are the trails and wooden boardwalks through the wetland restoration project minimizing human impact and maximizing participant learning?

To accomplish some of your projects, can you participate in local and regional conservation projects that encompass

TOOL 6.2 Walk-Through: Natural Resources and Land.

Be aware of the scientific studies being conducted in your area. They can inform your organization's plan, and are possible resources for you to tap.
© Maron Shields/Aurora Photos

multiple public and private lands? These community efforts can achieve results that individuals cannot, such as total watershed protection, the creation of **wildlife corridors,** the improvement of forest health, the conducting of scientific studies, habitat protection, and species preservation.

For many of these areas, you'll probably need to consult outside experts. Contact a private forester, biologist, ecologist, botanist, the USDA Forest Service, or the state department of natural resources. To build the knowledge of your staff, have staff check Web sites, join local conservation organizations to get their newsletters, attend local workshops, use library resources, and talk with your neighbors. With care, you can take what other people have learned and apply it wisely to your property.

4. How will you translate your list of projects into a yearly implementation plan?

Having identified the short- and long-term natural resources management projects you want to begin or maintain, you will need to plan for their implementation. A single comprehensive plan may be enough to encompass all the projects and projected time lines for your organization. But you may find you need multiple written plans, one for each large-scale effort such as a wetland preservation project or an invasive species removal project.

Your plans should include an implementation schedule with critical times for you to initiate action and monitor progress. For example, in April do you need to kill the spring growth of a noxious weed species? Will you reinventory rare species every year or every other year? Will your annual **incident report** analysis include problems from nuisance animals?

Ultimately, your list of projects, subprojects, and time lines should translate into a detailed annual operating plan that provides for incremental progress each year.

Beyond Nature Identification

Living in the natural environment of your property, participants enjoy a unique setting in which to learn about natural systems. Using your existing programs, you can guide participants in a formal or informal study of nature. On the CD-ROM you'll find resources that help you share the fascinating stories of the natural world with your participants.

When the property staff and programming staff work together on natural resources programs, the programs become more meaningful. Property staff can provide an understanding of the **ecology,** history, and technical facts about the property while programming staff teach this technical information to a nontechnical audience.

Because property staff are knowledgeable about the site, involved in the local community, and working with outside experts, they can point out specific examples, suggest programming ideas, and appropriately involve the participants in accomplishing program goals. Property staff might also assist in developing signage and construction for program activities, such as bird blinds for research studies that are conducted on-site.

The natural setting is a resource that is often underused. Simple plant identification trails are a beginning, but consider truly interpreting the meanings and the compelling stories inherent in your natural resources. Identification alone is not enough. Tell the story of why plants are important, interactions between plants and wildlife, the role of people in nature, and more. The field of interpretation is rich with resources.

To enhance participants' experiences at your facility, consider focusing on a limited number of educational messages or themes. These themes or messages should be repeated consistently in programming, signage, printed materials, and anything else you produce.

Your natural surroundings offer limitless opportunities for participants. Create experiences for hands-on science education, enlighten people with compelling stories about the natural setting, and craft life-changing experiences built around inspirational areas on your property.

Photo courtesy Ellen Sanner.

Children and adults need to experience nature through opportunities they wouldn't have in urban settings. By implementing your natural resources management plan, you can teach about natural systems and what you are doing on-site.

Your Memorable Place

Natural resources are key to your programming for inspiration and education. Managing the natural environment takes knowledge and time to develop a solid plan, but it is critical for the long-term health of the ecosystem and the economic viability of your operation. Learn as much as you can, find resources, use experts, and become involved in your community's work. Then make your long-term plans and implement, monitor, and adjust them throughout the years ahead.

BEST PRACTICES

✓ There is a current articulated natural resources management philosophy that is consistent with the mission and values statements.

✓ There is a current natural resources management plan with time lines and monitoring indicators that addresses the concerns of the site.

✓ The organization is aware of and involved in natural resources activities in the community.

✓ An inventory is conducted of the trees, plants, animals, fish, insects, noxious weeds, and invasive species on the site.

✓ Help is sought from professionals (foresters, county extension agents) when dealing with invasive species or endangered species.

✓ Erosion problems are continually monitored and addressed.

✓ The organization teaches about the natural site—beyond nature identification.

✓ A walk-through of the natural resources is conducted regularly.

FACILITIES

Your Visible Identity

Photo courtesy of Heartland Presbyterian Center, Parkville, MD.

Your facilities—the buildings, meeting rooms, equipment, furnishings, decor, sheds, and program areas—collectively represent the visual identity of your operation. The atmosphere they create is critical. Facilities establish the positive "sense of place" you want participants to experience. But to do so, your facilities must match your organizational mission and reflect a high standard of care. This is the province of your hardworking, dedicated maintenance staff, volunteers, and outside contractors.

You've heard people talking about it, and you've noticed it yourself: The tables in the dining room are getting old. Their appearance is not up to the organization's standard, and much time is spent repairing one or another of them every month.

You pull out your replacement schedule, and sure enough, it's time to replace the tables. With relief, you set about ordering new ones. Browsing through furniture catalogs and Web sites, you spot a style of table that would be easy to clean. Unlike the old model, this one would be easy to move, too—a desirable feature because tables are moved so frequently for activities. You are even familiar with this table: It's the same one you ordered for the cafeteria at your previous job with the school district.

You propose a budget, noting that the price of the new tables is well within the replacement amount allocated in the capital budget. You attach a printout of the Web page showing the table, with a note saying that you believe this will be the best table for the price. All that's left is for the committee to review and approve your request.

Or so it seems. During the budget discussion someone comments on your choice of tables. These long cafeteria-style tables won't really support the small-group interaction that is the focus of your mission. Once the statement is made, it becomes clear to all that institutional-style tables don't create the comfortable, group-building atmosphere the organization wants participants to experience. The group proposes more suitable tables.

Atmosphere: Reinforcing Your Mission and Values

A table is a table, right? Four legs, flat on top, stable, high enough so people seated in chairs can get their legs underneath. As the example illustrates, a table may need to be more than a place to eat or work. It may be the focal place around which people have discussions. If your goal is an intimate setting where people feel comfortable discussing issues in small groups, small, round tables are more conducive to talk than long cafeteria tables.

On occasion, you will wear the hat of an interior decorator, analyzing whether key elements of your facility create the right atmosphere. The interior decor—furniture, colors, flooring, and accessories—must have a look and feel consistent with your organization's aims and values.

> The lines of the ceiling, colors of walls and furniture, seating arrangements and the presence or absence of light all contribute to a worshiper's experience of God and the community of faith.
>
> *Thomas, 2002*

Look no further than your nearest upscale restaurant to see how important atmosphere is to the dining experience. White linen, polished silver, and fresh flowers—even on the plates!—establish a mood of luxury to match the upscale price tag.

Although you may not have white linen, the right atmosphere is just as essential for your organization. There should be no jarring notes in the decor's expression of the mission. Imagine what is needed to establish a professional atmosphere in a reception area at a nonprofit organization. The paint colors are subtle and not overpowering. Visitors find that the chairs are comfortable, the lighting is adequate, and the pictures on the walls show the excitement of the mission in action.

Atmosphere shapes what participants expect when they come. For instance, a visitor's center at a park may be upgraded with newly painted hallways and new carpeting in the latest style. But the details can convey other subtle but important messages. When the

Tables and decorations are selected as part of the ranch's mission.
Photo courtesy Twin Peaks Ranch.

facility is outfitted with the latest in energy-saving devices and fixtures, your participants can appreciate that your facilities offer the best of all worlds—modernization and good stewardship of the environment.

The exterior of your buildings is just as important as the interior for contributing to the right atmosphere. When renovating or upgrading a facility, be aware that building architecture, construction materials, and the external color scheme, among other design features, all contribute to the overall look and feel of your operation.

An increasingly popular way to shape the atmosphere at your organization is to adopt a green approach. By employing resource-efficient building techniques, recycling and composting waste, and adopting energy conservation measures, you demonstrate good stewardship of the environment and can reinforce the value of this philosophy with your participants.

Use all the expertise available to you when considering options for creating the atmosphere the organization wishes to achieve. Talk with the administrator, staff, board members, and participants. You may find a volunteer with a flair for design. Or, you may opt for the professional services of an interior designer, marketing or public relations branding expert, or **architect**, depending on the size and scope of the project.

EXPRESSING PROGRAM THEMES

Here are some ideas for elements of decor that create and sustain an atmosphere supportive of your mission and values:

- Display art and objects that illustrate program themes unique to your facility—for instance, music, sports, skis, paddles, farm tools, horse tack, and so on. See figure 7.1 for an example.

- Make sure your wall-mounted photographs are current or have historical significance and are related to the program. If the style of the picture frames is not historical or timeless, modernize them.

- Add nature to your building designs with leaf motifs, animal tracks (see figure 7.2), a mural of sea life, and the like. You can also use materials from the property during remodeling projects. For example, use trees and branches for banisters or supporting beams; use local rocks in the chimney, entryways, or landscaping.

- Replace your dated lighting fixtures with a timeless fixture style. While updating, consider fixtures that support the theme of your building or that enable you to use energy-conserving, compact fluorescent lightbulbs (see figure 7.3).

- Select furnishings with both ambience and maintenance in mind. This shows your commitment to programming and facilities working together. (See figure 7.4 for an example.)

FIGURE 7.1 Canoes are used as decorations and for functional uses throughout the camp, which has an extensive boating program.

Photo courtesy of YMCA Camp Chingachgook, Lake George, NY. Wynne Whyman photographer.

FIGURE 7.2 After the concrete was poured and while the cement was still wet, the workers imprinted these tracks on these outside stairs so it would look as though an animal walked up the stairs at Starsmore Discovery Center in Colorado Springs, Colorado.

Photo courtesy of Wynne Whyman.

FIGURE 7.3 A tree light fixture was chosen and used throughout the facilities. The style of the fixture complements the mission and environment.

Photo courtesy of Rainbow Trail Lutheran Camp. Wynne Whyman photographer.

FIGURE 7.4 Covering the lower half of a drywalled room with wood strips or paneling gives the building a camplike ambience and protects the drywall from chairs and wheelchairs, which minimizes maintenance. Campers can enjoy and fully participate in the programming without worrying about accidentally making a hole in the wall.

Photo courtesy of Easter Seals UCP, Timber Pointe Outdoor Center. Wynne Whyman photographer.

Sustainable Practices for Facilities

As part of your sustainability commitment, you and your participants can initiate small, incremental practices for your facilities. Other projects may take more time or money, and you can build them into your long-term plans. As a result, you can save money, make less of an impact on the environment, and teach participants the science behind the techniques employed. To generate excitement and inform your participants, you can describe your efforts in literature, in signage, and verbally.

Green Building Techniques

Green building means constructing healthy, resource-efficient buildings that minimally affect the surrounding ecosystem. You can use the principles of green building when you remodel, upgrade, or replace equipment in your existing facilities.

Following are some of the principles of green building (Adapted from BuildingGreen Inc., 2001). A wealth of additional information is available in the Resources section on the CD-ROM.

- *Safeguarding water and water efficiency.* Install low-flow toilets, showers, and faucet aerators. Where appropriate, use a natural wastewater treatment system. Minimize chemical usage in wastewater and protect the watershed. Consider incinerating or **composting toilets.** Use only biodegradable or nonphosphate soaps and detergents.

- *Energy efficiency and renewable energy.* Use designs that provide a high R-rating for walls and ceilings. Insulate your hot water supply lines. Install high-performance windows. Pay attention to power consumption when purchasing appliances and equipment. Use solar heating and high-efficiency lighting. Add and use devices that gather wind or solar power when possible, and capitalize on solar lighting systems as appropriate. Consider separate heating and cooling systems for large buildings, allowing selective use of energy based on current occupancy.

- *Conservation of materials and resources.* Minimize waste, spillage, pilferage, spoilage, and misuse of building materials during construction. Use recycled, renewable, and reused building materials. Avoid using materials that generate pollution or toxic materials during manufacture or use. Use lumber from Sustainable Forest Initiative (SFI) or Forest Stewardship Council (FSC) certified sources, indicated with a SFI or FSC label.

- *Sustainable site planning.* Locate new buildings to minimally affect the environment. Orient buildings to maximize winter sunlight and use natural cooling breezes in summer. Minimize the impact on trees and topsoil during construction. Design for timeless architecture and for opportunities to create communities of people.

- *Indoor environmental quality.* Design to achieve maximum fresh-air ventilation. This minimizes exposure to radon and mold and mildew problems.

Adapted from *Camping Magazine* by permission of the American Camping Association, Inc. American Camping Association, Inc. © 2003.

You'll need to make a commitment to do what is feasible, based on staff resources, monies, and time. Architects, land use planners, energy contractors, and local sustainable grassroots organizations are all good resources for learning about green building techniques.

The Living Machine is designed to accelerate nature's own water purification process through a series of biological cells that are integrated into indoor and outdoor garden spaces.

Photo courtesy of Bob Gratias, YMCA Camp Seymour.

This 70-year-old building, which has been a school, a convent, and elderly housing, was retrofitted and certified with a **LEED**-NC 2.1 GOLD Rating.

© denmarsh photography.

Recycling and Composting

Instead of paying for trash removal, organizations are setting up and maintaining cost-effective and easy-to-implement recycling and composting programs. This is also an example of putting the organization's values in action. Here are some of your choices.

- *Recycling or trash?* Your organization will generate a large amount of trash when the facilities are being used. You may want to institute a recycling program for materials that can be recycled in your community. Recycling should not be the sole responsibility of the site and facility team—engage the entire staff in carrying out your plans and educating participants. Multiple containers, clearly labeled for recyclables (plastic, aluminum, glass, cardboard, and so on) and placed next to conveniently located trash containers, will facilitate collection. Remember to have procedures to recycle any special materials, such as compact fluorescent lightbulbs and regular fluorescent straight tubes.

- *Composting versus garbage?* Flowers, shrubs, trees—in fact any of your landscaping—will benefit from a quarterly addition of freshly composted material. Although sometimes more difficult to institutionalize than recycling, collecting vegetable scraps from the kitchen and fallen leaves from the landscape can be incorporated into a successful program. Start with one of the excellent resources on composting and then analyze your collection opportunities. Coordinate with other staff to teach composting techniques and involve participants in organic gardening projects. Some organizations use their kitchen waste in farm animal programs.

Energy Conservation

Without question, you will realize the largest savings by efficiently managing energy consumption. A proactive approach to conserving electricity, heating fuel, and water can deliver real results. An energy conservation audit, such as the one in tool 7.1, is a good first step to saving money. The audit takes note of what you already do to conserve energy and suggests what more you could be doing.

Your electric company is a good resource for money-saving conservation measures. The employee who works with architects on new construction is likely to have the most up-to-date knowledge. Have this person help you evaluate the number and type of meters you use and your rate schedule. After this conversation, you may adjust the meter types or the number of meters you have. As an alternative, you may find it cost effective to supplement with a generator during peak times to avoid energy rate surcharges. Another resource is a state government organization that can help to evaluate your utility usage, offer alternatives, and inform you of rebate programs.

Tool 7.1 Blank
Energy Conservation Audit

Use this checklist to develop creative ideas for saving money by conserving energy. Customize and add items that are appropriate for your operation.

Name of person(s) completing this form _____ Date _____

Awareness of Energy Use

	Yes	No	Somewhat	N/A	Comments
A mechanism is in place for participants, staff, and volunteers to report needed repairs and suggestions for conserving energy.					
Gasoline consumption is recorded and evaluated.					
Heating fuel (propane, natural gas, heating oil) consumption is recorded and evaluated.					
Electricity consumption is recorded and evaluated.					
Water consumption is recorded and evaluated.					
Alternative energies are considered and used as appropriate.					
Energy Star products are used in all areas: appliances, heating and cooling, electronics, lighting, exit lighting, and office equipment.					
Old motors, compressors, and appliances are refurbished or replaced (older, unmaintained equipment can draw more energy).					

Vehicles

	Yes	No	Somewhat	N/A	Comments
Cars and trucks are warmed up while being driven rather than during a long warm-up idle.					
Vehicles are shut off, not idling, while the driver and occupants are talking with staff, volunteers, and participants.					
Vehicles are regularly tuned, and tires are inflated to their proper pressure.					
Vehicles are cost effective for the function they perform (e.g., golf carts or small utility maintenance vehicles are used instead of pickup trucks).					
Trips for supplies are consolidated into the minimum number.					

Tool 7.1 Blank Energy Conservation Audit. From W. Whyman, 2008, *Outdoor Site and Facility Management: Tools for Creating Memorable Places* (Champaign, IL: Human Kinetics).   1

TOOL 7.1   Energy Conservation Audit.

You'll also need to look at heating and cooling areas. If large auditoriums, conference rooms, activity areas, or religious areas are used only a few times a week, look to see how you can save money when they are not in use. If you are renting rooms when they are not being used for programs, always evaluate the cost of additional energy usage and staffing against the additional revenue. Sometimes it's not cost efficient.

One of the best ways to see whether your conservation efforts are making a difference is to log the monthly usage of your utilities. Logging utility usage is also a good way to monitor seasonal trends and utility expenses. A simple form for logging your electrical usage each month is shown in tool 7.2. With simple adaptations, you can use the tool to track gasoline and heating fuel consumption as well. If you manage your own water, whether you are required to or not for your water rights, a good practice is to have a meter on the well that will help you to monitor how much water you are using. Then calculate the gallons used per participant per day, both for educational purposes and to keep historical data for trends and potential future regulatory issues.

Safety Measures

Atmosphere is not the only thing you'll need to create through facility design and maintenance. In these safety-conscious times, organizations must place safety and security front and center.

Tool 7.2 Blank
Electric Meter Readings

Use this tool to record monthly utility expenses to analyze trends.

Meter # _____ Meter type _____ Location _____

Record the meter readings at the same time, either at the beginning of every month or when the meter is read (e.g., the 10th of the month).

	Year ____				Year ____			
	Beginning reading	Ending reading	kW used	Total cost	Beginning reading	Ending reading	kW used	Total cost
January								
February								
March								
April								
May								
June								
July								
August								
September								
October								
November								
December								

Tool 7.2 Blank Electric Meter Readings. From W. Whyman, 2008, *Outdoor Site and Facility Management: Tools for Creating Memorable Places* (Champaign, IL.: Human Kinetics).   1

TOOL 7.2 Electric Meter Readings.

Many of your guests likely come from urban settings. A stay at your outdoor property may be an altogether new experience for them, which naturally can trigger feelings of anxiety and insecurity. Just as you provide clear signage and adequate illumination for buildings and walkways, you should also give careful consideration to interior design elements that contribute to a sense of trust. Interior lighting and secure doors and windows can play a key role in making your guests feel safe and comfortable in unfamiliar surroundings.

A consideration of safety and comfort logically leads to the issue of security. Security, a concern for all organizations, involves much more than just the physical barriers on your site. It also involves the activities of staff. Staff members should make participants feel welcome and acquaint them with the facilities. Perhaps a staff person can sit at the entrance to both welcome people and provide security. Guests should find staff accessible, and every staff member should watch for unknown people at all times. The staff can implement safety procedures (such as the buddy system with children), conduct routine patrols, maintain proper adult–child ratios, periodically visit the less-used areas of the property, and rehearse emergency protocols that may include local authorities.

Another area to include in your security system is equipment such as mechanisms to summon help and alarms to make participants aware of immediate problems. The facilities and grounds can also be part of your security plan. See the Resources section on the CD-ROM for information on Crime Prevention Through Environmental Design **(CPTED)**, which covers facility design and location, lighting, maintaining fences, and trimming shrubs that obscure windows.

Setting up an appropriate security system is beyond the scope of this book. You will need to examine your circumstances carefully, as described in chapter 11. You might also consider getting the help of a professional to create a comprehensive security plan.

FIRST IMPRESSIONS

Ask a few of your first-time guests to tell you their first impressions of your facility. Note whether the overall appearance of your site and facilities increases their trust factor. Ask whether they feel safe and why or why not. A few questions can help identify areas in need of improvement.

Cleaning and Janitorial

Cleaning, cleaning, cleaning. It is ongoing. You clean to make a good appearance, but more than that, you clean for safety, such as cleaning the grease from a hood and vent over the stove in the kitchen to prevent a fire. Vacuuming helps the carpets last longer. You clean showers to remove pathogens. In all these areas and more, you want to be as efficient and effective as possible with your cleaning procedures to give your participants healthy surroundings.

But how clean is clean? Although there is not a nationwide standard for cleanliness, a five-tier system of expectations is emerging to help guide decision making. The figures are estimates. The actual number of square feet per shift a custodian can clean will depend on additional variables, including the type of flooring, wall covers, and the number of windows, all of which must be taken into account when determining workload expectations. The statistics in table 7.1 are for schools, but these emergent norms can be used for other types of organizations as well.

Table 7.1 Establishing Expectations for Custodial Efforts

Level	Description	Number of square feet per 8-hour shift
1	This cleaning results in a "spotless" building, as might normally be found in a hospital environment or corporate suite.	10,000-11,000
2	The uppermost standard for most school cleaning, and is generally reserved for restrooms, special education areas, kindergarten areas, or food service areas.	18,000-20,000
3	The norm for most school facilities. It is acceptable to most stakeholders and does not pose any health issues.	28,000-31,000
4	This cleaning is not normally acceptable in a school environment. Classrooms would be cleaned every other day, carpets would be vacuumed every third day, and dusting would occur once a month.	45,000-50,000
5	This cleaning can very rapidly lead to an unhealthy situation. Trash cans might be emptied and carpets vacuumed on a weekly basis.	85,000-90,000

U.S. Department of Education. Institute of Education Sciences, National Center for Education Statistics.

You'll need to determine your cleaning standards, schedules, and staffing based on the number of square feet and types of facilities you manage. Writing up these procedures helps with consistency and training new staff. Do you want to use green cleaning products in some areas? Remember also to include in your procedures the disposal of cleaning chemicals in keeping with your philosophy. As part of managing the cleaning function, you might want to look at some ways to decrease work, such as installing a recessed grate before the main entrance for outdoor facilities, which removes more dirt than a simple mat.

Managing Facility Maintenance

You have created a mission-appropriate atmosphere that builds participant trust in your organization's unfamiliar surroundings. As you are perhaps only too aware, your job is not over. To be attractive and safe, your facilities need to be well maintained. In fact, it often seems as though maintenance is a never-ending task. Here are some tips to help your maintenance work run as smoothly as possible.

To manage the tasks of facility **maintenance** effectively, think of them in terms of three categories:

1. Corrective, or breakdown, maintenance
2. Preventive, or scheduled, maintenance
3. Improvements or upgrades

Table 7.2 shows examples of each category. The first column lists typical fix-and-repair projects. The second shows tasks required to keep equipment and structures in continued working order. The third shows improvements or upgrades designed to eliminate or minimize maintenance problems in the future.

From a broad perspective, you need to know what types of projects are taking your staff's time. To find out, use tool 7.3. On the form, list all the major facility maintenance tasks you and your maintenance staff completed during the last month. Then classify each task

Table 7.2   Categories of Maintenance

Corrective or breakdown maintenance	Preventive or scheduled maintenance	Improvements or upgrades
Repairing	**Preventing it from breaking**	**A better way**
Reactive	*Proactive*	*Proactive*
Clean muddy carpets often	Install grates and mats outside of doors to minimize mud coming onto floor	Change a flat roof to one with a pitch to prevent water from sitting
Unclog sewer lines	Replace roof shingles that are in poor condition	Replace corroded waterline
Repair leaking roof	Restain the siding to preserve the wood	Bury a low-hanging electrical wire that delivery trucks can barely clear
Fix broken table leg	Tighten table legs monthly	
Replace damaged door gaskets because oven door isn't closing	Regularly change HVAC filters, oil motors, and so on	

by placing a check mark in the appropriate column. Do not include guest readiness or outside user tasks such as turning up the heat for an incoming group, restocking supplies, cleaning after a group leaves, and moving equipment.

Which of your columns has the most check marks? A goal for managing facility maintenance is to minimize as many items in the corrective or breakdown column as possible. Fix-and-repair is almost always unscheduled emergency work and usually not cost efficient. Pay close attention over a period of time to those tasks that showed up in the first column. Perhaps you can devise a plan for preventive maintenance that will eliminate several such emergency repairs.

Preventive maintenance (PM) is a proactive way of working that pays big dividends. PM is a continual process, a way of planning and looking at steps that prevent future problems by addressing maintenance issues *now*. It calls for regular servicing to keep equipment and facilities in satisfactory operating condition and involves a systematic program of inspection, detection, and correction of incipient failures.

Tool 7.3 Blank
Maintenance Work Analysis

Use this form to categorize the maintenance tasks that occupy a staff person's time. List the tasks performed last month, then mark the column that best describes the type of work.

Name of person(s) completing this form_____ Date _____

Maintenance tasks performed last month	Corrective or breakdown	Preventive or scheduled	Improvements or upgrades
Total			

Tool 7.3 Blank Maintenance Work Analysis. From W. Whyman, 2008, *Outdoor Site and Facility Management: Tools for Creating Memorable Places* (Champaign, IL: Human Kinetics).   1

TOOL 7.3 Maintenance Work Analysis.

BENEFITS OF PREVENTIVE MAINTENANCE

- Contributes to the comfort, health, and safety of participants, volunteers, and employees.

- Saves money. When you control the preventive maintenance, you control your expenses.

  - Saves energy. According to a Pacific Gas and Electric Company fact sheet for HVAC systems (1997), "Cleaning dirty refrigeration coils can save 25 percent in operating cost and help to prevent early compressor failure."

  - Extends the useful life of equipment and facilities.

  - Reduces the frequency of emergency repairs, which can be costly with labor overtime and overnight shipping.

  - Reduces the need for major repairs by keeping small problems from growing into larger ones. A rainwater drainage problem noticed during a building walk-through is easier to correct than a cracked foundation later.

- Keeps your warrantees valid. Some warranties are voided if there is a lack of maintenance.

- Prevents equipment failure by having staff inspect and replace worn components.

- Allows maintenance to be performed at convenient times. Who wants to service an air conditioning unit when it is 100 degrees outside?

- Enables you and your staff to use your time more efficiently. Cuts down on unexpected repairs and service calls.

STANDARD MAINTENANCE PROCEDURES

It's a good idea to develop standard operating procedures (SOP) for all preventive maintenance. Having written SOPs promotes consistency in maintenance tasks and enables the easy transfer of knowledge when staff changes. An SOP should include the following elements:

- Name of equipment or procedure
- Date when SOP was written or updated
- Maintenance interval recommended by the manufacturer or site manager
- Brief summary or purpose of the maintenance
- Special tools required
- Safety measures
- Description of maintenance steps

You can add this information to your individual building or equipment records (see tools 7.5 and 7.6) or put SOPs together in a portable maintenance manual for staff in the field.

Documenting and Scheduling Maintenance Tasks

Your secret weapon to managing facility maintenance may come as a surprise—it's paperwork! Being systematic and intentional about paperwork, that is. Your maintenance policy, the tasks you have scheduled, the maintenance that has been completed—documenting all these processes is valuable to effective management of the work flow. It also supports your risk management plan, as you will see in chapter 11. Here are some ideas for using paperwork to your advantage.

First, document as much as possible to help you evaluate recurring problems later. Have staff or participants complete a standard work request when they alert you to a needed repair, such as tool 3.1. Carry a recording device with you, such as a small notebook, a tape recorder, a cell phone with digital photo capabilities, or a PDA. Make daily notes of things-to-be-done as you see them, creating a comprehensive to-do list.

Next, combine the work requests and scheduled servicing into a master to-do list so you can prioritize your work. Include estimates of the time needed and two money columns for estimated costs and actual costs. Also include a place to record that the work has been completed.

Although you will want to develop your own system, tool 7.4 shows one example of how to do this, based on a week's worth of work. Anything from handwritten records to a structured

Tool 7.4 Blank
Master To-Do List

Use this tool to track all work and its status. Enter a dash if there is no information.

Week of _____ Year _____

Corrective or Breakdown Maintenance

Date requested and scheduled	Date completed	Project	Work to do	Requested by	Priority	Estimated time (hr)	Actual time (hr)	Estimated cost	Actual cost

Tool 7.4 Blank Master To-Do List. From W. Whyman, 2008, *Outdoor Site and Facility Management: Tools for Creating Memorable Places* (Champaign, IL: Human Kinetics). 1

TOOL 7.4 Master To-Do List.

computer database can work—whatever suits your personal and organizational work style. Just be sure to put it all together in one place on a regular basis to give you a total picture of the work required.

Whatever system you develop, keeping reasonable but detailed records will help you document how time is spent, reveal trends, and most important, provide the basis for a written history for each building or piece of equipment. The master list also provides the information to be compiled into a summary maintenance report to the organization's administration.

Logs for compiling information about specific equipment and buildings are shown in tools 7.5 and 7.6. Again, think about customizing these for your own needs. For example, in a larger facility you may want to adapt the forms for individual rooms. As another example, you may want to adapt the form for your program buildings or for specific areas such as the gymnasium or swimming pool. As maintenance tasks are completed, copy pertinent information from the master to-do list to the individual forms for buildings or equipment. This will give you easy access to building or equipment histories, which is important when determining life expectancies and whether warranties are current.

Do you need to log every project on the individual building and equipment records? Not necessarily, but you never know what will turn out to be useful. Replacing a light switch cover seems like a small task, requiring little time and little cost. But knowing that the same cover has been damaged twice a month might be important. On the other hand, replacing a rotting window frame is definitely important. Chapter 10 provides guidance to help you decide what information is important to log.

Completing the top sections of tools 7.5 and 7.6 provides a handy inventory of your buildings and equipment assets. These forms have multiple uses besides recording maintenance. For example, you may use them when renewing property insurance and for computing the total number of square feet that your site or facility staff maintains.

As an alternative to tools 7.5 and 7.6, many specialized software packages are available for your type of organization. This maintenance information can be recorded electroni-

---

Tool 7.5 Blank
Inventory and Maintenance Log: Equipment

Use this tool to record information about the purchase, equipment features, and maintenance performed.

Complete one form for each piece of equipment. Include appliances, office equipment, HVAC systems, power tools, hot water heaters, lawn maintenance equipment, well pumps, fire suppression systems, and so on.

Name of person(s) completing this form _____
Date or revision dates _____

Equipment name _____ Location _____

Manufacturer _____ Size or capacity _____
Model # _____ Serial # _____ Inventory item # _____

Manufacturer's Web site _____
Owner's manual storage location _____ Format: electronic ___ paper ___

Year manufactured _____ Date acquired _____ Vendor _____
Donated ___ Purchased ___ Original cost $ _____
Manufacturer warranty _____ Vendor warranty _____

Life expectancy _____ years   Replacement year _____

Maintenance Parts

Name	Brand	Number	Vendor	Comments

Preventive maintenance, inspection description, and service intervals:
_____
_____
_____

Tool 7.5 Blank Inventory and Maintenance Log: Equipment. From W. Whyman, 2008, *Outdoor Site and Facility Management: Tools for Creating Memorable Places* (Champaign, IL: Human Kinetics). Adapted from: Boy Scouts of America. 1975. *Camp Property Management.* Girl Scouts of the U.S.A. 1998. *Property Management in Girl Scouting.* Murray, J. 1980. *Facility Maintenance Systems.* YMCA. 1996. *Guide to Implementing Maintenance Scheduling Programs.*   1

Tool 7.6 Blank
Inventory and Maintenance Log: Building

Use this tool to record information about the building construction, major components, and maintenance performed.

Complete one form for each building.

Name of person(s) completing this form _____ Date/revision dates _____

Building name _____ Location _____

Function _____ Use: Summer only ____ Year-round ____
Dimensions _____ Total square feet _____ Capacity _____
ADA accommodation (description) _____

Roof material _____ Wall material _____
Floor material _____ Foundation construction _____
Fire suppression type _____
Distance from fire hydrant or other water supply _____ Describe water supply _____

Septic tank location _____ Size or capacity _____
Clean-out location _____ Grease trap location _____

National Register of Historic Places: Yes ____ No ____ Comments _____
Storage location of blueprints, plans, and warranty information:
Primary _____ Backup _____

Shelter for disasters (tornados, hurricanes, earthquakes, floods):
____ Yes, location in building _____
____ No, nearest location _____

Shutoff Locations

Electric	
Heating fuel (heating oil, natural gas, propane)	
Water	

Construction Information

	Year	Total cost	Architect	Contractor	Engineer	Soils test	Surveyor
Original							
Addition or remodel							
Addition or remodel							

Tool 7.6 Blank Inventory and Maintenance Log: Building. From W. Whyman, 2008, *Outdoor Site and Facility Management: Tools for Creating Memorable Places* (Champaign, IL: Human Kinetics). Adapted from: Boy Scouts of America. 1975. *Camp Property Management.* Girl Scouts of the U.S.A. 1998. *Property Management in Girl Scouting.* Murray, J. 1980. *Facility Maintenance Systems.*   1

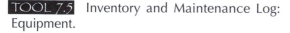

TOOL 7.5 Inventory and Maintenance Log: Equipment.

TOOL 7.6 Inventory and Maintenance Log: Building.

cally so you can easily update, copy and paste, search, and create long-range plans. Just remember to back up your electronic files regularly. You've invested valuable time in creating these records!

Tracking Equipment Maintenance

One of the items you will want to incorporate into your to-do list is regular servicing of equipment. Most owner's manuals provided with new equipment include a recommended equipment maintenance schedule. When you purchase equipment, record the details of where it was purchased, what it cost, the length of the warranty period, and the recommended preventive maintenance schedule on an individual equipment record such as tool 7.5.

If you have a great deal of equipment for which to track **preventive maintenance,** tool 7.7 can help you get organized. It's a list of all your equipment, the maintenance needed, and the recommended maintenance intervals. The form makes it easy to map out scheduled preventive maintenance tasks on a monthly, quarterly, or yearly basis. You can later transfer these scheduled tasks to your master to-do list, or just use this tool.

When mapping out your schedule, choose the best months for each type of maintenance, taking into account participant usage and your workload. For example, don't schedule the bulk of your equipment maintenance in May, when you are readying the facilities for the summer session. Try to do some of the work in April instead. In addition to maintenance tasks, many cleaning schedules must also be planned.

Tool 7.7 Blank
Equipment Preventive Maintenance Schedule

Use this tool to develop a schedule for equipment preventive maintenance.

Setup: Use the owner's manual and your knowledge to fill in the recommended maintenance interval for each item. Then shade the month best suited to such maintenance, considering weather conditions and staff availability.
Name of person(s) who scheduled the maintenance (gray portions) on this form _____
Date or revision dates_____

Workers: After you have completed the maintenance task, please fill in your initials and the date completed.

Year_____

Location	Equipment	Make and model	ID # or serial #	Maintenance task	Interval	Jan	Feb	Mar	Apr	May	Jun	Jul	Aug	Sep	Oct	Nov	Dec

Tool 7.7 Blank Equipment Preventive Maintenance Schedule. From W. Whyman, 2008, *Outdoor Site and Facility Management: Tools for Creating Memorable Places* (Champaign, IL: Human Kinetics).

TOOL 7.7 Equipment Preventive Maintenance Schedule.

Life Expectancy of Assets

Some of your maintenance tasks have to do with replacing equipment and facilities that are obsolete or worn out. Replacing items *before* they fail is a way to manage your workload and your budget and control your capital expenditures.

Most equipment and facilities have a definite life expectancy, also called useful life, that should enter into your long-term financial planning and work scheduling. Life expectancy information can usually be found in one of three places:

- Building and construction industry norms
- Product information or warranties
- Your own accurate property records

A number of references for industry norms are listed among the resources on the CD-ROM. Note that your own accurate property records are listed as a primary source. Your notes about conditions related to the item's performance, including temperature, use, materials, climate, and maintenance at your specific location, can be used to predict life expectancy.

Tool 7.5 includes a place to record the life expectancy of equipment. This information can later be combined in a yearly replacement schedule, such as shown in tool 7.8. Enter the year purchased and the useful life, and compute the year you should replace this item. Then place an X in the grid to the right to show when the item needs to be replaced.

Tool 7.8 Blank
Replacement Schedule: Facility and Equipment

Use this tool to keep track of the age and replacement of your facilities and equipment. For each asset, record the year purchased or replaced, then use published life expectancies to estimate when it will need to be replaced. Place an X in the replacement year to give a visual representation of how replacements will fall across years. See tool 9.5 to translate this into a schedule of expenses.

Name of person(s) completing this form _____ Date or revision dates _____

Asset	Purchase year	Useful life	Replacement year	'08	'09	'10	'11	'12	'13	'14	'15	'16	'17	'18	'19	'20	'21	'22	>'23
Buildings and equipment—main building																			
Equipment																			
Vehicles																			

Tool 7.8 Blank Replacement Schedule: Facility and Equipment. From W. Whyman, 2008, *Outdoor Site and Facility Management: Tools for Creating Memorable Places* (Champaign, IL: Human Kinetics).

TOOL 7.8 Replacement Schedule: Facility and Equipment.

USEFUL LIFE FOR BUILDING COMPONENTS AND APPLIANCES

Knowing the useful life of your assets is critical for long-term financial planning and work scheduling. These are approximate life expectancies for the more common items and depend on the quality of material, climate, proper installation for the particular locale, preparation, traffic patterns and participant volume, sun exposure, and preventive maintenance.

ROOFS

- Asphalt: 20-25 years
- Cedar shake, dry climate: 20 years; damp climate: 25-30 years
- Cement shingles: 40-50 years
- Fiberglass shingles: 20-25 years
- Metal: 30-50 years
- Tile: 40-50 years or more
- Gutters and downspouts, dry climate: 15-20 years; less in damp climate

BUILDING—OUTSIDE

- Wood siding: 20-25 years, if painted and maintained
- Stucco: 25 years, if maintained
- Metal: 25-30 years
- Vinyl: Life of building

FLOORS

- Hardwood floors (refinishing): 5-7 years
- Carpet: 3-4 years. Will begin to show a great deal of wear after about three years. Many motels remodel and replace carpet every three to four years.
- Soft tile (vinyl): 8-10 years

PAINTING

- Exterior: 4-5 years
- Interior paint, meeting rooms: Freshened every two or three years
- Interior paint, sleeping rooms: Sleeping rooms don't get as much wear and usually end up being repainted because of redecorating rather than any other reason.

APPLIANCES

- Air conditioners: 10-20 years
- Hot water heaters: 10-15 years
- Walk-in refrigerators: 20-50+ years; compressors: 10 years

Using the same walk-through principles described in chapter 5, you will need to visually check the condition of foundations, drainage, service points of utilities, and buildings on a regular basis. You can record your notes during your walk-throughs and inspections on tool 7.9. If you have a large operation, you may want to adapt the tool to include program facilities such as basketball courts, boating areas, or equestrian centers. While you are out, you can take digital pictures to update the **property portfolio.**

Working With Contractors

For larger or special projects you will often need to hire specialized experts. You may need to transfer the risk entailed in a repair by hiring a licensed technician who has separate insurance coverage. Or, there may simply not be enough time for the site and facility staff to do all the work.

There are several steps in the process of choosing and hiring a contractor.

Tool 7.9 Blank
Walk-Through: Facilities

Use this tool to assess the condition of and projects to be done with your facilities.

Note: Some of the items listed may need to be conducted by an external inspector; they are included on this list as a reminder. These external inspectors will usually provide their own written assessment forms.

Rate each listed area 1 = Poor, 2 = Good, or 3 = Very good. Note needed repairs, preventive maintenance, or improvements and upgrades. The time frame refers to how soon action needs to be taken.

Building or area _____
Name of person(s) making inspection _____ Date _____
Number of times each year this walk-through should be completed _____
The ideal month(s) to complete this walk-through _____

Area Immediately Outside Building

	N/A	Current condition	Project(s) to be done	Time frame
Entrance area				
Landscaping (plants, trees, shrubs)				
Parking				
Road				
Trail or sidewalk to building				

Tool 7.9 Blank Walk-Through: Facilities. From W. Whyman, 2008, *Outdoor Site and Facility Management: Tools for Creating Memorable Places* (Champaign, IL: Human Kinetics). Adapted from: Boy Scouts of America. 1975. *Camp Property Management.* Girl Scouts of the U.S.A. 1998. *Property Management in Girl Scouting.* Sharpe, G., C. Odegaard, and W. Sharpe. 1994. *A Comprehensive Introduction to Park Management.*

TOOL 7.9   Walk-Through: Facilities.

Planning and Preparation

For the project you need to have done by a contractor, you know best about the desired results. Before you start working with a contractor, put your initial thoughts to paper, being as clear as possible. Also, be as realistic as possible about your cost estimates, adequate budget monies, and the known applicable codes. Good planning is the start of a successful project.

1. Start planning the project by selecting the rough design and materials, keeping the organization's mission and theme in mind so the new work will complement existing work.

2. Incorporate ADA standards into renovations and new construction. Since the Americans With Disabilities Act (ADA) passed in 1990, many organizations have retrofitted their facilities or included physical accommodations in new construction, thus extending opportunities to previously excluded participants.

3. Develop a budget. For small projects, the history of similar efforts may provide sufficient guidance. For more costly projects, you should generally call a contractor and ask for a rough estimate. For very large projects, you may need to pay a contractor to come to the property and provide a detailed estimate, along with itemized comparisons if a number of options are being considered. Such estimates should provide separate pricing for major elements such as the foundation, structure, roof, and interior finishing.

4. Add at least a 10 percent contingency to your final estimate. This will cover changes to the design or materials and any unanticipated concerns.

5. Know how the project is to be funded. For example, your board may require that some or all of the construction costs for a building addition be in hand before beginning any work. If funding is coming from donors, the payout schedule for their pledges may affect your cash flow and in turn your construction schedule.

6. Be aware of applicable codes and their implications. Sometimes construction projects can nullify grandfathered exceptions to previous code requirements. Deed covenants and other land use requirements need to be checked before plans are designed, drawn, and implemented. Check all code requirements regarding fire, health, building, plumbing, and mechanical elements.

As a representative of your organization, you are responsible for ensuring compliance with all applicable codes, regulations, and standards. Many staff do not fully know all codes. Thus, it is important to always check with the local officials, no matter how small the project, to determine whether you need permits, what codes are applicable, what covenants apply, and the requirement for a licensed contractor to perform the work. When you hire an architect, you transfer this responsibility of knowing applicable regulations. Architects can be very helpful in interpreting the codes.

Selecting a Contractor

The contractor you select needs to be the best match for your needs, your budget, and the long-term implications of your project. Taking time to find the right contactor is critical to having your project built according to your previously laid plans and helps to minimize headaches during construction and after the project is completed.

1. Adapt a standard contract form to include your unique requirements, and have it reviewed by legal counsel for the organization. This becomes your template for a variety of contract projects.

2. Develop a written description of the project. The more specific you can be, the better—the contractor will clearly understand the project, and when it's done you'll

be happy that it is what you had in mind. If the description contains errors or fails to identify specifics, you may pay more to correct the resulting problems halfway into the project. Your project description should include the following:

- *Materials.* Note the type, quality, warranty, and brand names if you have a preference.

- *Design.* The drawn plans should incorporate details about location, materials, and specifications.

- *Schedule.* Be specific about the time frame to do the work, providing start and end dates. List any times that work must stop to accommodate normal hours of operation or participant needs. Specify when contract workers can be on the property and what locations on the property they have access to.

- *Penalty clause.* This optional clause can protect your investment if the project or subparts are not completed on time.

- *Delivery and drop-off locations.* Determine the best places to store building materials and where to permit truck access.

- *Permits.* Normally, the contractor arranges for applicable permits, but the description should confirm this.

- *Payment schedule.* Relate this directly to deliverables or completed subparts.

3. Ask several contractors for bids. Usually three bids will give you an acceptable range of choices. Select businesses that you have carefully researched to determine their reliability and the quality of their work. Business ethics dictate that you provide the same information to all bidders or run the risk of a lawsuit for unfair practices. This means sharing the answers to any individual questions with all bidders.

4. To evaluate the contractors and their bids, use a chart such as tool 7.10. The tool suggests several ways to compare the bidders. The three shaded areas are the most critical points in selecting a vendor:

   - To be certain that past work is of good quality, check references.

   - Review the written bids to be certain they are specific and complete.

   - Determine how long the firms have been in business and whether they have the appropriate licenses and certifications to do the work. Normally, bids are within range of one another. Any bid that is significantly above or below the others should be investigated carefully.

5. Adjust the contract, if necessary, and sign. For example, perhaps the contractor needs another week to prepare, and that's okay with your schedule. If you change the contract, make the change in writing and have both you and the contractor initial the change. *Always keep a paper trail when dealing with a contractor.*

Tool 7.10 Blank
Contractor Bid Comparison

Use this tool to evaluate which contractor to use. The three shaded areas are the most critical points in selecting a vendor.

Project _____
Name of person(s) completing this form _____   Date _____

Contractor characteristics and specifications	Bid 1	Bid 2	Bid 3
Name of contractor firm			
Principal contact and phone number			
Quality of similar past work (from site visits or talking to references)			
Completeness of written bid (responsiveness to your requirements; details of cleanup, care of landscaping, material quality)			
Company's financial stability, longevity, permanent address, insurance coverage, supervisor qualifications, individual licenses held			
Proposed bid price			
Completion date			
Past work experience with similar organizations (understands industry needs, limitations from regular hours of operations, conflicting uses)			

Tool 7.10 Blank Contractor Bid Comparison. From W. Whyman, 2008, *Outdoor Site and Facility Management: Tools for Creating Memorable Places* (Champaign, IL: Human Kinetics).   1

TOOL 7.10   Contractor Bid Comparison.

You have now done your due diligence in selecting a contractor, hiring based on the company's expertise and previous work. Although you will have unforeseen challenges when you begin the work, hopefully you have a contractor you can trust and who is willing to work with your needs and circumstances.

Overseeing Contract Work

Although you may have hired a good contractor, it is still important that you oversee the project. Interpretations may be needed, unexpected situations may be uncovered, and mistakes may happen. Overseeing the work helps to ensure that money is well spent and that the project meets its long-term intended purpose.

1. Know what the job is and how to measure its successful completion.

2. Designate a project manager. This person needs to have construction knowledge to oversee the quality of the contractor's work, inspect the materials, make sure the work happens according to plan, and oversee the progress of the project. This person may be a volunteer, the site manager, or, if it is a big project, an outsourced project manager. The project manager must focus on and act in the best interests of the organization.

3. Establish decision-making authority with the project manager. The project manager needs to have the authority to make decisions. You do not want the project stalled because it has to go back to the committee. Put in writing how far this person's decision-making authority extends, which staff member is authorized to make decisions on behalf of the organization, and when the organization's project manager needs to consult with the key staff member.

4. Sign and date any changes to the project plans as you go along. Change orders should be kept to a minimum, and they should be put in writing and recorded on drawings. Have the contractor bid on the change order separately. All details of the change must be in writing, and both parties need to sign the change order.

5. As you pay bills, withhold 10 percent to give yourself leverage in case negotiations become necessary. The project manager should review the quality of work and percentage of completeness before authorizing any payments. When components are quoted and billed individually, it is easier to monitor expenses and control the overall cost.

6. Make sure there is a financial checks-and-balances system in place. One method is for the project manager to review monthly financial statements from the accounting department. A second method might be to have the project manager keep a simple hand-ledger system for the major bills.

7. When the project is completed satisfactorily, and you receive the as-built plans (as applicable) and any maintenance and warranty documentation, pay the balance (the 10 percent that you withheld).

8. File the following documentation in a safe place:
   - Warranties
   - As-built plans
   - Contract
   - Electronic CAD files (if applicable)
   - Manufacturer and product description (type, color, grade), in case parts need to be replaced and colors matched later
   - Recommended maintenance intervals

9. Enter data on the appropriate inventory and preventive maintenance forms. Include service intervals, warranty information, and life expectancy.

You've invested a great deal of time and money in your project. Overseeing and knowing that the project met or exceeded expectations will give you peace of mind for years to come.

Facilities: Your Valuable Assets

Facilities are probably the most significant assets your organization maintains. Your organization invests significant funds in their construction and maintenance, and many of your programs take place within the facilities. To make the most of your facilities, create a memorable place that matches your mission. Then maintain it to a high standard by taking prompt corrective action, being proactive with preventive maintenance, hiring the best contractors, and continually monitoring to ensure that all facility needs are being addressed.

BEST PRACTICES

✓ Facilities are maintained and decorated to create a sense of place and an atmosphere consistent with the mission.

✓ Facilities and equipment are inspected regularly (at least once a year) based on regulations, weather, the needs of the site, and the risk management plan.

✓ Building and equipment inventories and maintenance logs are written and kept up-to-date.

✓ A written preventive maintenance schedule is followed for the facilities and equipment.

✓ Sustainable practices are used for buildings and saving energy.

✓ An energy conservation audit is conducted every year.

✓ Records are kept of energy usage (gasoline, heating fuel, electricity, water).

✓ The process for selecting contractors is systematic and thorough.

✓ A qualified project manager, representing the organization, oversees outsourced construction projects (as appropriate).

TIME

Making the Most of It

Property directors and their staff face an endless succession of things to do—burned-out lightbulbs to replace, water samples to collect and have tested, leaky faucets to fix, budget work to complete, seasonal staff to hire, grass to cut, and much more. The number of tasks alone is daunting, but even more challenging is finding the time to get everything done. Time is a lot like money: There's never enough of it to go around. You need to manage your time creatively and effectively to ensure an efficient operation.

Abraham Lincoln once said, "If I had eight hours to chop down a tree, I'd spend six sharpening my axe." A well-honed tool gets the job done quickly. You need a well-honed, system-based plan for getting the work done. Without such a plan, time can get away from you until what should take minutes takes hours if not days.

Smart time management is key to implementing your property management plan. Managing your time well delivers a range of benefits, some of them obvious, some less so. It improves your overall efficiency; it provides valuable strategic advantages; and it makes space for logical, creative thinking.

This chapter provides tips and tricks for effective time management. You will learn to do more in less time, be an efficient planner, and capitalize on each person's unique skills.

Learning to Be Proactive

You know the feeling. You're sitting at your desk, and you look at the clock. "Three o'clock already?! Where *does* the time go?" Another day spent working hard, but the tasks are not all done.

In the midst of all the activities, you may find yourself falling into task-focused thinking. Your list of repairs and maintenance keeps growing, so you focus more and more on running around trying to get each thing done. Or, you get bogged down in either–or scenarios, saying, for example, "I have time to do only the repairs. The more time I spend doing the repairs, the less time I have for preventive maintenance. But the more I do repairs, the more I need to do preventive maintenance."

If the majority of your time is spent doing and not planning, your work life might have a chaotic feel to it. It doesn't have to. If you feel as though you're just moving from one crisis to another—don't worry. You can change that by learning to deal with the tasks at hand in a systematic way. To have enough time on a regular basis to reflect, regroup, and plan, you need to be proactive rather than reactive.

Planning the use of your time is important because your time is valuable. Your skills should not be wasted on tasks done inefficiently or tasks that others could do. This is where planning comes in. Can you combine tasks to do them more efficiently? Can you delegate certain tasks to others? Can you devise a system to find staff or participants to help with some aspects of maintenance?

Using creative strategies to free yourself from the hands-on work will buy you time to spend on proactive work. With planning, you can identify, schedule, and perform preventive maintenance rather than being forced to react to the latest breakdown. Your focus can switch from doing specific tasks to keeping everything flowing smoothly, which is a better use of your specialized skills.

You will, of course, need to spend some extra time setting up the procedures, priorities, and work flow and discussing options with your team. As you will soon find out, however, planning time is time well spent.

Changing How You Spend Your Time

The next time you ask, "Where *does* the time go?" try answering the question for yourself. Keep a diary of how you spent your time for a whole week, or use your personal business organizer, such as a PDA or day planner, to refresh your memory, and compile your hours using the list provided in tool 8.1.

Because each person's job is unique and each organization does things differently, there are no rules for determining how much time spent in each category is enough. However, it is important to look at the bigger picture and review the list of hours spent at various categories of tasks. Are you doing work that matches your skills? Are you doing the work you were hired to do? Do the hours reflect the priorities of the job and the organization? Have you spent time doing proactive work?

Now look at your list at a finer level of detail: Which category of tasks takes up the most time? Do your hours for that category reflect reactions to complaints or last-minute requests? Which category seems to be the most frustrating? You need to take care of the reactive types of tasks, especially when there are health and safety concerns, but make a point of addressing the reasons you end up in reactive mode, and look for alternative strategies to use in the future.

If there is an area in which you would like to spend less time, choose a priority task from the list and set a goal for completion. List three specific actions that will help you accomplish this goal. For example, under "Maintenance and repairing—Facilities and Equipment," you might set as a goal, "Find ways to do things differently to save me time." Here are three specific actions you could take to move you toward that goal:

- I will find one volunteer to help five hours a month.

- With one staff person, I will discuss a task and ask for his or her suggestions for a different approach.

- I will read a book or listen to an electronic book on how to delegate tasks effectively.

When you take actions or make intentional changes in how you

Talking with another person gives you a different perspective regarding priorities, importance, and possible solutions. A dialogue can also help you garner support and integrate your work with other areas.

© PhotoDisc

Tool 8.1 Blank
Where Does Your Time Go?

Use this tool to determine where time is spent by a staff member.

Name of person completing this form _____ Date _____

Indicate the number of hours you spent last week doing the following:

Place
Mission or purpose statement _____
Other _____ _____

Participants
Guest and client services (check-in or out, moving gear, and so on) _____
Informing and training guests about the property (prior to participation) _____
Informing and training guests about the property (during participation) _____
Tours (informational) _____
Other _____ _____

People
Staff (supervising, interviewing, training) _____
Self-development (training, reading, doing online research) _____
Volunteers (managing, supervising) _____
Other _____ _____

Land
Community activities (meetings, reading, phone calls) _____
Maps _____
Water rights, mineral rights, easements, rights-of-way _____
Other _____ _____

Grounds
Landscaping and grounds (weeding, spraying, mowing) _____
Preventive maintenance and improvements (actual work) _____
Maintenance and repairing (actual work) _____
Purchasing supplies, placing delivery orders _____
Travel (to location, store) _____
Utility infrastructure _____
Vendors and contractors (supervision, soliciting bids, vendor calls) _____
Walk-throughs _____
Other _____ _____

Tool 8.1 Blank Where Does Your Time Go? From W. Whyman, 2008, *Outdoor Site and Facility Management:*   1
Tools for Creating Memorable Places (Champaign, IL: Human Kinetics).

TOOL 8.1   Where Does Your Time Go?

use your precious time, you become more proactive and less reactive. You become more effective in the work you do, and more significantly, you find the time to accomplish the important work. The important work cannot wait until tomorrow; the future of your organization's site and facilities depends on your ability to consistently find the time to address the important items.

Saving Time by Planning Ahead

Considering the range of management tasks and responsibilities you must master to be successful, you may frequently feel like the circus juggler trying to keep six assorted implements flying through the air. Even an excellent time manager may have to do some fancy juggling to keep everything airborne.

You can buy a lot of time by combining similar everyday tasks. If a project must be done on the third floor, the person can also bring tools for a project on the second floor so he won't have to return to gather more tools. Making a shopping list rather than going to the store separately for every item also saves time.

Clearly, saving time starts with planning. Another trick is to think ahead and let others help with the work at hand. For example, although the property manager may be convenient to lead a tour, a knowledgeable board member could lead the tour instead. If new lightbulbs and stepping stools are available in the main office, staff can replace the lightbulbs themselves without having to call maintenance workers. This saves time for maintenance workers to focus on projects that require more specialized skills —which is what they were hired to do.

A third way to plan ahead is to have an inventory on hand of commonly needed parts and supplies. However, this will only work if you install uniform fixtures, appliances, and equipment. Things like standard filter sizes and identical door handles allow you to have a smaller inventory on hand. With standard fixtures, maintenance workers can quickly ascertain what they need to do a job, and staff need only learn a few procedures rather than many.

The few seconds you save today can add up to minutes that add up to hours that add up to days of time saved over the course of a year. Come up with creative shortcuts and see how much time you can save.

Capitalizing on Each Person's Unique Skills

Each staff person was carefully selected and hired for his or her unique technical skills and work-related experiences and for being a team player. However, sometimes inappropriate tasks slowly creep into a person's job.

The administrator defines the boundaries of staff roles. Although the property director has a job description, the realities of the job still need to be revisited from time to time. The property director should discuss with the administrator the tasks she performs. She should be doing work that is unique to her role from the data in tool 8.1. If, instead, she is doing tasks that can be done by others, or the workload is too much, changes should be made.

The next step for the property director is to look at the work of the staff and ask the same question, Is everyone doing the type of work that is the best use of that person's time? Sometimes work needs to be shifted to another person, or even another department. Other times, if appropriate, staff could be asked to take responsibility for simple janitorial and upkeep tasks. For example, staff and volunteers can pick up trash outside on the grounds, rearrange tables and chairs, deliver clean or dirty linens, take the recyclables to the recycling bins, or transport program equipment to the storage shed so that maintenance personnel can focus on the repairs and upkeep that require a specialized skill set.

The property director's ultimate goal is to make sure that his staff members have time to do the work they need to do. Having the boundaries defined and periodically discussed maximizes the time site and facility staff have to do their important jobs. It also reaffirms the rest of the organization's commitment to protecting and preserving your site and facilities.

TIPS TO MAKE THE MOST OF YOUR TIME

- Set aside time for planning and scheduling.
- Perform several projects at one location, rather than making several trips.
- Give general work to the right staff member or volunteer.
- Identify and manage priorities.
- Do the work well to avoid future problems.
- Reward staff for time management and planning work.
- Call in experts for specialized projects.
- Learn new skills to become more productive.
- Take vacations to be rested.
- Keep your work area clean and organized.
- Encourage staff to increase their expertise in more specialized fields.
- Visit organizations similar to yours to see how they do similar tasks.
- Make a central knowledge bank. Share and document your work by writing standard operating procedures.
- Select for uniformity in purchasing equipment and parts.
- Extend your skills using appropriate technology.
- Take time to reflect before quickly jumping into a complicated project.
- Make preventive maintenance a priority.

Creating an inviting, well-constructed setting that requires minimal bush trimming, watering, and maintenance requires time to plan. Once the project is completed, you can reap the rewards and visit the labyrinth as you contemplate an upcoming project.

Photo courtesy of Life Enrichment Center, Florida Conference of the United Methodist Church. Wynne Whyman photographer.

Making Planning a Priority for All

If you supervise or oversee the work of others, make sure they understand the value of planning and scheduling in delivering efficient results. Use these ideas to make planning a priority with all staff:

- Does each job description clearly include the expectation that the employee will plan, prioritize, and schedule his or her assigned tasks? Giving employees responsibility for planning creates a way for them to build decision-making and planning skills. As a result, they can feel more empowered.

- Do staff feel supported in their efforts to plan and prioritize?

- In annual performance reviews, does planning count, or are staff rewarded only for hands-on work?

- If you are a supervisor, do you model the desired behaviors? Take time to plan, and then take time to meet with people to schedule their work or help them prioritize their tasks.

Remember, you're trying to build in your organization a commitment to making the best use of everyone's time. Let others know you are committed by adopting, demonstrating, and coaching people about the importance of planning.

Setting Daily Priorities

Your day is off to a bad start. The handrail along one set of steps is broken. A new staff person accidentally backed into the main speed limit sign and the post needs repair. Last night the wind cracked a major branch of a tree near the overhead power line. What's more, the spotlight for the stage is not working, and tonight is the final production. Your original plans for the day included doing a much-needed tune-up on the walk-in refrigerator and creating your work plan for next week. Where do you begin?

At hand are at least three competing needs and a host of other influences. To make a decision, you must weigh the risks of delaying the maintenance against the needs of the participants and against the need for proactive work that seems to always end up at the bottom of the list. You must also consider the availability of staff, the specific skills needed to do the job, the weather conditions, and the potential impact on people in various locations. How do you prioritize all the tasks lined up for the day?

A sample prioritization list is shown in tool 8.2. When you modify this list for your organization, make sure that your goals and the priority assigned to each one are in alignment with your organization's mission and the natural resources and priorities you created in chapter 6 (page 76). As you consider your pressing list of daily tasks, use these priorities to decide what is most important to do *now*. Remember to

Tool 8.2 Example
Work Priorities for Site and Facilities

Use this tool to create a standard priority system for the entire organization. Then all staff can use the same guideline to decide the daily work priorities and the rationale behind them.

Name of committee who decided these priorities _____ Date _____

Priority	Goal	Example of problem	If not done . . .
1 Emergency	Safety of occupants	No utility service (water, gas, electricity), broken stair, chemical spills, natural disasters, security problems, malfunctioning refrigerator	Will people be harmed or potentially harmed?
2 Imperative	Regulatory compliance	Items not in compliance or having the potential to violate various regulations or standards	Will this increase the organization's risk? Will accusations of mismanagement result? Will there be external or internal repercussions (or both)?
3 Critical	Protection of assets	Roof shingles blown off in windstorm, peeling paint on outside of building, clogged toilet, dense forest in danger of burning	Will assets degrade?
4 Urgent	Quality experience of participants	Program equipment malfunctioning, air conditioning unit in room not working	Will participants' experience be degraded?
5 Routine	Maintenance, effectiveness, efficiency	Dull chain saw, worn carpet, dripping faucet, preventive maintenance not done, recycling dumpsters full	Will a more costly project be needed in the future? Will resources be wasted?
6 Routine	Appearance	Dirty windows, scuff marks on floor	Will it eventually detract from the sense of place you are creating?

Tool 8.2 Example Work Priorities for Site and Facilities. From W. Whyman, 2008, *Outdoor Site and Facility Management: Tools for Creating Memorable Places* (Champaign, IL: Human Kinetics). 1

TOOL 8.2 Work Priorities for Site and Facilities.

let staff know how projects are prioritized so they can consistently support your property management work. Sometimes you also need to tell your participants that the concern has been logged, the estimated time required to complete the repair, and why everything cannot be done at once.

Let's examine how your prioritized goals might help you organize your response to the day's problems. With priorities lined up as in the sample shown in tool 8.2, if you were a property manager, you might direct your maintenance assistant to put up cones and tape the area with the broken handrail and then begin repairing. After the handrail is repaired, the assistant can then move on to repair the spotlight. The handrail repair addresses safety, a top priority; the spotlight repair addresses participant experience, which is a lower priority. While your assistant is attending to these tasks, you would immediately call the utility provider about the electrical line concerns and then call a tree trimmer. This project also addresses the top priority of safety. When these projects are done, then you'll take a look at the speed limit sign.

Importance and Urgency

Looking at a list of projects and prioritizing based on a predefined list is a great first step, but sometimes projects need to be categorized more broadly. A two-by-two matrix can help to classify the projects and give you a way to think about where site and facility time is being spent by staff and volunteers (adapted from Covey, 1989 and 1996). Sample activities for site and facilities are listed in figure 8.1.

- *Quadrant I.* These tasks are high in urgency and high in importance. These are significant tasks that require immediate attention, because the situation has caused a crisis.
- *Quadrant II.* These tasks are low in urgency and high in importance. They include planning, preparation, relationship building, and personal renewal.
- *Quadrant III.* These tasks are high in urgency but low in importance. Tasks in this quadrant are often based on other people's priorities and expectations and masked as quadrant I tasks.
- *Quadrant IV.* These tasks are low in urgency and low in importance. These tasks are classified as time wasters when a person spends time on unneeded tasks.

	Urgent	Not Urgent
Important	**I – Quadrant of necessity** • Waterline break • Unannounced visit by inspector • "Spend it or lose it" monies at the end of fiscal year	**II – Quadrant of leadership** • Designing and implementing the maintenance and replacement schedule • Developing relationships with surrounding property owners • Strategic planning • Professional development • Vacation and time off • Analyzing data to develop trends
Not Important	**III – Quadrant of deception** • Unsolicited sales calls or e-mails • Expected to "drop everything" for a person or project	**IV – Quadrant of distraction and time wasters** • Longer-than-necessary phone calls • Several trips, instead of a few, to purchase supplies • Excessive perfectionism on project

FIGURE 8.1   Two-by-two categorization of tasks.

Adapted from S. Covey, *First Things First* (1996) and *The 7 Habits of Highly Effective People* (1989).

Because of the nature of sites and facilities, there will always be work to do in quadrant I. Faucets eventually leak, a windstorm creates a hazardous tree that needs to be removed—the list goes on and on. However, if the site and facility staff are spending the majority of their time in this quadrant, your organization will never get ahead. It may even slip further behind in the work that needs to be done.

Being on top of things, being efficient in the work, and saving time are the work of quadrant II. Your goal is to maximize the time you spend on activities in quadrant II, but doing so is not easy. Tasks in the three other quadrants will eat away at the time you spend in quadrant II. Work to shrink your time in the other quadrants to have enough time for tasks in quadrant II.

Getting Out of Crisis Mode

Prioritizing daily tasks using tool 8.2 is kind of like performing triage in an emergency room. You may have succeeded in keeping the roof from caving in, but not because you found a problem and took care of it before it became a crisis! Somehow you must plan for those maintenance items that tend to fall to the bottom of the priority list in the crush of daily concerns. Only then can you stop acting in crisis mode and start being proactive.

Moving from reactive to proactive mode may take some time, and there may be a couple of steps along the way. One quick-fix technique is to review your daily or weekly to-do list and prioritize the top three projects. Consider the time needed to complete those projects and the availability of parts, supplies, resources, and tools. When your top three projects are taken care of, return to the list and determine the next three priorities. This saves you time from reprioritizing a long list frequently and helps to give you a clear focus for your immediate work.

When all the emergency projects have been handled, it's time to work on a more proactive **schedule.** One technique is to schedule all the tasks in your master to-do list of work using tool 7.4, Master To-Do List. Estimate the time required to do each task, and write this next to each item. Using these estimates, schedule all the projects over the next month. First add your higher-priority projects to the calendar, then the next-highest-priority projects, and finally the lowest-priority projects. Be realistic and spread projects out over time.

Be sure to leave one to two hours blank each day. Even the best planning cannot avert all crises, and you need to build in time to handle those.

Once you've blocked out specific time for all the work on your list, including your lower-priority maintenance and appearance projects, take satisfaction in the fact that you have embarked on a proactive approach.

SCHEDULING AIDS

A written plan of attack for each day or week is essential. Unplanned time tends to slip away and becomes a series of lost opportunities. Using some of the following scheduling tools can help you keep your focus and show people what you are working on:

- *Calendars.* Hang flipchart-sized blank monthly calendars and write the projects directly on the calendars, or put projects on individual sticky notes and attach them to the calendar.

- *Dry-erase board.* Use a dry-erase board that has a generic month preprinted on it. Fill in the days of the month, and add your projects for each day. Adjust projects as you go based on the accomplishments of each day. At the end of the month, you will have a record of all the work you've done, and you can take a digital picture of it.

- *Storyboards*. Using index cards, make three titles—To Do, Doing, and Done—and pin them on a large bulletin board. Put each task on a separate card, and pin it under the appropriate column (Forster, 1998, 2007).

- *Spreadsheets*. List tasks in the first column, grouping them by the type of project or by location (e.g., preventive maintenance, main building). Across the columns put either the days of the month (microlevel) or the names of the month (macrolevel). You can then color-code projects, putting an X in the column when you plan to do the work, or list the person's name who is assigned to the project. You can also use a spreadsheet to make a simple project management (Gantt) chart using arrows or shading to show when different phases of the project will start and stop. A sample **Gantt chart** is provided in tool 8.3.

- *Project management software, such as a Gantt chart, **PERT**, or **CPM***. See the glossary for definitions of these terms. Choose a software application that matches your needs.

- *Room and building use or scheduling software*. Using the same software that your registrar uses to book groups looking to use specific rooms, buildings, and equipment, you can notify the property staff when to prepare buildings for guests or clean up after guests leave. The software enables them to work around the registrar's schedules so maintenance projects do not interfere with building activities. Or, if there is not enough downtime for bigger projects, they may want to notify the registrar not to schedule guests when they need time to work on a disruptive project such as refinishing the main building's floor.

- *Facility maintenance scheduling software*. Using this type of software, you can assign your staff to projects on specific days. Some systems are also tied into **work order** systems or have a feature to print out a calendar. If your operation is small, you may be able to use a regular electronic calendar, such as Microsoft Outlook. Larger operations need special software that allows multiple people access to the information from multiple locations.

Tool 8.3 Blank Gantt Chart

Project Name _____

Use this tool to list the tasks of a project, develop a schedule, and give a visual timeline.

Name of person(s) completing this form _____ Date _____

Project activities	Involved	Week 1					Week 2					Totals	
		Day 1	Day 2	Day 3	Day 4	Day 5	Day 1	Day 2	Day 3	Day 4	Day 5	Total hours	Total project cost
Personnel hours													
Site manager													
Director													
Board													
Legal													
Purchasing													
Contractor(s)													
Total hours													
Labor cost at $50/hr with fringe benefits													
Cost of materials													

Tool 8.3 Blank Gantt Chart. From W. Whyman, 2008, *Outdoor Site and Facility Management: Tools for Creating Memorable Places* (Champaign, IL: Human Kinetics).   1

TOOL 8.3   Gantt Chart.

A public display of projects scheduled lets staff and volunteers know what needs to be done within a larger context. It can also be an educational tool, informing participants of the magnitude of the work required to run the operation.

Photo courtesy of Wynne Whyman.

Status and Priorities of Long-Term Planning

Looking beyond your day-to-day priorities, you need to consider how you can manage your time and that of your staff over the longer term so that your operation runs at peak efficiency while protecting your staff from burnout. Planning, prioritizing, and scheduling are critical to protecting and improving your site and facilities over the long haul. So where do you begin?

The starting point is to analyze where you are now. Begin by creating a baseline profile of your current operation using tool 8.4. It lists the areas of site and facility management corresponding to the chapters in this book. It also provides a scale of stages in the development of a planning and implementation effort. Use the tool to determine which stage each aspect of your operation has reached so far.

Now you will need to interpret your organization's results. Just because an area

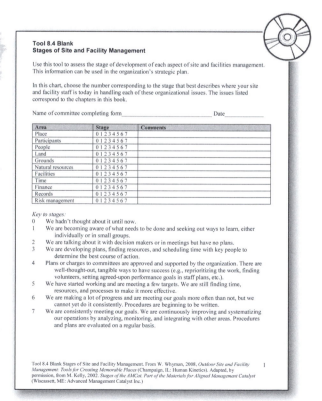

Tool 8.4 Blank
Stages of Site and Facility Management

Use this tool to assess the stage of development of each aspect of site and facilities management. This information can be used in the organization's strategic plan.

In this chart, choose the number corresponding to the stage that best describes where your site and facility staff is today in handling each of these organizational issues. The issues listed correspond to the chapters in this book.

Name of committee completing form_____ Date_____

Area	Stage	Comments
Place	0 1 2 3 4 5 6 7	
Participants	0 1 2 3 4 5 6 7	
People	0 1 2 3 4 5 6 7	
Land	0 1 2 3 4 5 6 7	
Grounds	0 1 2 3 4 5 6 7	
Natural resources	0 1 2 3 4 5 6 7	
Facilities	0 1 2 3 4 5 6 7	
Time	0 1 2 3 4 5 6 7	
Finance	0 1 2 3 4 5 6 7	
Records	0 1 2 3 4 5 6 7	
Risk management	0 1 2 3 4 5 6 7	

Key to stages:
0   We hadn't thought about it until now.
1   We are becoming aware of what needs to be done and seeking out ways to learn, either individually or in small groups.
2   We are talking about it with decision makers or in meetings but have no plans.
3   We are developing plans, finding resources, and scheduling time with key people to determine the best course of action.
4   Plans or charges to committees are approved and supported by the organization. There are well-thought-out, tangible ways to have success (e.g., reprioritizing the work, finding volunteers, setting agreed-upon performance goals in staff plans, etc.).
5   We have started working and are meeting a few targets. We are still finding time, resources, and processes to make it more effective.
6   We are making a lot of progress and are meeting our goals more often than not, but we cannot yet do it consistently. Procedures are beginning to be written.
7   We are consistently meeting our goals. We are continuously improving and systematizing our operations by analyzing, monitoring, and integrating with other areas. Procedures and plans are evaluated on a regular basis.

Tool 8.4 Blank Stages of Site and Facility Management. From W. Whyman, 2008, *Outdoor Site and Facility Management: Tools for Creating Memorable Places* (Champaign, IL: Human Kinetics). Adapted, by permission, from M. Kelly, 2002. *Stages of the AMCat. Part of the Materials for Aligned Management Catalyst* (Wiscasset, ME: Advanced Management Catalyst Inc.).

TOOL 8.4   Stages of Site and Facility Management.

116

Appropriate software can be a tool to increase your efficiency and do more complex tasks that are not possible on paper.
© PhotoDisc

is at a lower stage does not imply that it is a higher priority. Moreover, your organization did not reach the various stages (both high and low) overnight. A successful site and facility plan takes time—often several years. A productive approach is to view long-term planning as a process. With each advance to the next stage, you are moving from your present situation to a more organized, efficient operation. Identifying where you are sets a baseline—one that you can revisit in a year or two to reassess your progress.

Ideally, organizations would like all the site and facility areas addressed promptly to move them to stage 7. This rarely happens. Because everything cannot be done at once nor at the same speed, your organization will need to determine what to emphasize. Tool 8.4 can also be used to determine the priority the organization places on different site and facilities aspects in its broad 5- to 10-year strategic plan. By including the site and facilities in its strategic plan, the organization shows that it understands the importance of the property within the organization's work. With that done, the staff is free to create yearly operational plans to reach the strategic goal. Each year chips off another piece.

To help you make decisions about which areas need more or less emphasis in the coming year, tool 8.5 builds on the analysis performed with tool 8.4. This tool gives you a way to say, "start here" and can feed into the operation's annual plan. This exercise gives you the opportunity to step back and look at all the site and

---

Tool 8.5 Blank
Annual Priorities for Site and Facilities

Use this tool to determine the tactical objectives for the year in each area, after you have completed tool 8.4.

Look at tool 8.4, the broad goals of your organization, your various plans (such as a financial plan or a wetland restoration plan), and the work that needs to be done in the upcoming year. Write down one to three broad objectives that you are exploring for each area. Then evaluate which area needs more or less emphasis this year, and assign it a priority.

Key to priorities:
1   Highest priority. Many parts will receive extra effort and work this year.
2   Medium priority. Some parts will receive additional effort, and some parts will be left as they are.
3   Lowest priority. Our work and procedures are effective; this year we will continue to use them as they are.

Name of person(s) completing this form_____   Date _____

Area	Description	This year's objectives	Priority
Place	Including the importance of site and facility areas in the mission, vision, and value statements and ensuring that the mission permeates throughout all the operations.		1 2 3
Participants	Meeting participant site and facility needs. Sharing site and facility information in a variety of ways.		1 2 3
People	Carrying out the site and facility responsibilities and ensuring that all roles are administered.		1 2 3
Land	Managing the real property: legal documents, air rights, water rights, mineral rights		1 2 3
Grounds	Managing the roads, trails, and utility infrastructure.		1 2 3
Natural resources	Managing the natural resources of the site, teaching beyond nature identification.		1 2 3
Facilities	Managing buildings, major equipment, and energy conservation.		1 2 3
Time	Prioritizing, planning, scheduling, using maintenance cycles, and finding time for site and facilities.		1 2 3
Finance	Managing the organization's site and facility finances, both short term and long term.		1 2 3
Records	Knowing what site and facility records to keep, developing procedures for storage and retrieval, maintaining archives.		1 2 3

Tool 8.5 Blank Annual Priorities for Site and Facilities. From W. Whyman, 2008, *Outdoor Site and Facility Management: Tools for Creating Memorable Places* (Champaign, IL: Human Kinetics).   1

TOOL 8.5   Annual Priorities for Site and Facilities.

facility areas as a whole. You can also share this information with staff, volunteers, board members, and participants.

Cycles of Your Operation

Much of your property management work will be controlled or deeply affected by the cycles of your organization. The weather, the season, the financial fiscal year—any of these factors can determine the critical points for work on your site or facilities. Everyone involved, from the local administration to general laborers coming in for a specific job, needs to understand these cycles and how they can affect your work schedule.

When you move from a task-centered crisis mode to a planning mode, you will take the longer view, which allows you to consider these yearly cycles. The basis for your work plan will be a yearly overview that minimizes crises by avoiding work-flow bottlenecks and ensuring that funds are available when you need them.

What are your organization's crucial points for getting certain work done? For example, early spring may be the best time to start working on a large drainage problem. When should funds be solicited so that cash is available to begin construction when the ground thaws? Water systems need to be closed for the winter at the end of the fall season. Will staff be busy with other duties at this time? When does the fiscal year end? What is the slowest month for getting to projects that keep slipping?

You should consider these and other questions when creating your yearly cycle. Record your responses on tool 8.6, and then use the tool to help guide other planning initiatives throughout the organization.

Tool 8.6 Blank
Understanding Your Time Cycles

Use this tool to record key time periods to do various projects. To anticipate time-sensitive influences on project scheduling, record your organization's major milestones and events for each category.

Name of person(s) completing this form_____ Date _____

	January	February	March	April	May	June
Participants						
People						
Land						
Grounds						
Natural resources						
Facilities						
Finance						
Records						
Planning						
Risk management						

Tool 8.6 Blank Understanding Your Time Cycles. From W. Whyman, 2008, *Outdoor Site and Facility Management: Tools for Creating Memorable Places* (Champaign, IL: Human Kinetics).

TOOL 8.6 Understanding Your Time Cycles.

Time to Create Your Memorable Place

Managing your time is essential. It brings efficiency and cost savings to your property management plan. Effective time management facilitates planning, scheduling, and realizing the dreams that support your property's future. Protecting your valuable natural resources, planning green buildings, creating a unique atmosphere with your furnishings and accessories—these added touches that enrich participants' experiences can only be accomplished if you have the time to do them! Stay focused on your top priorities, move from crisis mode to proactive mode, and you'll find time to make your property the memorable place you want it to be.

BEST PRACTICES

✓ Staff are recognized and rewarded for planning and saving time.

✓ A method for setting project priorities is in place and understood by all staff (see tool 8.2).

✓ All site and facility management areas are assessed and prioritized annually (see tool 8.5).

✓ The strategic plan includes site and facility management.

✓ The organization's yearly cycles are used during planning.

9

FINANCES

Constructing the Future

Shorebird Park Nature Center, City of Berkeley, CA. Wynne Whyman photographer.

There is no doubt that property management requires money. Site and facilities are big-ticket items for any organization, and with them goes a responsibility to see that they hold their value. It's essential that property directors and administrators speak the language of finance to communicate your needs, effectively make plans, and have the needed funds for the future.

This chapter shows you how to assess your current financial situation and identify how much money you need to maintain or improve your site and facilities. Creating accurate operating and capital budgets will tell your team how much income is needed from a variety of sources and help you set project priorities as conditions change. But budgeting is not all you need to do. For the long-term viability of your property, you need long-term plans and strategies to fund needed replacements and improvements.

To achieve success with your property finances, you'll need determination, resourcefulness, and a few proven strategies, ideas, and techniques. This chapter begins with some ways to look at your current operation.

Four Perspectives

Relying on one view can be limiting and keep you from seeing the big picture. By analyzing your data from several perspectives, assessing your operation according to national and industry standards, and comparing your own trend data, you'll gain insights that will help you determine a good direction for your future. You can also use the results of your analysis to support funding strategies to help pay for what you need.

Property Expenses as Part of the Whole

Looking at the property **operating budget** and actual numbers continually is crucial. Are actual expenses at or below budget? Are the amounts budgeted and funded increasing over the years for all site and facility accounts? In addition, because the property is a part of the entire organization, what is the relationship between the property expenses and the total operating expenses of the organization? Asking these questions can yield some interesting data.

Pie charts are a good big-picture tool to help you visualize how your organization allocates its funds. The size of your wedge in comparison to that of other wedges in the pie gives a specific area to further analyze. Once you have your own pie chart, you can compare your organization with others in your industry. Figures 9.1 through 9.4 show the financial pie charts of various organizations and industries. You can also find data for your industry by contacting your professional association.

The information for the pie charts in figures 9.1 through 9.4 was collected from member surveys or government-required data reporting. Each pie chart represents total expenses including operating expenses; it may or may not include some capital expenses. It is important to point out that each data set was collected a little bit differently, depending on the needs of the organization. The pie charts differ in the names of categories, the line items included in each category, and how capital expenses were accounted for. With that in mind, when you compare the data for your organization with these figures, make sure you are comparing "apples to apples." Answering the following questions can help:

- Are maintenance wages included in the overall salaries and benefits category or in the maintenance expense category?

- Is replacement equipment included in the maintenance category? Some organizations erroneously classify replacement equipment as new equipment, because it is new. The new equipment category should be for items that have not been previously owned.

- Is the property insurance included as a stand-alone item or included with other insurance?

- Are you interpreting your data against the industry statistics in the correct way? Sometimes industry data are rich in information, but that information has to be interpreted. Because table 9.1 on page 126 uses median data rather than average data, you cannot

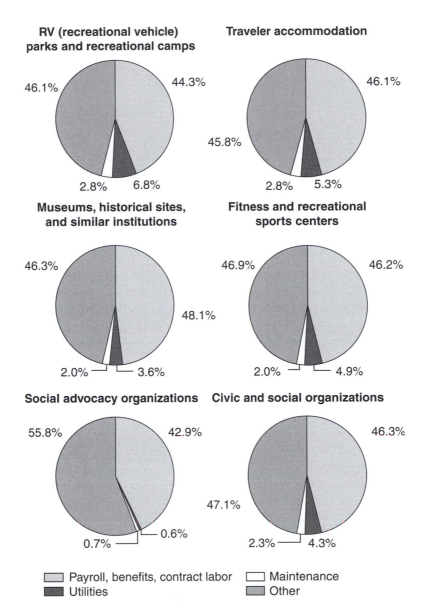

RV (recreational vehicle) parks and recreational camps

46.1%
44.3%
2.8%   6.8%

Traveler accommodation

46.1%
45.8%
2.8%   5.3%

Museums, historical sites, and similar institutions

46.3%
48.1%
2.0%   3.6%

Fitness and recreational sports centers

46.9%
46.2%
2.0%   4.9%

Social advocacy organizations

55.8%
42.9%
0.7%   0.6%

Civic and social organizations

46.3%
47.1%
2.3%   4.3%

☐ Payroll, benefits, contract labor   ☐ Maintenance
■ Utilities   ▨ Other

FIGURE 9.1 Percentages of total expenditures in various industries.

U.S. Census Bureau, 2002.

make it into a pie chart. However, you can compare your data to each variable and see how close you are to 50 percent of the population for each category.

- Does the pie chart represent an operating budget or a combined operating and capital budget? If an expansion project is included in an operating budget, rather than in the capital budget, it could skew the data. Similarly, if debt retirement is included, it could skew the yearly operating expenses picture.

Schools (K-12)

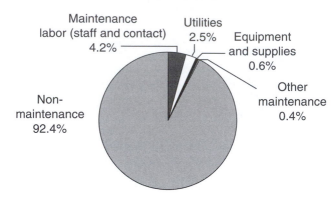

Maintenance labor (staff and contact) 4.2%

Utilities 2.5%

Equipment and supplies 0.6%

Other maintenance 0.4%

Non-maintenance 92.4%

Two-year colleges

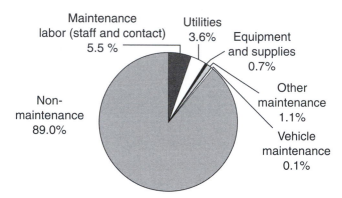

Maintenance labor (staff and contact) 5.5 %

Utilities 3.6%

Equipment and supplies 0.7%

Other maintenance 1.1%

Vehicle maintenance 0.1%

Non-maintenance 89.0%

Four-year colleges

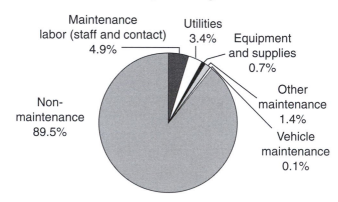

Maintenance labor (staff and contact) 4.9%

Utilities 3.4%

Equipment and supplies 0.7%

Other maintenance 1.4%

Vehicle maintenance 0.1%

Non-maintenance 89.5%

FIGURE 9.2 Percentages of total expenditures in educational institutions.

Adapted from Argon, 2006a, and Argon, 2006b, *American School and University.*

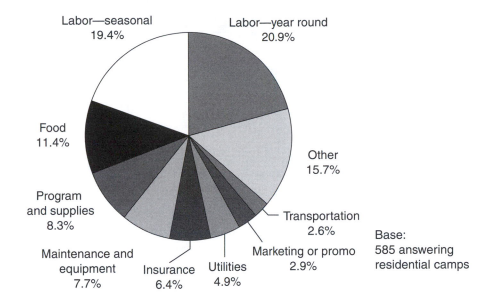

Labor—seasonal
19.4%

Labor—year round
20.9%

Food
11.4%

Other
15.7%

Program
and supplies
8.3%

Transportation
2.6%

Maintenance and
equipment
7.7%

Insurance
6.4%

Utilities
4.9%

Marketing or promo
2.9%

Base:
585 answering
residential camps

FIGURE 9.3 Percentages of total expenditures in camps.

Adapted from American Camp Association, by permission. Business operations profile survey: Residential camp summary (2006).

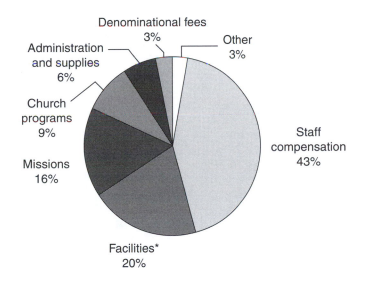

Denominational fees
3%

Other
3%

Administration
and supplies
6%

Church
programs
9%

Staff
compensation
43%

Missions
16%

Facilities*
20%

*Rent, mortgage, utilities, upkeep

FIGURE 9.4 Percentages of total expenditures in churches.

Adapted, by permission, from P. Ten-Elshof, 2000, "Church budgets: You are what you spend," *Your Church* 46(1): 70-75. © Christianity Today International.

Table 9.1 Median Amounts Spent for Various Budget Categories

	Median*
Maintenance and replacement supplies	4%
New construction and equipment	6%
Utilities	7%
Debt retirement and interest (capital)	5%
Debt retirement and interest (operations)	1%
Year-round personnel	34%
Food service	13%

*A median is the middle, where half the population has values less than the median and half have values greater than the median.

From *CCCA 2005 Industry Survey of Christian Camps and Conferences,* published by Christian Camp and Conference Association (CCCA). 339 respondents. Copyright © 2005. Christian Camp and Conference Association. Used with permission.

Keep in mind that slices in a pie chart show *average* data representing organizations of all sizes, types, and locations. Your own data should not look exactly like any pie, because each organization has its own priorities based on its strategic plan. Nor does a pie chart depict the best-performing organizations for that particular industry. It is simply an average of the organizations that responded to each survey.

A pie chart can help you visualize how your organization spends money. The easiest way to create a pie chart for your organization is to convert tool 9.1 from the CD-ROM into an electronic spreadsheet. First, fill in the numeric data. Then, using your spreadsheet's graphing tools, select the fourth column, "% of total operating expenses," and click on the tools in your spreadsheet to make a pie chart. The labels for the pie chart come from column 1, "category."

Industry data can be very useful as a benchmark to begin analyzing your own data. With your own pie chart in hand, you're in a position to analyze it on three

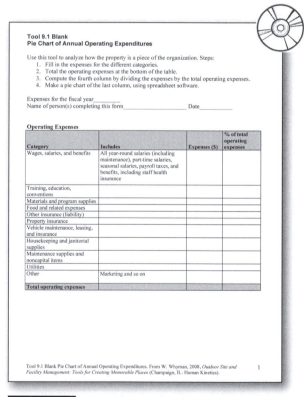

TOOL 9.1 Pie Chart of Annual Operating Expenditures.

levels: You can compare the wedges within your organization, compare a current pie chart for your organization with one from five years ago, or compare your current pie chart against industry standards.

Comparing the wedges within your organization.

- For most organizations, the salaries and benefits are the largest wedge. What is the next largest wedge?

- What makes sense about the sizes of the wedges? What surprises you?
- How does the maintenance wedge compare to those of other expense areas in your chart, such as program supplies?

Comparing your current pie chart with one from five years ago.

- Is the maintenance percentage lower, higher, or the same? Was there an intentional reason, or did it just happen?
- With utilities fluctuating and steadily increasing in price, what trends do you notice from your utilities data? Perhaps the monies spent on utilities are staying steady as a result of utility conservation measures.
- How do the relative sizes of the wedges compare against the organization's strategic plan for site and facilities?

Comparing your current pie chart against applicable industry standards.

- How do the wedges of your pie chart compare with the industry benchmarks? Are your percentages higher or lower than the national average? Why? The underlying reasons for the data are probably more important than the data themselves.
- If your maintenance expenses are less than the national average, do you have other data that indicate that your organization may not be funding maintenance adequately? It is important not to act on one piece of data. Instead, gather data from many sources, develop themes from the data points, and then act on the data.

Tell your "story" of how numbers translate into creating a memorable place: Ample funds for staffing and supplies are necessary and here's why . . . .

In addition to the analysis for your own work, the pie chart can be useful in sharing your needs and concerns with others in the organization. Consider the following:

- By showing where the money goes, the chart graphically represents your organization's priorities and needs. This may be helpful to show during a staff meeting for a broader understanding of the entire operation—with site and facilities as an integral part.
- A pie chart visually illustrates an area that may need more emphasis or resources. For example, a very small maintenance wedge may indicate that maintenance needs more resources. A very large utilities wedge may indicate that conservation, energy redesign, or additional insulation is needed.
- A pie chart attached to your budget proposal for the administrator, board, or finance committee can support your request for a needed budget increase. Comparing your chart against the industry averages can provide additional support. A graphic sometimes sends a stronger message than just numbers.
- A pie chart and the summary numbers provide evidence in a form familiar to financial people and funders. These detailed explanations are more effective than the general claim that "we need more money."

The overall goal of graphic representations such as pie charts is to translate "just the numbers" into meaningful information. An illustration or graphic gives people a broader perspective or presents a trend to discuss further. To get your financial message across, look at your data, the trends, and industry standards and create a visual that explains the meaning behind the numbers.

Total Facility Budget: A Percentage of Replacement Value

Your pie chart tells what your organization is spending on various expense categories, but it does not tell whether those are the *right* amounts. For that, another technique is needed. The origin of this assessment comes from the Building Research Board of the National Research Council's study on public buildings (schools, health care facilities, government administration buildings) (Commission on Engineering and Technical Systems, 1990).

This quick assessment determines whether you are spending the right amount of money for facility maintenance and repair. Begin with an analysis that expresses maintenance and repair as a percentage of replacement value.

$$\frac{\text{Total maintenance and repair}}{\text{Current replacement value}} = \underline{\hspace{1cm}}\%$$

The numerator—total maintenance and repair—should include the following operating and capital expenses for one year: preventive maintenance, major maintenance, and routine repairs.

Do *not* include any of the following in the numerator total: utility supply costs, custodial services, snow removal, pest control, refuse collection and disposal, environmental operations, landscaping, record keeping, security services, fire protection services, or any expansion projects (Federal Facilities Council, 1996).

The denominator—current replacement value—is the amount it would take today to replace the buildings. This number can be determined from a recent property insurance schedule or an appraisal.

For example, an organization is spending $50,000 for the maintenance and repair of its facility. The current replacement value of the facility is $4.5 million.

$$\frac{\$50,000}{\$4,500,000} = 1.1\%$$

Carrying out the division, the maintenance is 1.1 percent of the replacement value. Computing the percentage is only the first step; the second step is interpreting the percentage. The resulting federal report recommended a target of 2 to 4 percent each year for maintenance and repair as a percentage of replacement value (Commission on Engineering and Technical Systems, 1990).

According to the federal benchmark, this organization could justify spending more on maintenance to preserve its assets. If the organization has been putting off certain maintenance and repair tasks, the percentage may need to be even higher than the federal benchmark of 4 percent to take care of its backlog of **deferred maintenance.**

What is the percentage for your organization? Use your maintenance and repair total from this year's operating budget and replacement items in the capital budget. Remember to include only the items described earlier. Use your insurance schedule to determine the current replacement value. If your percentage is less than 2 percent, and your building is not brand new, you are likely not investing enough in maintenance.

Including this simple calculation and its interpretation can carry real weight when submitting your budget requests or when discussing the long-term financial plan.

Facility Condition Index (FCI)

How would you describe the current condition of your facilities? Good? Run down? In need of a bit of sprucing up? Perhaps a more precise description would help.

The Facility Condition Index (FCI) is a handy assessment tool used to describe the condition of your buildings. The FCI was developed by the National Association of College and University Business Officers (NACUBO) and Applied Management Engineering, Inc. (AME) (Brooks, 2004). The FCI has become a standard benchmark in the building industry for all sectors. The FCI replaces informal condition assessment—"It looks like the roof needs to be replaced"—with a solid evaluation. It also assigns *a degree of condition,* which is important in an accurate overall assessment of needed maintenance.

The FCI objectively calculates the condition of your building.

Photo courtesy of Camp Alexander Mack, photographer Erin Kauffman.

The FCI for a particular building is simply the ratio of deferred maintenance to replacement value.

$$FCI = \frac{\text{Cost of maintenance and repair deficiencies}}{\text{Current replacement value of the facility}}$$

The percentage is used to rate the condition of the building as follows:

0–5%	Good
5.01–10%	Fair
>10%	Poor

As you can see, the higher the percentage (ratio) is, the worse the condition of a building is.

As an example, if the deferred maintenance on a small house converted into a nonprofit's office space were as follows,

$ 7,000	Roof work
5,000	Painting, caulking, repairing water damage
5,000	HVAC system
$17,000	TOTAL

and the replacement value of the building were $250,000, the FCI would be

$$\frac{\$17,000}{\$250,000} = 6.8\%.$$

Referring to the FCI rating system, the building in this example would be rated in fair condition.

The FCI is useful because it lets you quantify the condition of very different buildings using a common measurement—the total dollar amount needed and the condition of each building. With these data you can plan your operating and capital budgets and have a tool to describe the degree of work needed.

Tool 9.2 shows the calculations for various buildings. Note that the amount of money spent in proportion to the value can paint quite a different picture. Although $2,000 for the cabin doesn't sound like a lot, it is a lot when you compare it to its replacement value.

Using the blank tool on the CD-ROM will enable you to calculate the FCI for each building on your site. This will give you a standardized and objective look at the condition of each one; some sample buildings are shown.

If you have several buildings and need a summary report, tally all the ratings to get an overall picture of the scope of needed

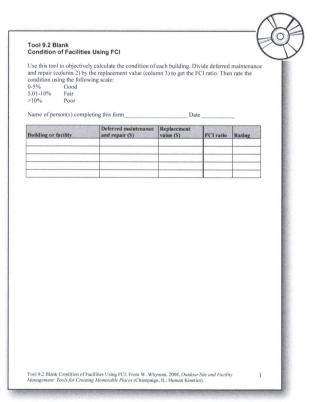

Tool 9.2 Blank
Condition of Facilities Using FCI

Use this tool to objectively calculate the condition of each building. Divide deferred maintenance and repair (column 2) by the replacement value (column 3) to get the FCI ratio. Then rate the condition using the following scale:
0-5%   Good
5.01-10%   Fair
>10%   Poor

Name of person(s) completing this form_____ Date _____

Building or facility	Deferred maintenance and repair ($)	Replacement value ($)	FCI ratio	Rating

Tool 9.2 Blank Condition of Facilities Using FCI. From W. Whyman, 2008, *Outdoor Site and Facility Management: Tools for Creating Memorable Places* (Champaign, IL: Human Kinetics).

TOOL 9.2 Condition of Facilities Using FCI.

maintenance—for example, 14 buildings are in good condition, 5 are in fair condition, and 2 are in poor condition. Putting your tally into a visual form can convey a much more meaningful message, as shown in figure 9.5.

Needs Index

Using deferred maintenance financial numbers, the FCI tells you the condition of the building, but it doesn't tell you whether the buildings are up-to-date, meet the needs of today's participants, and fulfill the mission. For example, a 1950s

FCI category	Number of buildings
Good	
Fair	
Poor	

= one building

FIGURE 9.5   A graphic summary of FCI assessment is easy to understand. Include an explanation and data as well.

building could be immaculately maintained, but the style is not current, and the existing space limits the types of activities. The **Needs Index** addresses the "total need—sufficiency, suitability, and condition." Or said another way, it adds the programming and mission needs to the equation. The Needs Index was published in APPA's 1999 *The Strategic Assessment Model* (Cain and Kinnaman, 2004). The revised FCI equation is as follows:

$$\text{Needs Index} = \frac{\text{Cost of maintenance and repair deficiencies} + \text{capital renewal} + \text{renovation or modernization}}{\text{Current replacement value of the facility}}$$

Capital renewal is the total amount of expenditures that would be required to restore the buildings to an optimal condition based on the life cycle and the assessed condition of facilities to adequately support programs. Renovation and modernization is the total amount of expenditures required to meet evolving technological, programmatic, and regulatory demands (APPA Web site, n.d.).

The Needs Index will take more work than the FCI to compute, because you are involving more than just the facility staff. The upgrades need to be aligned with the mission and meet the needs of the participants. The administrator, board members, facility staff, and key staff will need to agree about the types of upgrades needed throughout the organization, often by working on a master plan or long-range plan. Once there is a strategic direction, the financial numbers can be calculated. The resulting number will often be higher than that reached with an FCI calculation. In the end, with the Needs Index, you will have a more realistic view of your needs by accounting for modernizations, renovations, and upgrades.

Crafting a Budget

The assessment tools just reviewed can help you evaluate your financial commitment to your site and facilities and the condition of your assets. Each one gives you industry perspectives to apply to your organization and information that may help you present a case for increased funding for areas that need additional emphasis. However, these analyses do not provide the specific dollar amounts needed for your budget.

How should you go about budgeting for your site and facilities? In a word: systematically. The next sections present the basics of preparing a budget. You will create two distinct budgets: an operating budget for the yearly expenses it takes to run your operation and a capital budget for major expenditures such as replacing buildings, remodeling, and purchasing replacement vehicles.

Chart of Accounts

For the operating budget, you'll first need a **chart of accounts,** which is a list of categories to which various expenses are allocated. Your organization probably already has an established chart of accounts that it uses to track expenditures and develop budgets.

Study your chart to determine which accounts pertain to the site and facilities. Compare your accounts with those listed in tool 9.3 and note the differences. If you see some additional accounts that would be useful, bring your recommendations to your finance director to find out what the process is for adding another account. Depending on the type of your organization, there may be additional considerations in selecting the categories, to be in alignment with the organizational or legal reporting requirements.

Getting the chart of accounts right is tricky, but essential. You need enough

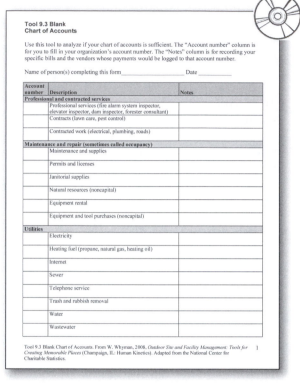

Tool 9.3 Blank
Chart of Accounts

Use this tool to analyze if your chart of accounts is sufficient. The "Account number" column is for you to fill in your organization's account number. The "Notes" column is for recording your specific bills and the vendors whose payments would be logged to that account number.

Name of person(s) completing this form _____ Date _____

Account number	Description	Notes
Professional and contracted services		
	Professional services (fire alarm system inspector, elevator inspector, dam inspector, forester consultant)	
	Contracts (lawn care, pest control)	
	Contracted work (electrical, plumbing, roads)	
Maintenance and repair (sometimes called occupancy)		
	Maintenance and supplies	
	Permits and licenses	
	Janitorial supplies	
	Natural resources (noncapital)	
	Equipment rental	
	Equipment and tool purchases (noncapital)	
Utilities		
	Electricity	
	Heating fuel (propane, natural gas, heating oil)	
	Internet	
	Sewer	
	Telephone service	
	Trash and rubbish removal	
	Water	
	Wastewater	

Tool 9.3 Blank Chart of Accounts. From W. Whyman, 2008, *Outdoor Site and Facility Management: Tools for Creating Memorable Places* (Champaign, IL: Human Kinetics). Adapted from the National Center for Charitable Statistics. 1

TOOL 9.3   Chart of Accounts.

Inform people of how their money is being used as well as the upcoming improvements they can look forward to when they return.

Photo courtesy of Wynne Whyman.

categories to allow a meaningful analysis of your expenditures, but not so many that your record-keeping system bogs down. For example, you may decide to split your maintenance and supplies account into *equipment* maintenance and supplies, *building* maintenance and supplies, and *grounds* maintenance and supplies. This will let you evaluate and compare expenses for equipment, buildings, and grounds separately. However, some would argue that splitting these types of accounts is problematic. When you go to the store to purchase supplies and then submit the receipt, you have to break out which items are considered equipment, which are for building maintenance, and which are for grounds maintenance. You'll need to weigh how you will use the details against how much input will be required.

Tracking expenses may be simpler with just a few accounts, but the budgeting process is usually easier and more accurate if you have a fair amount of detail in your site and facility expense accounts. You can precisely monitor each account and budget accordingly. For example, if your generic utilities account is increasing, you won't know whether the increase is coming from natural gas or electricity unless you pull out all the bills and tally them separately. By having separate utility accounts for gas and electricity, you know exactly which utility is increasing and can put more realistic numbers in the budget for each utility account.

The value of separate accounts becomes especially apparent when using past data to project next year's budget. An example of a utility budget is given in tool 9.4, which shows accurate tracking and prediction of expenses. Note that the budget has multiple accounts under utilities. The sample budget shows four years: two past years of historical data, this year's projected spending, and next year's budgeted amounts. A comments column is useful to record brief explanations that help others understand the budget.

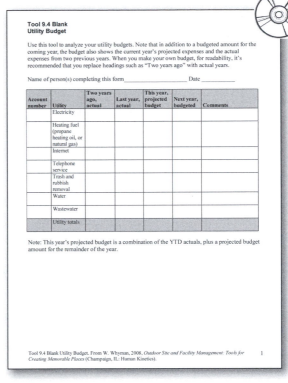

TOOL 9.4 Utility Budget.

BUDGETING TIPS

- Your chart of accounts determines which data you can analyze later. For example, if you need to track the costs of leased vehicles versus owned vehicles separately, by all means establish separate accounts.

- Maintenance keeps your current assets working and can extend the life of assets. Reflect the importance of maintenance in your budget by making it a central focus. Although maintenance usually covers several accounts, remember to look at the aggregate—is the total maintenance budget in alignment with your earlier analysis and your long-term financial plan?

- If you manage natural resources on your site, make sure at least one account covers maintenance of the various natural resources. This will help you assess whether

continued

continued

you are spending adequately on such projects as restoring streams, thinning trees, planting trees, removing hazardous trees, controlling erosion problems, removing noxious weeds, or protecting endangered plant or animal species.

- Include enough historical data in your budget to enable you to see trends. If you compare next year's budget (budgeted) only with this year's budget (budgeted or projected actuals), you miss an opportunity to consider past expenditures, which are generally your most accurate data. Include at least the two previous years' actual expenses to provide a better basis for your budget projection.

- Monitor changes and trends in your county that may affect your site and facility costs, such as utility rate increases, conservation work, lumber prices, and construction costs.

- Keep your budget steady, or steadily increasing, from year to year. Having relatively steady operating and capital expenses for your property will facilitate working with budgets and planning income-generating activities. Unexpected peaks (surprises) in expenditures are generally harder to fund.

- Make your operating budget comfortably tight and build in a contingency. Because of the nature of sites and facilities, you cannot foresee every expense. Calculate the best number you can, based on past expenses, trends, external conditions, and upcoming projects and needs. Then add a contingency amount to each line item of your budget. It's acceptable for this contingency fund to be somewhere between 1 and 10 percent. The amount of the contingency depends on the type of account; some accounts will require a greater percentage than others.

Annual Operating Budget

Now that you have a general sense of the format of the budget, this section gives some specifics about developing the operating budget.

Some of your operating budget for the coming year is determined by recurring expenses such as utilities (see tool 9.4), general supplies, landscape maintenance, taxes, and insurance. These accounts need to be budgeted based on historic data, along with any planned or anticipated changes in the upcoming year due to inflation, rate increases, or conservation initiatives.

The rest of the annual operating budget is determined by the maintenance projects you intend to complete in the coming year, and this entails setting some priorities.

Your first step is to develop a list of possible projects. This is where some of the tools presented in other chapters come in handy. Assemble the following reports and forms to help you judge which operational projects need to be budgeted for in the coming year:

- Tool 5.1 Walk-Through: Grounds
- Tool 5.2 Walk-Through: Utilities
- Tool 6.2 Walk-Through: Natural Resources and Land
- Tool 7.4 Master To-Do List
- Tool 7.9 Walk-Through: Facilities
- Inspection reports received from outside sources (electrical, fire, health)
- Strategic or long-range plan

From this list, compile project names, descriptions, anticipated times to complete, target dates for completion, and projected costs. As you analyze all the projects to set priorities, remember to think realistically. Determine what you, your staff, contractors, and volunteers can accomplish in a year, and put the associated costs in your operating budget. Once the numbers are compiled, you will need to assess what is financially realistic to accomplish.

Budget Addendum

When submitting a proposed budget, attach an addendum with essential explanations and background information. Skip the details, because your aim is to put your budget in its big-picture context. Keep your addendum small, one to two pages at most. If it's overwhelming, no one will bother to read it.

- State where the organization stands in relation to the financial part of the strategic plan; for example: "Our five-year goal is to spend 2 percent of the total replacement value on maintenance. Last year we spent 1.1 percent. This year's budget reflects 1.3 percent."
- Describe the facts, including both short-term and long-term results of decisions made in the current budget. For example, if the maintenance budget was cut the previous year, and there is only a modest increase this year, show both the short-term increase and the long-term deficit caused by a burden of deferred maintenance. For example: "Because of tight circumstances last year, we cut $8,000 from the maintenance budget. This year we are requesting our current needs, plus the $8,000 from last year." This helps others see that a growing deferred maintenance number could put the organization in financial jeopardy.
- Provide market data that is affecting costs; for example: "A 4.5 percent increase in electricity rates by the local energy company will go into effect October 1."
- Highlight the effects of any planned initiatives; for example: "We anticipate a savings of 2 percent on utility costs as a result of implementing our energy conservation program."

The budget addendum gives a written rationale to help bring clarity to the numbers. It is a tool to highlight the important changes in the budget and a way to emphasize important strategies. By having the commonly asked questions already addressed, the budget review discussions can change from an information inquiry ("Could you please explain . . .") to something that is more strategic ("In the long run, does the 1.3 percent . . .").

Five-Year Capital Budget

A capital budget is constructed somewhat differently than an annual operating budget. The capital budget is where money is set aside to purchase big-ticket items that can then be capitalized (depreciated) throughout their life expectancy. You will need to consult with your organization's finance department to determine the requirements for **capitalized** expenses in your organization.

Typically, capital expenditures are budgeted over a longer term than one year. Because they are costly items, try to work out at least a five-year plan to allow plenty of time to create plans for funding strategies and staffing.

To begin developing your budget for capital expenses, use tool 7.8, Facility and Equipment Replacement Schedule. This shows the year when you purchased equipment or did major maintenance or repair and the life expectancy of each asset. To determine your capital budget needs, start with these items and add the projected costs as explained next.

To transform tools 5.3 and 7.8 into a budgeting tool, you can use tool 9.5. Take the original costs and the expected replacement dates of your capital assets from tools 5.3 and 7.8. Add this information to tool 9.5, selecting just those replacements expected in the next five years.

Now calculate what it will cost to replace each asset when its useful life has expired. Compute the best estimate for the work in the future, remembering to account for trends in the construction market, inflation, and the cost of materials. Develop estimates from similar work you are currently doing. Or, if it's a larger, complicated job, you may want to pay a contractor to give you a realistic estimate.

You now have your replacement items and costs logged in tool 9.5. Now, pull together your walk-through reports, preventive maintenance schedule, inspection reports, and other documents you used to develop your operating budget, and find any other items that are capital budget projects. Add them to tool 9.5. When you are finished, tool 9.5 will show five years' worth of capital projects you anticipate, with associated costs. Simply total the items by year to complete your five-year capital budget.

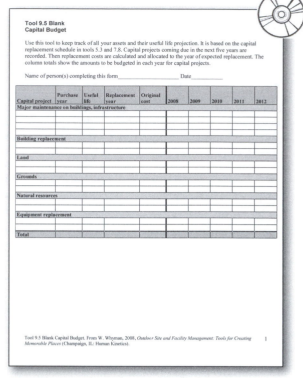

Tool 9.5 Blank
Capital Budget

Use this tool to keep track of all your assets and their useful life projection. It is based on the capital replacement schedule in tools 5.3 and 7.8. Capital projects coming due in the next five years are recorded. Then replacement costs are calculated and allocated to the year of expected replacement. The column totals show the amounts to be budgeted in each year for capital projects.

Name of person(s) completing this form_____ Date_____

Tool 9.5 Blank Capital Budget. From W. Whyman, 2008, *Outdoor Site and Facility Management: Tools for Creating Memorable Places* (Champaign, IL: Human Kinetics).

TOOL 9.5 Capital Budget.

CALCULATING REPLACEMENT AMOUNT

There are many formulas to calculate **replacement amount.** The formula shown here is a simple one that you can use to calculate the approximate replacement amount of an asset in the future, using interest compounded annually. In the formula, the interest is an approximate average rate of change based on a projected inflation rate, changes in the market, and special local conditions.

$$\text{Replacement amount} = \text{original cost } (1 + i)^n, \text{ where}$$

$$i = \text{interest percent each year}$$

$$n = \text{number of years}$$

For example, an organization replaced a vinyl floor in 2001 at a cost of $3,000. The new flooring has a life expectancy of 20 years. When it's time to replace the flooring in 2021, with an estimated 2 percent interest rate each year, this same floor will cost about $4,458, calculating as follows:

$$\text{Replacement amount} = \$3,000 (1 + 0.02)^{20}$$

$$= \$3,000 (1.02)^{20}$$

$$= \$3,000 (1.4859)$$

$$= \$4,458$$

This simple formula gives you a ballpark figure to work with. Ask your accountant or financial planner if he or she would prefer that you use a different formula.

Should you rely solely on your five-year capital budgeting? Definitely not. You need to update your estimated costs periodically, based on changing conditions in your area and the costs associated with your most recent projects. Your walk-throughs will also determine which year you actually do the work. Patterns of use and weathering may dictate that the project be done earlier or later than anticipated.

By projecting your capital budget at least five years out, you not only proactively manage your workload but also generate a key piece of the financial picture that no one else has—the needs that have a big price tag. Knowing what your site and facilities need, and when, gives you and others time to plan and develop funding strategies.

SITE AND FACILITY INCOME

Preparing realistic operating and capital budgets is only the first step toward meeting your financial goals. You also need to work with the financial team to investigate ways to fund site and facility needs, then team up with others to make things happen. Here are some potential sources of income to consider:

- *Participant or user fees.* Accurate operating and capital budgets for site and facilities can be part of a formula for determining participant or user fees. When your operation determines its fees, the process should accurately build in the full needs of the site and facilities.

- *Grants and **gift-in-kind** donations.* Property directors and fund developers can work together to identify grant and gift-in-kind opportunities based on property needs. Several site and facility projects can be a good match with many funders, because the results of their donation are often clearly visible. The key is to find the right fit between the organization's needs and the funder's interests or stated priorities. Property directors are well placed to help the development professional who has identified a grant opportunity. The rationale, plans, and budgets for specific projects will provide much of the substantiating data that funders typically require.

- *State, federal, and local funds.* These monies, which come from lottery dollars, property taxes, and city operating budgets, each have their own qualification requirements, budgeting processes, and reporting rules. Funds are usually designated for specific uses. Access this information through your organization.

- *Donations.* You can suggest a variety of appealing projects and then work with the team to decide on a featured project. The chosen project can be communicated to the participants on the Web site or through registration forms or donation cards.

- *Maintenance endowment.* Your organization can invest funds in an endowment, the earned interest from which is earmarked for maintaining the facilities. This funding mechanism is attractive to funders who would like to support infrastructure improvements, *and* it adds an important revenue source specifically for property-related projects. For example, when one organization raised money to construct a new building, it also raised enough money to set up an ongoing maintenance endowment—a percentage of the new building's cost.

Plaques are a way to show donors that their contributions count. As part of your plaque program, you will need to determine which projects qualify for a plaque and when you can retire a plaque over time.

Girl Scout Camp Ginger Cascades.

Preparing for the Future

Tracking expenses and creating budgets are only half the job of managing your organization's finances. The other half is planning to maintain the current and long-term health of your site and facilities. These two parts have many names, but they can simply be called short-term management and long-term management; they are shown in table 9.2. Each plays an important role in ensuring your organization's financial health.

The last few sections have focused on short-term financial management, which takes a historical view of your finances. This practice sets up accounts and records what is spent using common language, financial statements, and acceptable practices such as **generally accepted accounting principles (GAAP).** A yearly **audit** performed by an independent firm informs the board whether the organization conforms to GAAP requirements.

Short-term management and accounting practices are essential for projecting and tracking expenses, but they do not tell you whether you have adequate funds for site and facility needs. The next sections focus on long-term management, or how to plan to address present and future needs and map out strategies to reach long-range goals.

Reserve Funds

Some organizations barely make ends meet at the end of the fiscal year. Even thinking about putting aside money for a reserve fund seems impossible. Yet, no matter how small the fund amount, it's good to incrementally develop a reserve. You never know what unplanned

Table 9.2   Two Types of Planning

Short-term management	Long-term management
Historical orientation	**Current and long-term orientation**
Budgeting: Operating and capital budgets	Long-term view: Determining what financing is needed for future projects
Auditing: Evaluating annually whether accounting methods are acceptable and figures are accurate	Funding reserves: Providing for planned and unplanned financial needs, including operating reserves, a capital replacement fund, and endowments
Comparing: Showing actual amounts spent versus budgeted amounts and explaining which factors caused variances	Planning: Developing strategies to reach financial goals, including income and expense priorities
Current status: Financial statements show a snapshot of the current value of the site and facilities, based on recorded assets and any outstanding debt	

projects will suddenly appear for the site and facilities. Figure 9.6 is an example of a visual to show the progress toward your goal.

Although people agree that it's important to have some money set aside for unplanned and planned future purchases, they sometimes have different views on what constitutes a rainy day and how the money can be used. Consider, for instance, a church that owns a camp. Money is tight, and many believe that because the camp has a reserve fund, it doesn't need as much subsidy from the overall organization for this year or subsequent years. The camp is obviously running in the black. In this case, if a natural disaster strikes before the camp can rebuild its reserve fund, it will have little means to repair damage, keep the operation open, and generate income.

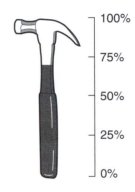

FIGURE 9.6 A meaningful visual conveys how the money from the successful campaign will be used in carrying out the mission. Choose a graphic that matches the overall campaign theme.

SAFEGUARDING YOUR RESERVE FUNDS

These tips will help to ensure your reserve funds are used as intended:

- Write a description of each account. Include the purpose and scope, the approval process for adding or spending funds, how the account will be monitored, any investment guidelines to be followed, and how the interest from each account will be used.

- Be as clear as you can with the account descriptions. For example, if the funds are intended to go toward capital expenditures, call the account something like "building replacement fund" instead of "reserve fund" or "contingency fund."

- Account for each reserve fund clearly. Ideally, each account should have its own checking account to facilitate clarity in accounting.

continued

continued

- Show regular summaries and brief explanations of all accounts in prominent locations, such as financial documents, management reports, and board manuals.

- Through board training and management practices, everyone should be aware that frequent borrowing of cash and not replenishing these funds can jeopardize the future. These accounts are critical to the organization's future existence.

- Maintain a clear distinction between funds destined for maintenance and replacement (capital replacement fund) and funds destined to purchase something new (capital improvement fund). A new furnace may appear to be a new purchase, but because it actually *replaces* a nonfunctioning furnace, it should be funded from the capital replacement fund. A capital improvement fund would hold money for a new building or tennis court that currently is not part of your property. You should not use your capital replacement fund to build these new assets.

- In reports describing the reserve accounts, include both the dollar amounts *and* the percent funded. For example, saying that you have $900,000 in an operating reserve sounds as though your organization is in good financial condition. However, if this is only three months' operating reserve and the goal is six months, then the reserve is only 50 percent funded! That's quite a different perspective.

- If you receive funding from a parent organization, such as an agency or religious organization, specifically designate where their funds are to go, such as the capital replacement fund. The parent organization that owns the assets should invest in protecting assets for the long term, rather than subsidizing only participant programming fees.

Borrowing reserve money must be done with care. First, the board or committee must have a clear agreement and in-depth knowledge of the issues. Second, plans must be made to replenish the reserves, and a mechanism should be in place to monitor the progress. On the other hand, if the board has a yearly discussion about borrowing from the reserve fund, it could be a symptom of a more serious problem that needs to be addressed. Perhaps the administrator, finance committee, or board does not know about the long-term financial needs of the property. People take a risk when they borrow against the future.

The word *reserve* can have different interpretations for different people. Thus, instead of having one reserve account, you might want to set up three accounts—an operating reserve, a capital replacement fund, and a capital improvement fund. Tool 9.6 shows the various components of a capital replacement fund.

Tool 9.6 Blank
Capital Replacement Fund Considerations

Use this tool to discuss and then agree upon how the long-term needs of the property will be funded. People who may be involved in this discussion include property directors, administrators, board of directors, and financial planners.

The proper amount to place in a capital replacement fund depends on the policies of your organization, the age of your facilities, and the decisions your organization makes.

Name of person(s) completing this form_____ Date_____

Component of capital replacement fund	Organization policy	Amount
Insurance reserve fund. Your property insurance has a deductible to meet each time a claim is filed. How many incidents are normal for your operation? If you estimate two each year, and your deductible is $1,000, then $2,000 would need to be in this fund. Some organizations do not put monies aside, preferring to find the monies when they are needed.	❑ Included in fund ❑ Not included in fund	$_____
Emergency capital fund. If you have a fully funded annual maintenance operating budget and a capital budget, you're in pretty good shape. However, you will still have unexpected projects. For example, suppose a water well's productivity decreased by 50%. You may need to pay for work done on the well and engineering time—a project not planned. Another example is if the organization carries flood insurance, but there may be exclusions on the policy that the organization would need to pay for in the event of a flood. Some organizations do not put monies aside, preferring to find the monies, conduct a special campaign, or solicit grant monies when they are needed.	❑ Included in fund ____ % of the replacement value ❑ Not included in fund	$_____
Planned capital expenses. Per the industry norm, about 2 to 4 percent of the replacement value should be set aside each year to cover capital and operating expenses. Determine the percentage you need each year for the capital expenses portion only. Capital expenses can be paid for in one of two ways. 1. *Cash basis.* You fund the full amount of the capital budget each year through participant fees, support from the parent organization, grants, and so on. 2. *Payment plan.* If you expect to replace a roof in 20 years, you make 20 yearly deposits to set aside the calculated replacement amount, taking into consideration projected inflation, construction market increases, interest on the account, and so on. When the roof needs replacing, the money is already in your account.	❑ Cash basis ❑ Payment plan For either option: ____ % of the replacement value	$_____
Total		

Tool 9.6 Blank Capital Replacement Fund Considerations. From W. Whyman, 2008, *Outdoor Site and Facility Management: Tools for Creating Memorable Places* (Champaign, IL: Human Kinetics).

TOOL 9.6 Capital Replacement Fund Considerations.

THREE ACCOUNTS TO PROVIDE FOR THE FUTURE

- *Capital replacement fund.* Designated to cover capital *repairs and replacements* due to the expired useful life of assets or to capital emergencies. Can also be used to fund unplanned annual capital expenses during the fiscal year. Examples:
  - *Insurance deductible.* A property loss occurs, and you need to cover a $2,500 deductible on your property insurance.
  - *Emergency capital projects.* As a result of extreme use conditions over several years, the septic system needs to be replaced before its useful life was scheduled to expire.
  - *Anticipated capital expenses.* Based on life expectancies, the shingles on one building and the oven in the kitchen are due to be replaced this year.
- *Capital improvement fund.* Designated for the purchase of *new or additional* capital assets that require long-term funding. These projects are beyond the scope of this book. Examples:
  - Expanding the capacity of a building
  - Purchasing an additional truck or minibus
  - Purchasing additional land to allow for future expansion
- *Operating reserve.* Designated to cover operating expenses in case the organization cannot operate. Also covers emergency expenses not fully covered by insurance policies (you'll need to know exactly your limits and types of coverage). Example:
  - A tornado closes a nonprofit for five weeks, so no income is generated. Before reopening, repairs must be done. Meanwhile, salaries and other site and facility operating expenses not covered by insurance must be paid. (*Note:* The operating reserve does *not* include anticipated or unanticipated capital expenses for the site and facilities.)

Developing a Financial Plan

For property management, significant benefits lie in developing a detailed, comprehensive plan that outlines how funds will be sought and spent and how priority will be assigned to the work at hand. You must determine and then articulate your needs. Then, you must build a step-by-step plan to fund the needed repairs, replacements, and improvements for your site and facilities.

Put together the best financial plan you can. Your long-term goal is to have adequate monies for current expenses (yearly operating and yearly capital budgets) and funds to ensure the long-term health of the organization (operating reserve, replacement fund, capital improvement fund, maintenance endowment, and so on).

For planning, it's critical that you have an accurate sense of your property's future needs and are able to articulate them in financial terms. With the help of others in your organization, tool 9.7 leads you through the process of

Tool 9.7 Blank
Site and Facility Financial Plan Outline

Use this tool to develop a comprehensive financial plan. Add other useful pieces of information as needed, keeping in mind the importance of keeping the plan succinct so people will use it. Much of this information is available from the tools you have created in chapter 9 (finances) and other chapters. Below is an outline you can customize for your organization.

Name of person(s) who developed this financial plan_____ Date_____

Section I. Current Assessment
1. Description of the site and facilities
   - Number, condition, and age of buildings and capital equipment items
   - Acres of land and current condition of the site
   - Year the land was purchased
   - Any additional comments that give an overview of the property, including water rights, mineral rights, and easements

2. Description of current financial conditions
   - *Historical expenses.* Show three years of actual financial data to present the overall picture rather than a single extreme year (high or low). Separate historical expenses by operating and capital budget accounts.

	Three years prior	Two years prior	One year prior
Operating expenses			
Capital expenses			

   - *Income sources.* List separately all income sources that cover operating expenses and all income sources designated for site and facility capital expenses. In each case, indicate the biggest source of income.
   - *Reserve funds.* Show operating reserves, capital replacement fund, capital improvements fund, maintenance endowments, and so on. In each case, indicate the percentage funded.
   - *Assessment tools.* Include a pie chart of the organization's overall expenses, with a comparison to industry benchmarks (tool 9.1). Show maintenance expenditures as a percentage of value. Show ratings of the condition of your facilities (tool 9.2).

Section II. Where You Want or Need to Be
   - *Summary.* Overall summary of where you want the organization to be and why.
   - *Maintenance as a percentage of replacement value.* What is your ideal percentage? Usually this goal is higher than the percentage you computed in section I.
   - *Five-year capital replacement schedule.* This may have more items listed than allowed for in the approved capital budget.

Tool 9.7 Blank Site and Facility Financial Plan Outline. From W. Whyman, 2008, *Outdoor Site and Facility Management: Tools for Creating Memorable Places* (Champaign, IL: Human Kinetics).   1

 TOOL 9.7 Site and Facility Financial Plan Outline.

FUNDING DEPRECIATION IS NOT ENOUGH

If you simply put aside the yearly **depreciation** amount every year, you will not have adequate resources for replacement. For example, if a roof cost $2,000 in 1995, and you project that it will last 20 years, then you can depreciate it $100 each year ($2000 / 20 years = $100) using the straight-line method. If you put $100 each year in a capital replacement fund to fund that depreciation, you will not have enough money in 2015 to replace the roof. Why? You are funding the historical cost, not the future replacement cost.

Work with your accountant or financial officer to make sure you set aside the proper amount to allow for inflation and fluctuations in the construction market. It is important that you regularly monitor the balance to make sure your payments are on track.

developing a financial plan by providing an outline that you can adapt to your organizational needs.

You should be able to complete the majority of sections I, II and III from your own knowledge and records, perhaps in consultation with the finance person, the fund development person, or the administrator. Section IV may be completed in partnership with the administrator, then submitted to the finance committee for approval; or, it may be a collaborative effort between staff and board members. Either way, the board is responsible for the overall direction and finances of the site and facilities, so they'll need to review and approve the recommendations.

You may not accomplish this plan in one year, and maybe not even in five. Getting started is the most important thing. Then you can celebrate your successes as you progress toward your goals. You will probably need to recalibrate and update your plan every three to five years as your planning continues to evolve.

Interpreting data and implications with financial, administrative, and property experts can give a rich, broad perspective to determine the best options for the financial future of the organization.

© PhotoDisc

FINANCIAL STRATEGY EXAMPLES

Here are examples that might be converted into milestones and goals in section IV of the financial plan:

- Hire a part-time maintenance person to give the property director time to do management work.

- Do a cost analysis to see whether contracting work out is financially sound. Then weigh the results against the risk management plan.

- Designate money saved from utility conservation toward a specific project.

- In all grants, build the case that the organization has the capacity to be a good steward and is capable of maintaining the property. A grantor is usually more interested in contributing toward the success of the mission than in bailing out an organization.

- Have a special campaign to create the maintenance endowment.

Making It Happen

Once you have your approved financial plan, focus on implementing and reporting incremental progress toward the plan objectives. Discipline is required. The temptation to borrow from the reserve funds is strong, especially when unplanned operating expenses are needed. Reserve funds are hard to replace and should be used only when necessary. You should focus on making savings in smaller areas, which will add up in the long run. Tool 9.8 lists tips for saving money.

Make sure your capital replacement fund is substantial enough to withstand all but the most grievous of emergencies. The people starting the fund may not be around to see the full cycle of the fund, so the protection should be institutional. Many organizations build in several layers of control to adequately protect their long-term funds. These frequently include board, management, and executive checks on any large expenditures.

One thing is sure: If you don't take control now, dealing with next year's financial planning will be even more of a challenge. If you are in a hole, the first thing to do is stop digging. A systematic approach to the problem that begins with a baseline to determine your current state is required to move ahead.

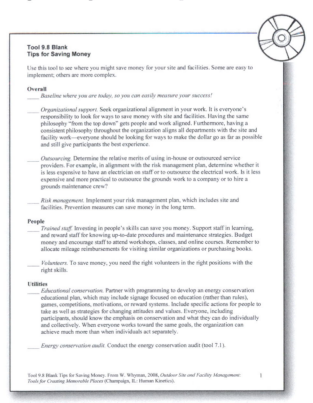

Tool 9.8 Blank
Tips for Saving Money

Use this tool to see where you might save money for your site and facilities. Some are easy to implement; others are more complex.

Overall
____ *Baseline* where you are today, so you can easily measure your success!

____ *Organizational support.* Seek organizational alignment in your work. It is everyone's responsibility to look for ways to save money with site and facilities. Having the same philosophy "from the top down" gets people and work aligned. Furthermore, having a consistent philosophy throughout the organization aligns all departments with the site and facility work—everyone should be looking for ways to make the dollar go as far as possible and still give participants the best experience.

____ *Outsourcing.* Determine the relative merits of using in-house or outsourced service providers. For example, in alignment with the risk management plan, determine whether it is less expensive to have an electrician on staff or to outsource the electrical work. Is it less expensive and more practical to outsource the grounds work to a company or to hire a grounds maintenance crew?

____ *Risk management.* Implement your risk management plan, which includes site and facilities. Prevention measures can save money in the long term.

People
____ *Trained staff.* Investing in people's skills can save you money. Support staff in learning, and reward staff for knowing up-to-date procedures and maintenance strategies. Budget money and encourage staff to attend workshops, classes, and online courses. Remember to allocate mileage reimbursements for visiting similar organizations or purchasing books.

____ *Volunteers.* To save money, you need the right volunteers in the right positions with the right skills.

Utilities
____ *Educational conservation.* Partner with programming to develop an energy conservation educational plan, which may include signage focused on education (rather than rules), games, competitions, motivations, or reward systems. Include specific actions for people to take as well as strategies for changing attitudes and values. Everyone, including participants, should know the emphasis on conservation and what they can do individually and collectively. When everyone works toward the same goals, the organization can achieve much more than when individuals act separately.

____ *Energy conservation audit.* Conduct the energy conservation audit (tool 7.1).

Tool 9.8 Blank Tips for Saving Money. From W. Whyman, 2008, *Outdoor Site and Facility Management: Tools for Creating Memorable Places* (Champaign, IL: Human Kinetics).   1

TOOL 9.8   Tips for Saving Money.

Financing Your Mission

Protecting your site and facilities is essential for your organization. Indeed, many would argue that ensuring the long-term viability of the property is one of the most important duties of every governing board. You need to budget well, plan for the future, manage the finances skillfully, and make well-researched and well-documented recommendations. With care, your memorable place will survive to continue providing those life-changing experiences.

BEST PRACTICES

✓ Financial tools are developed that show all organizational expenses and provide a way to evaluate site and facility expenses as a part of overall operating expenses.

✓ Annual operating budget worksheets show four years: two actual, one projected, and one budgeted.

✓ Capital budgets cover a minimum of five years.

✓ Projects eligible for grant funding are identified on a yearly basis.

✓ Reserve fund accounts are reported in prominent locations, showing both the dollar amounts and the percentage funded.

✓ The site and facility financial plan is updated every three to five years.

✓ The board is regularly informed of progress toward the long-term financial plan for the site and facilities.

10

RECORDS

At Your Fingertips

Can you find what you need when you need it? Do you have ready access to blueprints, expense receipts, vendor contracts, newspaper clippings, site photos, legal documents, and maps? Whether kept in manila folders and metal file cabinets or on computer disks and hard drives, the records of your organization are essential to your business of property management. Life will be easier if you can establish an organized system for filing and retrieving those records.

Keeping good records, and keeping them well, offers measurable benefits. Complete, well-organized records provide solid documentation on everything from costs and expenditures to maintenance schedules. Systematic record keeping saves time and money and helps you better manage risks. Implementing one centralized system throughout the entire operation makes the integration and retrieval of important information from all areas easier.

But what sort of system is right for your operation? What level of detail do you need? And how can you set up and manage such a system? This chapter answers these questions and several more.

Whose Job Is It?

A key step in establishing a good records management system is deciding who is best suited to keep the records for your site and facilities. Start by talking with the appropriate staff. Look at the record-keeping systems that already exist, such as attendance, event, finance, or historical alumni records. Could these systems be adapted to also manage the site and facility records?

The person designated for the records management job may be an on-site staff member or an office person who organizes all the records of the organization. Maybe it's a volunteer who has the skills and time. What responsibilities does the property director have for ensuring that proper record keeping is done? The property director or administrator is the best one to decide what makes sense for your organization.

Choose your records manager carefully. When considering who should manage your records, look for someone who

- is familiar with the site and facility operation,
- is willing to research legal requirements to find out how long records must be kept,
- knows or can learn archiving techniques, and
- is well organized and detail oriented.

You need someone who will develop consistent document management procedures and manage them in an integrated fashion with other operational areas, such as accounting, management, and other records of the organization. The person managing your records should have record-keeping or archiving responsibilities, or both, included in his or her job description.

Keep or Purge?

"Well, I might need this someday," you say to yourself as you open the drawer and file the paper in a folder. You're playing it safe. You don't need this contractor estimate now. But later? *You never know.*

You may know a "keeper." You may even be one yourself. A keeper keeps it all—every paper that crosses her desk. Her file cabinets are overflowing, stacks of files teeter precariously on her office shelves. Her favorite phrase is something like, "One of these days, when things are slow, I'll start digging out." Or perhaps you're more of a purger. Maybe you send every piece of paper or e-mail that comes your way to the trash file faster than you can say, "Get this *out* of here!" Whether you are a keeper or a purger, if your job focus is site and facility maintenance, record storage and retrieval can be as daunting as it is fraught with challenges.

VALUE OF KEEPING
WELL-MANAGED PROPERTY RECORDS

- *Enables knowledge sharing.* When records are well managed, they can be shared among staff. This is especially important when staff turnover occurs.

- *Meets legal responsibilities.* Records document your maintenance and inspection activity. This helps demonstrate that you are running a safe operation for your constituents.

- *Manages risk.* Records give you the documentation you need to help safeguard your organization from legal liability and other risks.

- *Tells your operation's story.* Records show building changes over time, including additions and remodeling. These data and pictures can come in handy when putting together fund-development case statements. For example, to show your accomplishments from the past year in the dishwashing room, you can show pictures and describe the waterline repairs and improvements. A written description combined with before and after photos makes a strong statement.

- *Enables data monitoring.* Records help you keep track of a range of operational data, everything from the current state of the forest's health to trends in electricity consumption. Monitoring trends and looking for patterns are key components of effective management.

- *For urban sites.* By knowing the approximate location of buried utilities and easements, you know what disturbances may occur in your landscaping. When you call for utility marking for a new project, you begin a verification process that helps you avoid surprises later in the project.

- *For rural sites.* Saves money. Knowing the locations of the buried utility lines before digging gives the backhoe operator a targeted location for work, as well as knowledge of other lines in the same location to avoid accidental severing and subsequent costly repairs. In addition, by avoiding accidental loss of service, you are preventing a loss of participant usage revenue and an interruption in the delivery of programming.

When it comes to records management, you need to be both a keeper *and* a purger. The trick is to know what to keep and what to throw away—and when. Some records, such as your legal title, should be kept indefinitely. Many need to be retained for a prescribed number of years. Others you can throw away immediately.

The last thing you want is a piecemeal approach to records management in which you decide the fate of individual documents or digital data as they cross your desk or computer screen. A systematic approach is much more effective. The principles outlined in this chapter will help you create such a records management system.

What to Keep and for How Long

What essential data and information should you keep? And how long should you keep it? It is almost impossible to give a standard answer to this because each organization is subject to unique statutory requirements and organizational needs. You'll need to do some research to find out what is needed for your organization.

A good way to establish a minimum list of records and learn how long to retain them is to ask regulatory agencies, records experts, accountants, and your legal counsel. Another good source of information is your organizational risk management plan (see chapter 11). Frequently, risk management plans include rather comprehensive sections on record keeping. Finally, your personal knowledge of your operation can help you determine what you should keep.

Remember to include visual records as well as written records. For example, you'll want to archive the various site maps outlined in chapter 4. Also consider the value of keeping detailed photographic records. Photos can help you get an overview of the changes to both the structures and the land.

For example, comparing the views of the lodge in figures 10.1, *a, b,* and *c* over 70 years, you can see that the porch has been screened in, the balcony railing has been rebuilt, the underside of the porch has been enclosed, and the vegetation is denser both in the foreground and behind the lodge. Rather than just reading the list of construction materials, you can see the work that was done. Another example of when photographs over time are practical is when a second roof has been built over the original roof. When the second roof leaks, a photo of the original roof might be invaluable to troubleshoot the problem. You can also compare how the vegetation has changed for better or worse after implementing natural resources management plans.

FIGURE 10.1a Lodge at Green Mountain Falls, Colorado, in the 1930s.

Photo courtesy of Girls Scouts-Wagon Wheel Council.

FIGURE 10.1b Lodge at Green Mountain Falls, Colorado, in 2002.

Photo courtesy of Friends University, Rockcleft Camp. Wynne Whyman photographer.

FIGURE 10.1c Lodge at Green Mountain Falls, Colorado, in 2003.

Photo courtesy of Friends University, Rockcleft Camp. Wynne Whyman photographer.

Using expert advice from various sources along with your own written and visual records, the designated record keeper will be able to set up a record retention schedule. You and the records manager can work through the complexities by using tool 10.1. After the team has decided what is important to keep and for how long, write it down. Then prioritize the list so you know where to begin. Committing the list to a written plan helps ensure thoroughness and brings clarity to the process.

Tool 10.1 Blank
Record Retention Worksheet

Use this tool to create a records retention schedule.

Solicit expert advice and discuss with your team which records to keep and how long to keep them. Use this worksheet to create a permanent record of retained records and the dates to pitch them.

Name of person(s) completing this form_____ Date _____

Area	Examples	Authoritative source used	Property records to keep	How long?
Participant and program activities and equipment. What are industry standards and regulations for various program areas?	Challenge course inspection, testing water in the lake for swimming			
Land. What legal responsibilities do you have?	Encroachment from adjacent property owners, water rights, easements, mineral rights, aerial photos			
Grounds. What records are needed by local ordinances?	Spraying for insects and pests, soils testing, health of the trees around the buildings			
Utilities. What do you or your utility companies need to use for maintenance and liability?	Location for maintenance, shutoff location, installation information, water consumption, sewage discharge amounts, electrical and gas inspection reports, lease agreements for heating fuel tanks			
Natural resources. From your mission statement, what type of a site do you want? What aspects are you monitoring?	Watershed management, walk-throughs, inspections, hydrologist visits, forester visits, geologist visits			

Tool 10.1 Blank Record Retention Worksheet. From W. Whyman, 2008, *Outdoor Site and Facility Management: Tools for Creating Memorable Places* (Champaign, IL: Human Kinetics).   1

TOOL 10.1 Record Retention Worksheet.

Organizing Information So You Can Find It

In his book *Information Anxiety,* Richard Wurman (1989) described five ways to organize information:

- *By category:* Buildings, waterlines, type of information such as photos or receipts
- *By time:* Date built or serviced
- *By location:* Geographic area or room number
- *Alphabetically:* By the name of the equipment
- *In a continuum:* Appraised value

Successful organizing processes can be developed in a variety of ways. One organization may use the category method by keeping its photographs together and creating subcategories by location (main building, maintenance area, and so on). A different organization may use the time method to keep all its paid invoices in chronological order and the location method to provide each building with its own set of records as a spreadsheet of recorded projects and costs. Yet a third organization may use a database to organize its information, which can be queried using multiple methods.

There's really no right way to organize information. Think about how you'll need to use the information, and organize it accordingly. Remember, though, that changing the orga-

Numbering utilities and buildings can be helpful for record keeping; it should be done attractively.

Pike's National Forest. Wynne Whyman photographer.

WHAT ABOUT MISSING DATA?

If some of your information has ever gone missing, your organization is not alone. Changes in staff, simple error, even natural disasters can claim records. When you need to find missing information, check these backup sources to help you reconstruct what you need:

- The finance department for a list of depreciated assets or invoices
- Alumni, including former staff members
- Adjoining property owners
- Local organizations such as the county seat, utility companies, soil conservation districts, forest service, local organizations protecting the watershed, historical society, and the local library
- Previous contractors, architects, or master planners (they may have blueprints or computer renderings)
- The organization's bank safe deposit box
- Aerial photographs from local landowners, agencies, the U.S. Geological Survey (USGS), or satellite images from the Web

nizing system is not the same as changing the color of your building. If you begin keeping receipts chronologically but later start to file them by the type of project, finding them will be difficult. This can limit the value of your system.

Preserving Your Records

The life span of an archival object depends on many variables including the original quality, the quality of the media used, the amount of use the item receives, and storage conditions. Life span is hard to quantify. A poorly stored picture may still be recognizable but not of the original quality. Similarly, a CD may have usable blocks, but some may be unreadable.

Whether your organization is small or large, you'll need a safe place to store your records on-site and backups of your important records off-site.

To protect your documents, computer files, and photographs, you need to ensure that your storage procedures and facilities are conducive to document longevity. Tool 10.2 provides an overview of professional archiving techniques in chart form.

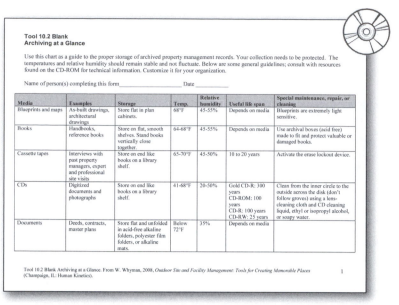

**Tool 10.2 Blank
Archiving at a Glance**

Use this chart as a guide to the proper storage of archived property management records. Your collection needs to be protected. The temperatures and relative humidity should remain stable and not fluctuate. Below are some general guidelines; consult with resources found on the CD-ROM for technical information. Customize it for your organization.

Name of person(s) completing this form_____ Date _____

Media	Examples	Storage	Temp.	Relative humidity	Useful life span	Special maintenance, repair, or cleaning
Blueprints and maps	As-built drawings, architectural drawings	Store flat in plan cabinets.	68°F	45-55%	Depends on media	Blueprints are extremely light sensitive.
Books	Handbooks, reference books	Store on flat, smooth shelves. Stand books vertically close together.	64-68°F	45-55%	Depends on media	Use archival boxes (acid free) made to fit and protect valuable or damaged books.
Cassette tapes	Interviews with past property managers, expert and professional site visits	Store on end like books on a library shelf.	65-70°F	45-50%	10 to 20 years	Activate the erase lockout device.
CDs	Digitized documents and photographs	Store on end like books on a library shelf.	41-68°F	20-50%	Gold CD-R: 300 years CD-ROM: 100 years CD-R: 100 years CD-RW: 25 years	Clean from the inner circle to the outside across the disk (don't follow groves) using a lens-cleaning cloth and CD cleaning liquid, ethyl or isopropyl alcohol, or soapy water.
Documents	Deeds, contracts, master plans	Store flat and unfolded in acid-free alkaline folders, polyester film folders, or alkaline mats.	Below 72°F	35%	Depends on media	

Tool 10.2 Blank Archiving at a Glance. From W. Whyman, 2008, *Outdoor Site and Facility Management: Tools for Creating Memorable Places* (Champaign, IL: Human Kinetics).

TOOL 10.2 Archiving at a Glance.

PHYSICAL STORAGE GUIDELINES

Here are a few practical tips that can help you avoid disaster when storing important records:

- *Archive location.* Locate storage facilities away from water pipes, leaky foundations, or basements if flooding is possible.

- *Clean air.* Make sure air is well ventilated with minimal dust contaminants and little or no use of chemicals (from cleaning or **insecticides)**. Storage areas should not be near cigarette smoking areas.

- *Fire protection.* Work with professionals to design a quality fire suppression and smoke and heat detector configuration for your collection and building.

- *Lighting.* Both the sun and fluorescent bulbs accelerate damage to items. Close window drapes and limit UV exposure.

- *Pest-free.* Prevention is the best pest control. Frequent cleaning and the elimination of damp, dark areas will deter pests. To avoid importing any problems, put new donations into white kitchen bags for a few days to make it easier to detect any insect eggs and droppings. Keep a close eye on sticky traps in less frequently accessed areas. Avoid the use of insecticides, because these chemicals may cause as much damage as the insects themselves (Colorado Archives).

- *Storage.* Store materials off the floor by using shelving or pallets. Use fire-protected file cabinets for extra protection of critical records.

- *Temperature and relative humidity.* Keep both the temperature and relative humidity constant and avoid fluctuations.

Cataloging What You Have

When you look for an item at the library, the first place you probably visit is the reference catalog. Central directories and catalogs, whether computer based or paper based, organize your records and make them easy to find. Catalogs are especially helpful when data are stored in several areas of your organization.

A simple plan for cataloging your records is to use a three-ring notebook with a bright color cover. In the notebook, record the following by hand or print from a computer list:

- A brief synopsis of each document or data file
- The location of the actual document or data file.

Store the notebook in a prominent location where everyone can see it and find the data quickly. The notebook becomes the organization's main brain, rather than having it in one person's personal memory—inaccessible when he or she is on vacation. One tool that is good to include is tool 4.1, Property Record Catalog.

In addition to cataloging your documents, you will also need to describe each cataloged piece. **Metadata** describe the characteristics of the data, such as the source, content, quality, condition, and date. In effect, metadata are data about data. For example, have you ever had a picture of a building that you could not identify? Maybe the building was torn down 10 years ago. Metadata describe the material in a consistent manner, with the same types of information being recorded about all materials. They can also serve as an inventory.

Three general categories of metadata need to be kept (adapted from Library of Congress, n.d.).

- *Descriptive.* Describing the content, indexing, or the material, and so on.
- *Administrative.* Background information such as donor information, source, author, restrictions, preservation of the image, or scanning resolution.
- *Structural and technical.* Describing the relationship among the parts, such as the page order in a book or the relationship between a thumbnail and the master image.

This information could be recorded in your master three-ring notebook or in a spreadsheet, database, or word processing document.

Creating Backup Records

Always have an extra set! This statement is good advice for records management. Consider updating your most important site and facility records, then storing a second copy at a different location. This will preserve your records in case one set gets damaged, lost, or destroyed.

For your on-site records, divide them into two key groupings: everyday use and archival use. In addition, make off-site backups of essential archival records. These groupings are described in table 10.1.

Consider, for example, a DVD. To minimize damage, store the original in a safe place (archival use) and make a copy for viewing (everyday use). Then you do not need to worry about people accidentally leaving the DVD in a hot car or losing it because of its small size. If they do, you simply make another copy. You can also put the archival version on a high-quality DVD that will last many years and use less expensive DVDs for copies.

Table 10.1   Archival and Everyday Records

Archival records	Everyday records
Limited use, limited access	**Frequent use, convenient access**
• *Original nondigitized materials:* Papers, photographs, as-built plans, videotapes • *Master digital files:* Original digital scans of photographs, with as much digital information as possible (use uncompressed formats, such as .tif formats) • *Acid-free master copy of original:* Newspaper articles copied on acid-free paper • *Original digitized materials:* Images from digital cameras or camcorders	• Copies of as-built plans to take out in the field • Copies of historical pictures for a fundraising event • Copies of videotapes to be checked out and viewed • Derivative digital files, such as a smaller file size in .jpg format to use on the Web

Photographs are another application in which backing up makes sense. Consider keeping the original photograph *and* an original scanned image in the archival use location. By creating such redundancy in the archival storage area, you ensure preservation of a copy, despite inevitable deterioration (archival use). Once **digitized,** the photograph can be used flexibly in other formats. For example, you can reformat an image for use in an alumni newsletter or add historical photos to your Web site (everyday use).

Managing Your Archives

To manage your archives, you and your organization will need to determine certain policies and procedures to follow. Here are some factors to consider:

• *Access to archives.* Determine who may have access to your archives and who has authority to check out, add, or dispose of archival materials. For controlled access, some organizations rent a safe deposit box off-site to store the originals of their most important documents. Again, create redundancy by putting a quality copy of these important materials in your backup storage.

• *Access procedures.* Stipulate in your access procedures that no food, drink, or smoking is allowed in the area and when gloves should be used (skin oil can cause damage to archival materials).

• *Acquisition policy.* Alumni staff or participants may offer you their memorabilia for the archives, such as old photographs, videotapes, employee agreements, uniforms, or signs. Know which donations you will accept and which you will not accept. After accepting such materials, determine whether the donor can check them out and for what type of use. As a courtesy, establish who will send the donor a thank-you letter. See the Archives Association of British Columbia Web site listed on the CD-ROM for policy samples.

• *Archival materials maintenance.* Based on authoritative sources, establish procedures to check for deterioration of physical storage media (e.g., warped or cracked CDs, moldy boxes, pests) and electronic content (e.g., unreadable disks). Spin video- and cassette tapes to tighten them. Establish conversion schedules to transfer electronic records onto new media—for example, copying aging videotapes onto new tapes before the videotapes deteriorate (Minnesota Historical Society).

- *Archival media.* Weighing the life span of your archived records, the cost and quality of archival supplies, and the type of materials you have to work with, determine the archival material type and quality to be used. For example, do you want to store electronic data on USB flash drives, CDs, or DVDs? What level of quality will you purchase? (Pay particular attention to the life expectancy.)

- *Archive storage facility.* Maintenance procedures should address regular cleaning (with chemicals that will not leave harmful residue or fumes), regular maintenance of heating and cooling equipment (furnaces, air conditioners, dehumidifiers), and monitoring temperature and humidity (Minnesota Historical Society).

- *Backup policy.* Establish how often you want to make backup copies. Determine which materials you'll be backing up and where you'll be storing your off-site backup materials. Remember to include backing up your computer's hard drive to avoid losing data as a result of computer virus attacks, computer crashes, and natural disasters.

- *Supervision, training, and monitoring.* You can have excellent procedures describing what needs to be done. However, the supervisor needs to ensure that the person in charge of archiving is trained in the organization's procedures and expectations, as well as deciding the amount of decision-making authority that person has to purge documents. The supervisor needs to ensure there is at least one backup person who knows as much about the archives as the primary person does, in case the primary person becomes ill, moves away, or becomes disgruntled with the organization. Finally, checks and balances should be set up to make sure the right records are kept and the organization's procedures are solidly in place. The integrity of the archives must be ensured over time.

ARCHIVAL SUPPLIES

Archived material can deteriorate faster than normal if the right archival supplies are not used. Use archival storage materials for the following:

- *Enclosures or folders.* Excessive alkalinity can damage photographs, blueprints, some artwork on paper, and textiles. Use plastic-based archival sleeves to hold documents, never magnetic or self-adhesive albums. Size enclosures appropriately to protect each item and give the item the proper support (New York State Archives).

- *Pens.* Use acid-free pens for identification purposes. Do not use a ballpoint pen or a regular permanent marking pen.

- *Storage boxes.* Use acid-free boxes to store collections of materials. Do not use regular cardboard boxes.

- *CD storage.* Store CDs in protective cases. Do not use a label on archival CDs. Instead, write an identifying note on the CD's clear center near the hole. Write on the top surface using a water-based permanent marker (MAM-A, 2003).

- *Picture matting.* Use acid-free adhesive tape, not Scotch tape or glue.

- *Dusting cloths.* Use lint-free dusting cloths.

- *Gloves.* You may need special cotton gloves for handling sensitive media.

Developing Integrated Procedures

Many others in your organization may need access to the records you keep about your site and facilities. To help you think about how to integrate your property records system with other parts of your operation, look closely at the following issues and address them as necessary:

- *Finance and property records.* The receipts from purchases are required in the finance department. However, site and facilities need the same receipts. When you need a copy of a receipt, you can simply ask for a copy from the finance department. However, when people in the finance department are purging their records, they should come to you to determine what records to keep. If a piece of equipment fails in its warranty period, you don't want to find out that the proof of purchase was shredded two years earlier! An alternative choice is for a finance staff person to make copies of the essential site and facility receipts, and for you to maintain a separate system.

- *Program and property inspections.* Equipment safety checks are regularly done by the programming staff for areas such as climbing walls, ropes courses, and other high-risk areas. If something needs repair, the site and facility staff person often completes the maintenance. On a sheet of paper, you can put the programming safety check at the top and the maintenance performed at the bottom. An administrator can quickly review the log and see the inspections and corrective action taken. This shows diligence in ensuring the safety of participants.

- *Inventory and inspections.* For staff completing a year-end inventory, consider adding a column for "recommended repairs and purchases for next year." This accomplishes both the inventory and an inspection of the equipment at the same time—in written form.

Another record-keeping method is to record parts information or the installation date directly on the equipment. But still keep the owner's manual!

Photo courtesy of Wynne Whyman.

The work of program and properties inspections can be integrated in a couple of other ways. First, the site and facility staff member can monitor that the programming staff are completing the safety checks. This serves as a checks-and-balances system. Second, both the programming and site and facility staff can put in their schedule that an outside inspector is needed annually. If one of them misses the reminder, the other can pick up on it.

Electronic Record Keeping

Every organization maintains a paper-based record-keeping system, and most also use a variety of electronic-based methods. Many software tools are available to record and store site and facility data. Some are quite complex and require the services of a consultant, centralized expertise, or a nearby college or university to help you determine what functionality you need, develop and set up your system, and perhaps provide ongoing support.

Usually organizations use a combination of electronic files from various software applications. These can be organized like paper files, with digital folders mimicking paper folders. Organizing and naming the digital folders to match the paper folders makes finding things easy. Table 10.2 lists the pros and cons of going digital.

Following is a list of several major software applications and how they might be used for record keeping. Remember, the best system is not necessarily the most expensive. It's the one that records useful data and makes it easy to retrieve it.

- *Word processing* is good for transcribing handwritten notes that can later be inserted into various documents. You can insert pictures into documents to associate images with the text.

- *Spreadsheets* are useful for calculating numbers, sorting, formatting, and setting up a basic maintenance record. Consider using one file for the equipment. Inside each file, make a separate worksheet for each piece of equipment. The top of the worksheet can list the description (e.g., name, date built or purchased, manufacturer,

Table 10.2   Pros and Cons of Going Digital

Pro	Con
Accessibility: Gives people access to materials that would not be otherwise accessible because of age, value, or damage.	*Obsolescence:* Software and hardware formats are continually changing. A format may become obsolete and thus inaccessible in a few years.
Searchability: Converting an interview from a cassette tape to a written transcript makes it possible to search for a keyword.	*Cost:* Conversion to digital format takes time, money, and possibly technical support.
Quality: Saves wear and tear on original records.	*Skills required:* Staff or volunteers may not be fully skilled in digital conversion.
Space: Electronic records take up less physical storage space than paper records do.	*Quality:* If done incorrectly, the quality of electronic copies may be less than that of the originals. Electronic records may degrade faster than the originals, requiring periodic recopying.
Flexibility: Documents and visuals can be used for multiple purposes (brochures, case statements, reports).	

serial number), and the bottom can provide the maintenance record. Similarly, make a separate file for each building.

- **Rational databases** enable you to easily pull (query) various assortments of data together after entering the information once. A query might be: "Show me a list of the roofs replaced between 1993 and 2005," or "Show me a list of all volunteer projects." Databases are very helpful for organizations that have multiple buildings or multiple properties. Certain staff and volunteers may have the skills to build a basic database. However, to make the most of your system and to allow for growth and change, you will probably need someone with professional database design skills. It is very difficult to redesign an inadequate system once data have been entered.

- *Digital images and video* are excellent for visually documenting your property and how it has changed over time. Digital images are also an excellent way to record the locations of septic tanks and buried utilities when you undertake excavations. These images are especially useful if you include a physical reference in the picture such as a tape measure extended from a recognizable landmark.

- *Computer-aided design (CAD)* software lets you draw building and utility layouts for locations that do not have maps or blueprints. A range of CAD software is available. Architects use CAD software for drawing building plans. When using architect services, if possible, write into the contract that at the end of the project you would like a CD of the data and their naming convention. You can then copy the data for use with your next project or give a copy of the CD to the next architect you hire.

- A *geographic information system (GIS)* is not only a way to create maps, but also keeps all your information in one place. It can combine informational elements (e.g., your maps and information records), freeing you from the need to use separate systems. See chapter 4 for a further explanation of how a GIS works.

You have many choices of software to choose from to design, create, and store your electronic information. You'll make decisions about the capabilities of the software, its cost, and the stability of the product. However, your success is not based on the software alone. Having skilled staff and volunteers who can properly design the system and maintain it over time is critical. The records are vital for future reference; you do not want to be handicapped by a poorly designed system. Sometimes you will need a professional to help with your digital work, computerized systems, and maintaining your paper records.

USING THE WEB

What can you find by searching on the Web?

- *Equipment:* Owner's manuals and servicing instructions
- *Equipment photographs:* Professional photographs of new equipment
- *Flora and fauna:* Inventories for your region
- *Information:* Material specifications, green products
- *Maps:* Aerial maps, county maps, water district maps
- **Material safety data sheets (MSDS)**
- *Online learning modules*
- *Public meetings or hearings:* Agenda and minutes

- *Regulations:* County, state, and federal
- *Safety procedures*
- *Soils data*
- *Training materials and quizzes that you can tailor for your staff*
- *Water quality test results (public water systems)*
- *Watershed information*
- *Wetland area information*

Enter your property name into a couple of popular search engines. You might be surprised where your property name appears or how others are using your property's information.

Once you have found the information, download it to your network or hard drive for safekeeping. It's helpful to make electronic folders to hold similar types of information, such as "equipment," "natural resources," or "buildings."

Getting Professional Assistance

When archiving records for your site and facilities, you may want to perform most of the work yourself but use professional help when you go beyond your level of expertise. Professionals who understand the intricacies of organizing systems can help you create systems that provide an impressive range of functionality.

Working with a professional archivist can give you long-term preservation *and* ensure the everyday usability of your materials. Use the skills of a professional archivist, conservator, restorer, records management consultant, or computer specialist to do the following:

- Address observed changes in an object, such as a flaking surface, fading, insects, or mold (American Institute for Conservation of Historic and Artistic Works).
- Clean, restore, or repair an object (American Institute for Conservation of Historic and Artistic Works).
- Set up an archival system for the materials.
- Change the display of an object (such as removing pictures from frames) (American Institute for Conservation of Historic and Artistic Works).
- Convert from one medium to another.

To find these experts, contact your local genealogical society, historical society, library, archival associations, heritage programs, computer graphic professionals, and museums. You can also find experts using the resource section on the CD-ROM.

Finding What You Need

Keeping good records is a vital component of good property management. You can derive satisfaction from the fact that 50 years from now people will be able to easily access your records to find information about a building remodeling project, read about warranty information, locate utilities, or locate an old mine shaft. In the meantime, your record-keeping system will place at your fingertips the records you need to create a comprehensive maintenance plan or forecast expenses 5 to 10 years out, thus helping you be proactive and plan for the future.

BEST PRACTICES

✓ A systemized, integrated record-keeping system is instituted for site and facilities.

✓ Decisions about what records to keep and for how long are documented in a record retention schedule and consistently implemented.

✓ Duplicate copies of essential records are made for everyday use to preserve the archived originals.

✓ A second set of essential records is regularly backed up and stored off-site.

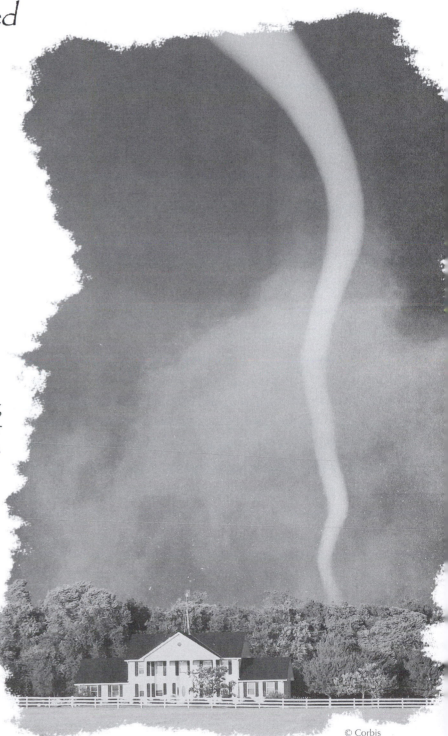

RISK

Managing to Be Prepared

Site and facility concerns are a critical part of your organization's overall risk management strategy. Managing site and facility risks and preparing for natural disasters and other emergencies ensures participant safety, creates a safe work environment for staff, and protects your physical assets. Risk management and emergency preparedness require a team effort and a lot of technical expertise, but the plan you implement will give you a level of comfort that you have done all you can to ensure the safety of people, the organization's reputation, and its financial security.

© Corbis

What are the risks to your site and facilities? And how do you manage those risks? Risk management is all about preparing for worst-case scenarios. It involves thinking through harmful situations that can occur and how to avoid their individual, organizational, and financial consequences. Can accidents be prevented? Does the organization have adequate insurance coverage? Should some risks be transferred by hiring an outside firm that has its own insurance? How can the organization develop emergency protocols to avoid confusion and keep people as safe as possible? These are the kinds of questions that risk management considers.

Site and Facility Risk

Sites and facilities carry multiple degrees of risk; some activities may have a minor impact on the organization or individuals, whereas others may have severe consequences. Some examples show the range of possibilities:

- Faulty electrical wiring installed by a nonlicensed electrician causes a building fire.

- The boiler is improperly maintained, thus voiding the warranty and causing an additional expense.

- A participant has an encounter with a rabid bat, and the parent files a lawsuit.

- A pond accumulates trash and debris, necessitating pond remediation and the elimination of the fishing program.

- A staff member is injured by an older power tool that did not have the proper safety devices.

- A hurricane weakens the structural integrity of a building.

- Two staff people give contradictory media messages, resulting in a questionable reputation for safety in the community.

- The old hot water heater floods the records room, causing water damage to several important records.

Thinking of all the possibilities that could happen to sites and facilities can seem like an endless and daunting task. A risk management plan uses the list of possibilities, applies risk management principles, and develops ways to provide a safe operation.

A comprehensive risk management plan is essential to providing a safe experience for staff, volunteers,

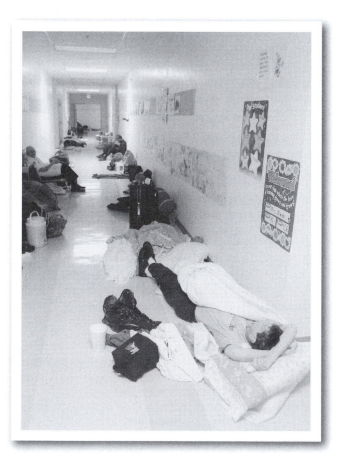

During an emergency, people are generally more calm if they know what to do as part of a well-orchestrated plan.

© Corbis

and participants—and to safeguard site and facility assets. Your organization has probably already developed a risk management plan for the entire organization. Read your organization's plan, keeping an eye on how site and facility risks are addressed. To enhance the site and facility portions in your existing risk management plan, this chapter gives you several areas to examine.

During the development of your site and facility portions of your risk management plan, you will be deciding the best measures to put in place. You will probably do some of the work yourself and also work with other people who bring various kinds of expertise. You may work with board members, insurance representatives, financial experts, local disaster professionals, and others. In addition, extensive resources on the CD-ROM give you reputable information to include in your site and facility procedures and risk management plan.

What Is Risk Management?

The goal of risk management is to improve performance by acknowledging and controlling risks. It puts you, not the risk, in charge. It's about protecting and conserving your organization's resources and providing goods and services sensibly. With prior planning and effective procedures in place, your organization can pursue its mission by accepting more—not less—risk. Ideally, risk management creates an environment in which an organization can take informed risks.

Risk Management Process

A risk management plan is no small undertaking. Before incorporating site and facility information into the existing risk management plan, it is good idea to thoroughly analyze all aspects of your site and facility operation, because it is easy to overlook something. The Nonprofit Risk Management Center (Oliver, 2003) has five steps to follow to identify and address risks (see figure 11.1).

FIGURE 11.1   Risk management process.

The "Risk Management Process" description and diagram are adapted and reprinted with permission of the Nonprofit Risk Management Center from *Managing Facility Risk: 10 Steps to Safety* by Barbara B. Oliver, The Nonprofit Risk Management Center, www.nonprofitrisk.org, is a nonprofit serving other nonprofits through articles, books, online training, workshops, conferences and consulting with a nonprofit's slant on managing risk.

Step 1 Establish the Context

What role does risk play within the organization? Does the leadership live on the edge and feel comfortable taking chances, or is it unwilling to move outside known parameters that it considers safe? Score your organization on the following scale.

Risk averse   −9   −6   −3   0   +3   +6   +9   Extreme risk taker

How important is the practice of risk management to the organization? If risk management is important, the organization budgets for and spends monies on risk management, and the staff are continuously having the time to work on risk management. To evaluate whether your organization is committed to risk management, you might ask these questions: Is the risk management function defined? Does a committee or point person oversee the fulfillment of risk management goals? Or, on the other side of the continuum, is risk managed on an as-needed basis (when the insurance claim or lawsuit is filed or the negative news airs) because the organization believes there isn't time, money, or personnel to devote to managing risk on an ongoing basis? Rank your organization on the following scale:

Poorly financed   −9   −6   −3   0   +3   +6   +9   Well financed
and understaffed   and staffed
to meet goals   to meet goals

With your committee, collectively write down the answers to these questions:

- What is the relationship of the organization to its environment?
- What community needs does it meet?
- What legal and regulatory parameters must it operate within?
- What are other considerations (language, cultural, political)?
- What are the organization's overall strengths and weaknesses, the opportunities it has, and the threats it faces (**SWOT analysis)**?

Step 2 Acknowledge and Identify Risk

Brainstorm with a committee answers to the following:

- What can happen that will put our mission at risk?
- Why would this happen?
- How would it affect the mission?

You can organize the brainstorming around the following:

- How the consequences or impact of the activities could affect vari-

Evaluate the level of risk inherent in each activity and determine ways to manage the risk so activities can be done in a safe manner.
© Corbis

Tool 11.1 Blank
Brainstorming Site and Facility Risks

Use this tool to revise the site and facilities component of the organization's risk management plan.

Brainstorm different areas of concern your organization may encounter. Then determine their severity and frequency by writing down a 1 or 2 (1 = low; 2 = high). After you have brainstormed, decide how you will best manage this risk. You may manage the identified risk in more than one way.

Name of person(s) completing this form _____ Date _____

Area	Specific area(s) of concern	Risk assessment (severity) [1 or 2]	Risk assessment (frequency) [1 or 2]	Method to manage: Avoidance Modification Sharing Retention	Techniques to implement to address risk	Monitoring techniques
General overview						
Participants						
People— staff						
People— volunteers						
People— volunteer boards						
Site—land						
Site— grounds						
Utilities						
Site— natural resources						
Site— natural disasters						

Tool 11.1 Blank Brainstorming Site and Facility Risks. From W. Whyman, 2008, *Outdoor Site and Facility Management: Tools for Creating Memorable Places* (Champaign, IL: Human Kinetics). Based on ACA. 1

TOOL 11.1 Brainstorming Site and Facility Risks.

Tool 11.2 Blank
Risk Management Checklist for Site and Facilities

Use this tool to verify you have these specific site and facility areas covered in your organization's risk management plan.

After reviewing each question, determine whether the item is applicable to your organization. If it is applicable, use the process described in the book to determine practices you might incorporate to manage your risk.

Name of person(s) completing this form _____ Date _____

General Considerations

_____ **Best practices.** Are the best practices implemented? Use this book, industry standards, your insurance agent, your agency or organizational resources, and land management resources to ensure a good understanding of best practices in risk management and emergency preparedness.

_____ **Business continuity planning.** Are the site and facilities addressed in your plan?

_____ **Conflict of use.** Will participants be on the property while projects are worked on? Will the work interfere with participant activities? How will use conflict be avoided or minimized?

_____ **Contracts.** Are there guidelines for reviewing and signing contracts? Does one person sign the contracts, or do different people sign contracts, depending on the financial risk (dollar amount) or project risk (specialization or potential for problems)? When do attorneys review contracts?

_____ **Emergency plan development.** Have you reviewed and integrated your site and facility plans with local experts, community procedures, and building codes? Include fire departments, law enforcement agencies, community disaster planning agencies, natural disaster experts in your region, the Red Cross, and local search and rescue organizations.

_____ **Emergency supplies.** Are supplies on hand for participants in the event of emergencies? Examples include food, a method to warm food and water, drinking water, lanterns or flashlights (with extra batteries), two-way radios (in case cell phone towers become overloaded or do not reach remote locations).

Tool 11.2 Blank Risk Management Checklist for Site and Facilities. From W. Whyman, 2008, *Outdoor Site and Facility Management: Tools for Creating Memorable Places* (Champaign, IL: Human Kinetics). 1

TOOL 11.2 Risk Management Checklist for Site and Facilities.

ous aspects of your organization, such as people, property, income, and reputation (goodwill)

- Risk inherent in departments or operational units, such as administration, finance, governance, development and fund-raising, conferences and events, communications, client services, and information technology

- Types of events, such as natural disasters (hurricanes, mudslides, floods), human-induced disasters (fire, power outages, major traffic jams), or damage to property records

To organize your brainstorming for your site and facilities, use the first two columns in tool 11.1. The areas follow the categories of this book. As you go through the areas in tool 11.1, refer to the checklist in tool 11.2.

Step 3 Evaluate and Prioritize Risk

Not every risk you've identified is likely to materialize. For each potential risk, ask the following:

- How likely is this risk to occur? Sometimes it is helpful to classify the possibilities in terms of frequency and severity, as shown in figure 11.2. Frequency is the number of times the incident may happen as well as the likelihood of its occurring. Severity is the degree of harm to people, finances, intangibles, or physical property. For instance, if you're located in the midwest,

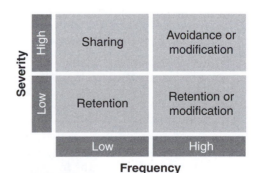

FIGURE 11.2 Ways to categorize and manage risk, based on the amount of risk.

the likelihood that your building will be swept away by a tsunami is infinitesimal. A building may suffer some damage from sewer backup or basement flooding following a downpour, but the building is still standing and can be cleaned up and repaired. This type of building risk has a higher probability of occurring, but less repair cost than a tsunami.

- What damage would it likely inflict?

Examine statistics in your type of organization or type of work. What are common types of accidents? For example, by looking at the following **OSHA** statistics, you can determine the likelihood that some of these accidents may happen at your organization. For construction workers in 2004, here are the types of nonfatal injuries and illnesses involving days away from work (Meyer & Pegula, 2006):

OSHA Claim Percentages

- Overexertion (20%)
- Struck by an object (18%)
- Fall to lower level (14%)
- Fall to same level (8%)
- Struck against an object (8%)

Step 4 Implement Risk Management Techniques (Manage Risk)

Decide how to manage your risks and implement a risk management program using available tools. Have the committee working on the plan develop strategies to minimize the likelihood of a risk materializing and develop responses that it could activate should that incident occur. The completed matrix from step 3 gives you a starting place in addressing the various types of risks. The tools in the risk management process are as follows:

- *Avoidance.* Activities the organization will not undertake because the risk outweighs the benefits. Examples: Not purchasing or accepting a gift of property in a **floodplain,** not allowing participants under the age of 18 to participate in service projects that involve power tools.
- *Modification (also called reduction or control).* Actions the organization will implement to reduce the severity of the risk. Examples: Installing a sump pump in the basement and having the ground sloped away from the building's foundation, performing preventive maintenance, keeping records, training staff, supervising, performing regular inspections, informing participants of dangers such as posting signs at cliffs or near wet floors.
- *Sharing (also called transfer).* Actions the organization will carry out with another organization to reduce the severity of the risk. Examples: Purchasing fire insurance through an external company to share the cost of damage should it occur, contracting with an outside vendor to regularly maintain the HVAC system.
- *Retention.* The organization accepts the full risk. Examples: Planning to pay for minor vandalism damage to avoid paying a higher insurance premium.

Your next task is to test your strategies. Low-priority risks should be accepted and monitored, and high-priority risks should be evaluated against the organization's mission before being rejected or accepted. Some organizations couldn't exist without accepting high-priority risks. Consider residential treatment programs for juvenile offenders (boot camps), mentoring programs for physically or mentally challenged children or adults, and sports programs on city playgrounds.

Now take your identified risks in tool 11.1, and finish completing the columns. This is where facility risk management comes into play. By analyzing what is needed to protect the service recipients, employees, volunteers, vendors, and organization, you can reduce the chance the risk will occur and cause extensive damage to your organization's finances, reputation, and existence.

Step 5 Monitor and Update the Program

Risk management is a circular process. Each stage of the process is connected to the one before and the one after. You will continually monitor all incidents, whether small or large. To monitor and continually address various incidents, you will use discussions, anecdotal comments, participant evaluations, and formal incident reports. After each incident, you'll analyze how it could have been prevented or minimized. What procedures worked? What didn't work? What do you need to do differently another time? As a result, you might modify the risk management plan; retrain staff, volunteers, and participants; revise procedures; or consult with an external expert.

In addition, it is very important that you regularly step back and look at the overall themes, the types of incidents, and what you have learned. Use objective data from your incident reports, usage statistics, and other organizational data. At least once a year, the risk management committee members should review and revise the techniques it has implemented, as well as identify new areas that need attention.

The "Risk Management Process" description and diagram are adapted and reprinted with permission of the Nonprofit Risk Management Center from *Managing Facility Risk: 10 Steps to Safety* by Barbara B. Oliver, The Nonprofit Risk Management Center, www.nonprofitrisk.org, is a nonprofit serving other nonprofits through articles, books, online training, workshops, conferences, and consulting with a nonprofit's slant on managing risk.

Techniques to Reduce or Modify Risk

As noted in step 4 of the risk management process, one way to manage your risk is to take actions that will decrease or minimize the risk. Almost all organizations do this by providing safety measures when engaging in risky activities. There are several methods for working with your assets, staff, volunteers, and participants.

Depending on your activities and facilities, your plan needs to include ways to assist those who need additional attention during an evacuation.

ENABLING HELICOPTER EVACUATION

For remote sites, a critical part of your emergency procedures will be to identify the nearest helicopter landing site, either on your property or at a nearby property. If you determine that your property might be a possibility for a helicopter evacuation site, following are some steps to guide the development of your site.

- Determine (with **GPS** coordinates) two or three possible locations that are flat, grassy or paved (to minimize airborne dirt), away from trees, and accessible by vehicles.

- Ask your medical evacuation organization to visit the site to determine the preferred helicopter landing site and the nearby location where injured people will be held until they can be transported to the helicopter.

- Work with your county, adjacent landowners, and back country organizations to collaborate and possibly share any costs for clearing or developing the site to enable helicopter evacuation.

- Mark the helicopter evacuation site on your maps and incorporate it in your written emergency procedures.

- *Physical projects.* Access to a swimming pool can be minimized by installing fences around the pool, locking the entrance gate or door, and posting a sign that states "no admittance without permission." A moisture barrier in the basement can prevent moisture from entering and causing mold. Creating a helicopter landing site would decrease evacuation time (see the Enabling Helicopter Evacuation sidebar).

- *Written documentation.* Describe what important actions people need to take, what you expect to happen, precautions that are important, and contact information. Written plans and procedures are important communication methods. You can train people to use these documents as reference sheets during a crisis. With these documents in hand, people will be less likely to panic in a crisis situation because they know what to do, they have the same information as fellow staff so they can help each other out, and they know how the organization will be taking care of them. You, as a planner, will have peace of mind knowing that you've thought through many of the "what ifs" ahead of time, consulted with experts, and determined the best course of action.

Use the organization's past experiences, community experts, national organizational resources, surrounding landowners, books, and national resources to develop your written procedures. Three information-packed resources will help you develop procedures and protocols for your site and facilities. See tool 11.3, Workplace

Tool 11.3 Blank
Workplace Safety Operating Procedures

The following points can be incorporated into your procedures.

Name of person(s) completing this form_____ Date _____

____ Employees are responsible for their personal safety and do not do work they cannot perform in a safe manner.

____ Employees do only work for which they have the licenses, skills, or training to do so.

____ All equipment safety devices and features are used.

____ Maintenance areas are kept clean and organized.

____ Personal protective devices are provided and worn. These include gloves, safety glasses, protective clothing, respirators, and back support belts.

____ Work is done in compliance with Occupational Safety and Health Administration (OSHA) standards.

____ A lockout or tagout program is implemented. *[Describe your organization's procedures.]*

____ The organization provides access to material safety data sheets (MSDS). *[Describe your organization's location of these sheets, accessibility, updates, and any organizational procedures.]*

____ Chemicals are stored properly, and staff and volunteers use them following manufacturers' guidelines and training received.

____ Dangerous work is performed only when following the organization's procedures. The number of staff who must be present when performing dangerous work is identified.

____ Accidents or incidents are reported using the policies identified in the personnel manual. The personnel manual also describes workers' compensation regulations.

Tool 11.3 Blank Workplace Safety Operating Procedures. From W. Whyman, 2008, *Outdoor Site and Facility Management: Tools for Creating Memorable Places* (Champaign, IL: Human Kinetics). 1

TOOL 11.3 Workplace Safety Operating Procedures.

Tool 11.4 Blank
Evacuation of Building (On-Site Emergencies)

Use this tool to develop your on-site evacuation procedures.

Name of person(s) completing this form_____ Date _____

Writing Clear Evacuation Procedures

When writing evacuation procedures, make them as user-friendly as possible. You might write the documents, and then ask for others to review. It never hurts to find someone who has good editing skills to bring additional clarity. You will want procedures to be as clear as possible to minimize confusion. Following are some pointers:

- Make it readable. Use bold, italics, underlining, and capital letters sparingly to emphasize only essential key points. Left justify the list.
- Keep the length short. The emergency procedure should be no longer than one regular-sized sheet of paper—and usually less.
- Use short sentences. Tell people directly what they need to do, such as "take your car keys with you," rather than "when exiting the building, make sure you take your car keys with you."
- Include only the critical information applicable to everyone in a single document. For example, create one main participant emergency evacuation procedure rather than one each for fire, bomb, and tornado evacuations. Additional information for administrators and other groups should be included in a separate document.
- Find the best location for information and use it only once. This brings clarity and makes it easy for you to update the procedures later.
- Number the items. People need to know the order in which they need to take action.

Your evacuation procedure should include the following:

_____ *A statement of commitment to safety.* For example, "The safety of our staff, volunteers, and participants is our first concern."

_____ *A designated central location.* This location needs to be outside, easily evacuated, away from the front doors where emergency services will be located, and away from any potentially dangerous areas such as heating fuel storage.

_____ *Equipment and supplies.* Essential items to bring such as vehicle keys, purses, cell phones, first aid kits, flashlights, and prescriptions.

_____ *Maps.* Evacuation maps prominently posted throughout the property, with "you are here" clearly marked. Show both primary and secondary routes to the central location.

_____ *Your location.* Next to emergency phones and communication devices should be a sign stating "Your location is . . ." with the property name, address, name of the county, driving directions, and phone number. This is useful because many people do not have this information memorized. In addition, new staff and rental groups especially will find this helpful.

Tool 11.4 Blank Evacuation of Building (On-Site Emergencies). From W. Whyman, 2008, *Outdoor Site and Facility Management: Tools for Creating Memorable Places* (Champaign, IL.: Human Kinetics).   1

Tool 11.5 Blank
Evacuation of Site

Use this checklist to be certain essential elements are included in your organization's written emergency procedures and plans.

Name of person(s) completing this form_____ Date _____

Property Evacuation

In the event of a flood, forest fire, or hurricane, the property may need to be evacuated. This involves two sequential steps:
1. Bring people to a central location on the property. An alternate central location should be predetermined in case the first location is not accessible. See tool 11.4.
2. Move people to a predesignated safe location off the property.

To coordinate these efforts, at least two people (usually administrators) need to be present at a communication center in close proximity to the central gathering place. For example, the designated central location might be an open area, and the communication center might be a building a few hundred feet away that has a telephone, computer access, two-way radios, and a way to activate the emergency warning system.

The administrators at the communication center will be in the best position to make decisions. They will see the whole picture and have access to all the information rather than just the present situation. They will serve as the air traffic control tower that directs people and information, both within the property and externally. Internally, they will keep track of where everyone is located and give groups permission to move within the property to the central location or to the off-site location.

The details of the evacuation procedure should be discussed with your team and detailed in written procedures. Areas for consideration as you develop your written procedures and preparations include the following:

_____ **Off-site evacuation area.** Has an area in the city or town been designated for the participants to be evacuated to in the event of a natural disaster? Make sure you have permission, verify that there is enough physical room, know whether it is an evacuation point for other organizations, and have at least two people's contact information.

_____ **Communication with an outside person.** A remote person or group can help communicate with emergency services, the media, and participant families. What resources does this person need, such as an evacuation map, telephone tree list, or access to participant records?

_____ **Transporting people.** Will organization-owned vehicles be used to transport people? Private vehicles? Bus service providers?

Tool 11.5 Blank Evacuation of Site. From W. Whyman, 2008, *Outdoor Site and Facility Management: Tools for Creating Memorable Places* (Champaign, IL.: Human Kinetics).   1

TOOL 11.4   Evacuation of Building (On-Site Emergencies).

TOOL 11.5   Evacuation of Site.

Safety Operating Procedures; tool 11.4, Evacuation of Building (On-Site Emergencies); and tool 11.5, Evacuation of Site.

Once you have written operating procedures and emergency procedures, they cannot sit in a file or fade on the wall. You need to implement them with your staff and practice them on a regular basis.

- *Training.* Training might be offered for all staff, including the site and facility staff. On the other hand, individual staff members might take specialized training in a regular classroom locally or online. Courses may address controlled chemicals, water treatment, or skills in a particular area. You will need to identify which courses support your risk management plan, and provide the time and payment of the registration fee for staff members to attend (see chapter 3 on benefits). Once staff people have completed the course, you will need to document their training in a written format.

- *Training resources.* One resource for training staff is the insurance companies that hold your policies. You can work with your agent to evaluate and develop strategies for managing your risk. Some insurance companies offer materials for training and sample forms. Training and education are commonly available through your **workers' compensation** insurance carrier in such areas as proper lifting techniques, hazard communication, and accident analysis. Although the intent of the procedures and training is to increase worker safety, the employer may also receive a slight discount in workers' compensation insurance premiums when training documentation is provided.

- *Practice and rehearsal.* Training is only the first step as people learn what they need to do. To make the training stick, they need to practice. The organization also needs an opportunity to assess the effectiveness of the written documents and procedures. To see how things are working, you might rehearse during different times of the day or night, create different scenarios, and rehearse different locations of disasters. Practice shutting off utilities. After the rehearsal, conduct an evaluation to make improvements to your procedures.

- *Supervision and support.* Safety is a philosophy that needs to permeate everything that is done from using stepladders appropriately to wearing safety goggles. To reinforce a safety mindset, supervisors need to be aware during all discussions and when they are in the field. For example, if you have determined that safety back belts are needed when lifting anything over 25 pounds, you will want to make sure they are being used. To reinforce their use, you might say something like, "Great to see you wearing your safety back belt. Is that brand working out for you?"

On an ongoing basis, work with your staff and organization to keep the safety of all staff and volunteers paramount in everyday tasks.

Practicing an evacuation so everyone knows what to expect. Afterward, meet with everyone involved to evaluate what worked and what did not.
© Corbis

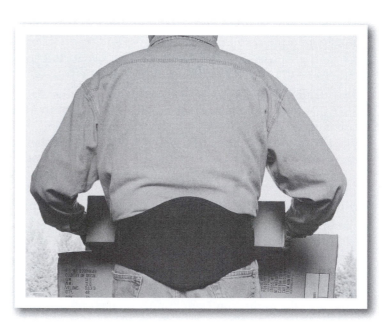

Protect your staff and volunteers with appropriate safety devices.
© Corbis

Safety First

Including site and facilities in your organization's risk management plan shows that you are prepared for unexpected property incidences. You do not need to do all the work yourself. Form a committee to use the many available resources, including your insurance company, local community resources, books, trainings, and Web sites. By reviewing plans and procedures regularly, training new staff promptly, working with experts, and becoming involved in the community plans, you are providing the safest environment you can for your participants, staff, and property.

BEST PRACTICES

✓ Safe working conditions are maintained for the site and facility staff.

✓ Volunteer work projects are designed and implemented with safety paramount.

✓ The organization's risk management plan includes site and facility risks.

✓ Technical expertise is sought to develop safety plans for the facilities and to protect the site.

✓ Staff, volunteers, and participants are trained to follow the emergency protocols.

✓ Evacuation routes are posted at strategic locations.

✓ A detailed emergency protocol with appropriate maps is available on-site, off-site, and on file with local authorities (for remote sites).

SITE AND FACILITY JOB DESCRIPTIONS

When you are writing your job description(s), pick a title that best describes the type of work the person will be doing. A basic list and high-level overviews of the job titles are provided below. Once you have selected an appropriate title, adapt the following job descriptions to meet your needs. Since the responsibilities of a caretaker or site ranger vary greatly among properties, select phrasing from the other job descriptions that matches your needs. An electronic version of the job descriptions is available on the CD-ROM.

Staff for Sites and Facilities

property director—Responsible for all natural resources, grounds, and facility activities, including management functions of one or more properties.

facilities manager—Alternative titles: Maintenance director, facilities director, or buildings and grounds director. Responsible for buildings and grounds only. The position does not include the natural resources management responsibilities.

site manager—Responsible for all site and facility activities, including management functions of one site. Oversees and performs extensive maintenance.

site ranger—Alternative title: Ranger. Responsible for most site and facility activities, but does not perform extensive or specialized work. Oversees and performs moderate maintenance.

caretaker—Responsible for security and checking people into and out of the site and facilities. May be responsible for janitorial work. Oversees and performs light maintenance.

grounds assistant—Responsible for grounds work and tasks as directed.

maintenance assistant—Responsible for minor maintenance as directed. Examples include minor participant requests, such as heating and cooling adjustments and minor plumbing.

Grounds Assistant

Paragraph about the organization: ownership, year-round schedule of operation, number and description of participants, location.

Paragraph about the site and facilities: number of acres, number of buildings and total square feet, grounds or natural resources philosophy.

Desired Qualifications

- Driver's license and good driving record
- Ability to use and repair small motors preferred
- Previous maintenance or grounds experience preferred

Responsible to

Site manager

General Responsibilities

- Be a team player and relate positively to participants, volunteers, other staff, and visitors.
- Consistently strive to maintain a clean and attractive facility.
- Implement safety standards and practices.

Specific Responsibilities

- Perform grounds work: lawn mowing, watering, edging, applying weed control and fertilizer.
- Trim brush and grass away from buildings.
- Maintain trees, bushes, and plants—planting, trimming, watering, and weeding.
- Perform janitorial work: emptying garbage, sweeping, and so on.
- Complete written reports and work summaries.
- Attend and participate in staff meetings.
- *Optional: When maintenance work is not required, participate in organization activities.*
- Other duties as assigned.

Essential Functions

- Minimum age: 18 years old
- Ability to climb ladders
- Ability to lift a minimum of 50 pounds without assistance, which may include chemicals and buckets of water
- Ability to work independently
- Ability to operate power mowers, trimmers, and other small equipment
- Stamina to work outdoors in various weather conditions in two- to four-hour blocks
- Ability to assess visually the cleanliness of the grounds and buildings

Maintenance Assistant

Paragraph about the organization: ownership, year-round schedule of operation, number and description of participants, location.

Paragraph about the site and facilities: number of acres, number of buildings and total square feet, grounds or natural resources philosophy.

Desired Qualifications

- Driver's license and good driving record
- Ability to use and repair maintenance tools preferred
- Previous experience in minor building care and maintenance preferred
- Previous painting or repair work preferred

Responsible to
Site manager

General Responsibilities

- Be a team player and relate positively to participants, volunteers, other staff, and visitors.
- Consistently strive to maintain a clean and attractive facility.
- Implement safety standards and practices.

Specific Responsibilities

- Perform minor maintenance services such as painting, minor carpentry, and repair of programming structures and equipment, such as *(list for your organization).*
- Perform services for participants, such as replacing lightbulbs and screens, *(list other tasks such as moving gear and delivering supplies).*
- Perform janitorial services, including emptying garbage, sweeping and mopping floors, buffing floors, cleaning bathrooms, *(list programming or activity areas for janitorial services).*
- Inspect, clean, and restock buildings and units after use.
- Purchase supplies as needed.
- Follow cleaning procedures and schedule; perform deep cleaning of facilities on a regular basis.
- Complete written reports and work summaries.
- Attend and participate in staff meetings.
- *Optional: When maintenance work is not required, participate in organization activities.*
- Other duties as assigned.

Essential Functions

- Minimum age: 18 years old
- Ability to climb ladders
- Ability to lift a minimum of 50 pounds without assistance, which may include gear, chemicals, inventory, and buckets of water
- Ability to work independently
- Ability to operate power tools and equipment, such as drills, saws; may be supervised for use of dangerous power tools
- Ability to use a mop, broom, and other cleaning tools
- Stamina to work outdoors in various weather conditions in two- to four-hour blocks
- Ability to assess visually the maintenance and janitorial services needed by the buildings and equipment

Site Manager

Paragraph about the organization: ownership, year-round schedule of operation, number and description of participants, location.

Paragraph about the site and facilities: number of acres, number of buildings and total square feet, grounds or natural resources philosophy.

Position Summary

This position maintains the land, grounds, natural resources, structures, and equipment so as to ensure the safe and efficient operation of the organization's programs and to protect the long-term value of the assets.

Description of the schedule, expected hours, and benefits. Example: This full-time exempt position requires 50-hour workweeks in the summer and offers the flexibility to work fewer hours per day or week during the other seasons. This position requires weekend work and occasional night work. Housing and benefits are provided.

Responsible to
Administrator or property director

Supervises
- Seasonal maintenance staff
- Volunteers

Desired Qualifications
- 3-5 years working in the site and facilities field
- Certifications and licenses (may obtain within six months of employment)
  - Driver's license and good driving record
  - General contractor's license preferred
  - Electrician's license preferred
  - First aid certification
  - EMT or advanced first aid certification preferred
- Experience operating a tractor with grading blade
- Ability to use and repair hand and power tools
- Experience working with vendors, suppliers, and service providers
- Previous broad experience in several of the trades—carpentry, construction (general), heating and air conditioning, painting (interior and exterior), fencing, plumbing, and electrical and mechanical systems—to maintain buildings and grounds, utilities, vehicles, and water supply systems
- Project management skills and the ability to resolve complex problems and issues
- Planning, organizing, and scheduling skills
- Experience using independent judgment and discretion in managing subordinates including handling emergency situations, determining procedures to be implemented, setting priorities, maintaining standards, and resolving problems
- Knowledge of site and facility standards, codes, and regulations
- Preferred experiences
  - Experience in environmentally sustainable technologies
  - Demonstrated interest in or knowledge of local flora and fauna

- Experience with word processing, spreadsheets, and databases
- Knowledge of the maintenance of some of the program or recreational activities *(Describe activities such as boating, mountain biking, and so on.)*

General Responsibilities

- Site and facility use
    - Develop and maintain an effective, positive working relationship with participants, parents, staff, volunteers, adjoining landowners, community members, inspectors, and local vendors. Represent the organization in a positive manner. Serve on internal or external committees.
    - Prepare and clean up participant use areas, which may include program areas, kitchen, living areas. Respond to requests from participants.
    - Health, safety, security
        - Monitor the arrival and departure of people on the property.
        - Minimize trespassing and vandalism and maximize safety by enforcing regulations and taking a proactive approach based on education, patrols, outreach, and training.
        - Act decisively and professionally in responding to, evaluating, and handling problems.
        - Respond to emergencies during and after hours, including inclement weather, fire, theft, and vandalism.
- Supervision
    - Select and supervise vendors and contractors.
    - Plan, prepare materials for, and supervise volunteer projects.
- Regulatory
    - Keep up-to-date on and implement all applicable laws, ordinances, policies, regulations, and standards pertaining to the specific duties and responsibilities of the job.
    - Perform regulatory activities, such as water sample collecting for testing.
    - Arrange for external inspections including fire inspections, electrical evaluations, and health department inspections.
    - Keep accurate records of work performed by staff, volunteers, vendors, and contractors. Also maintain manuals, warranty information, and inspection reports.
    - Develop and revise written standard operating procedures.
    - Follow the organization's financial procedures.
- Natural resources
    - Implement conservation principles including controlling noxious and nonnative weeds and plants.
    - Use care so maintenance or program activities do not affect the watershed or wellhead, and enact erosion control measures.
    - Implement forest management plan.
    - Oversee wildlife habitat enhancement projects.
- General operations and maintenance
    - Consistently strive to maintain a clean and attractive facility.
    - Purchase maintenance and cleaning supplies.
    - Supervise the disposal of garbage and waste materials.

- ○ Keep plant, program, fire, and maintenance equipment, tools, and vehicles operational and in good repair. Maintain an accurate inventory.
- ○ Ensure that the trails, buildings, fences, gates, roads, plumbing, heating and air conditioning, and utility systems (including electrical, septic or sewer systems, telephone, and water system) are in good repair.
- ○ Implement ways to conserve energy and use alternative energy, where possible.
- ○ Implement a preventive maintenance plan.
- Planning for improvements and upgrades
- Plan and schedule daily, weekly, and monthly work
  - ○ Conduct an annual inspection of all site and facilities, as qualified.
  - ○ Annually develop a two- or three-year annual operating budget based on the strategic plan.
  - ○ Identify projects for fund development to secure funds.
  - ○ Update and implement a risk management plan regarding site and facility aspects.
  - ○ Develop and implement long-term site and facility goals as part of the larger organization's goals.

Essential Functions

- Ability to climb ladders
- Ability to lift a minimum of 50 pounds without assistance, which may include gear, chemicals, inventory, and buckets of water
- Ability to drive and maneuver heavy loads using trucks, skid loaders, and various equipment
- Ability to operate power tools and equipment, such as drills, saws, and cleaning equipment
- Ability to communicate effectively with diverse groups of people and to make and interpret written reports and documents
- Stamina to work outdoors in adverse weather conditions in two- to four-hour intervals.
- Ability to work independently and take initiative with minimal supervision
- Ability to plan ahead and adjust quickly to changing conditions and circumstances
- Ability to evaluate unsafe situations for self and others
- Ability to use independent judgment and discretion in the handling of emergency situations
- Ability to prioritize projects, maintain standards, and solve problems

Facilities Manager

Paragraph about the organization: ownership, year-round schedule of operation, number and description of participants, location.

Paragraph about the site and facilities: number of acres, number of buildings and total square feet, grounds or natural resources philosophy.

Position Summary

This position maintains the grounds, structures, and equipment so as to ensure the safe and efficient operation of the organization's programs and to protect the long-term value of the assets.

Description of the schedule, expected hours, and benefits. Example: This full-time exempt position based on a 40-hour workweek requires some evening and weekend work.

Responsible to

Administrator or property director

Supervises

- Seasonal maintenance staff
- Volunteers

Desired Qualifications

- 3-5 years working in the site and facilities field
- Certifications and licenses (may obtain within six months of employment)
  - Driver's license and good driving record
  - First aid certification
- Ability to use and repair hand and power tools
- Experience working with vendors, suppliers, and service providers
- Previous broad experience supervising outside contractors in several of the trades: carpentry, construction (general), grounds, heating and air conditioning, painting (interior and exterior), plumbing, electrical and mechanical systems
- Solid skills in basic maintenance
- Project management skills and the ability to resolve complex problems and issues
- Planning, organizing, and scheduling skills
- Knowledge of facility standards, codes, and regulations
- Knowledge of green building principles
- Preferred experience in word processing, spreadsheets, and databases

General Responsibilities

- Site and facility use
  - Develop and maintain an effective, positive working relationship with participants, staff, volunteers, adjoining landowners, inspectors, and local vendors. Represent the organization in a positive manner. Serve on internal or external committees.
  - Prepare and clean up participant use areas, which may include program areas and kitchen. Respond to requests from participants.
  - Health, safety, security
    - Be aware of different groups using the facility.
    - Minimize trespassing and vandalism and maximize safety by enforcing regulations and taking a proactive approach.
    - Act decisively and professionally in responding to, evaluating, and handling problems.
    - Respond to emergencies during and after hours, including inclement weather, fire, theft, and vandalism.

- Supervision
  - Select and supervise volunteers, vendors, and contractors.
  - Plan, prepare materials for, and supervise volunteer projects.
- Regulatory
  - Keep up-to-date on and implement all applicable laws, ordinances, policies, regulations, and standards pertaining to the specific duties and responsibilities of the job.
  - Perform regulatory activities, such as fire alarm testing.
  - Arrange for external inspections including fire inspections and electrical evaluations.
  - Keep accurate records of work performed by staff, volunteers, vendors, and contractors. Also maintain manuals, warranty information, and inspection reports.
  - Develop and revise written standard operating procedures.
  - Follow the organization's financial procedures.
- General operations and maintenance
  - Consistently strive to maintain a clean and attractive facility.
  - Purchase maintenance and cleaning supplies.
  - Supervise the disposal of garbage and waste materials.
  - Keep plant, program, fire, and maintenance equipment, tools, and vehicles operational and in good repair. Maintain an accurate inventory.
  - Ensure that the buildings, fences, plumbing, heating and air conditioning, and utility systems are in good repair.
  - Implement ways to conserve energy and use alternative energy, where possible.
  - Implement a preventive maintenance plan.
- Planning for improvements and upgrades
- Plan and schedule daily, weekly, and monthly work
  - Conduct an annual inspection of all grounds and facilities.
  - Annually develop a two- or three-year annual operating budget based on the strategic plan. Identify projects for fund development to secure funds.
  - Update and implement a risk management plan regarding site and facility aspects.
  - Develop and implement long-term site and facility goals, as part of the larger organization's goals.

Essential Functions

- Ability to climb ladders
- Ability to lift a minimum of 50 pounds without assistance, which may include gear, chemicals, inventory, and buckets of water
- Ability to operate power tools and equipment, such as drills, saws, and cleaning equipment
- Ability to communicate effectively with diverse groups of people and make and interpret written reports and documents
- Ability to work independently and take initiative with minimal supervision

- Ability to plan ahead and adjust quickly to changing conditions and circumstances
- Ability to evaluate unsafe situations for self and others
- Ability to use independent judgment and discretion in the handling of emergency situations
- Ability to prioritize projects, maintain standards, and solve problems.

Property Director

These are responsibilities of a property director's position. Since this position may be combined with an administrator's position, an operations director's position, or a site manager's position, below is phrasing you can use in other job descriptions.

General and Specific Responsibilities

- Protect site and facility assets for the long-term.
- Strategically position site and facilities within the organization's tactical plan.
- Supervise all property activities, from planning to implementation.
- Select, hire, train, develop, and evaluate employees.
- Integrate site and facility plans with fund development plans.
- Monitor regulatory, legislative, and community issues.
- Employ sound fiscal management of the property.
- Promote stewardship of the environment.
- Supervise regulatory compliance.
- Oversee a safe environment for participants, volunteers, and staff.
- Develop and implement a site and facility risk management component as part of the organization's risk management plan.
- Develop mechanisms for users and visitors to give input and participate in decision making and planning, as appropriate.
- Partner with the programming staff on appropriate projects.
- Use a variety of communication channels to inform the participants about the projects that have been done and those planned for the future.
- Analyze the following data on a regular basis:
  - Site and facility funding
  - Site and facility usage
  - Participant site and facility needs
  - Energy audits, consumption
  - Programming staff needs for site and facilities
  - Types of maintenance
  - Incident reports

Desired Qualifications

- Experience working with computer applications, such as Excel, Word, and Power-Point
- Strong background in project management, including finances, planning, and scheduling
- Experience in facilities management
- Superior interpersonal skills
- Knowledge of green building principles
- Supervisory experience

Qualifications Preferred, But Not Required

- Training or experience as an architect, contractor, or landscape architect
- Environmental education knowledge
- Natural resources management experience

GLOSSARY

abstract of title—The condensed history of title to a particular parcel of real estate, consisting of a summary of the original grant and all subsequent conveyances and encumbrances affecting the property and a certification by the abstractor that the history is complete and accurate. In the United States, the abstract of title furnishes the raw data for the preparation of a policy of title insurance for the parcel of land in question.

acre—A measurement of land, 43,560 square feet, or 208.71 feet × 208.71 feet. Historically from the land-measuring system for plowing, the rectangular amount of land a man and his horse could plow in one day. An acre is 90.75 percent of a football field. Without the end zones, a football field is 48,000 square feet.

acre-foot of water—A measurement of the volume of water, approximately 325,851 gallons, or equal to 1 foot in depth and covering 1 acre. Water rights are measured in acre-feet.

actual cash value—The cost of repairing or replacing damaged property with property of the same kind and quality and in the same physical condition, minus depreciation. See also *replacement cost.*

adjudication of water rights—A legal process to determine the validity and extent of existing water rights.

administrator—A person who is accountable for the management, operation, and oversight of an organization, such as the executive director or CEO.

aerial photograph—A photograph taken from an aircraft or satellite.

air rights—The use of air space above water, the ground, or a structure without impeding the original use of the property.

amps—The basic unit of electric current (amps = watts / volts). Electric fixtures and appliances consume varying amounts of amps; generally, heating items (kitchen toasters, hair dryers, ovens) draw higher amps. For example, a hair dryer might draw 1,500 watts, or 13.6 amps (1,500 / 110), and a 60-watt lightbulb draws only 0.55 amps (60 / 110). In an electrical panel, a typical household electrical circuit is rated for 15 to 20 amps. Commercial kitchen appliances, air conditioners, some large freezers, and refrigerators are rated 30 to 50 amps or more.

appropriative rights—The rights to divert a state's public water and apply it to a beneficial use. Water rights are administered in accordance with a temporal—"first in time, first in right"—priority system based on established priority dates. In other words, if there is a shortage of supply, junior (more recent) users are shut down until available supply is sufficient to supply remaining senior right holders. Generally applies to the western states. See also *riparian rights.*

aquifer—An underground water supply typically found in sandstone, limestone, or granite.

architect—A visionary, creator, coordinator, and communicator of a project's design and construction documents. Architects are licensed by the state. Services in-house or contracted out may include assistance in securing a contractor; evaluation of the progress and quality of construction; facility programming; marketing and economic feasibility studies; budgeting and financing packages; site use and utilities studies; environmental analysis; planning and zoning applications; preparation of materials for public referenda; special cost or energy analysis; tenant-related design; special drawings, models, and presentations; and facility operation services after project completion (www.wrenn. com/youparin/gloofter.html; http://www.aia.org/pub_yaya_identifyservice).

audit—The independent accountant's review of an organization's financial statements to ensure compliance with generally accepted accounting principles (GAAP) and to render an opinion on the fairness of the financial statements.

basal area—The cross-sectional area of a tree or of all trees in a forest stand, usually measured at "breast height," about 4 1/2 feet above the ground.

base map—A map that includes physical features (e.g., creeks, elevation contours) and any construction (roads, buildings, fences) within a specific property boundary. It usually doesn't include studies, such as soil analysis or drainage patterns.

biodiversity—The variety and variability among living organisms, including land-based and aquatic ecosystems, and the ecosystems of which they are a part. These include diversity within species, between species, and of ecosystems. A high level of biodiversity is desirable.

biology—The study of living organisms.

black water—Water containing liquid or solid human body waste generated through toilet use, or water in which decaying organic vegetation creates tannic acid, which is highly acidic and low in minerals and other nutrients.

board feet—A standard measurement for lumber or timber: 144 in^3 (1 inch × 1 foot × 1 foot) of wood. In a specific stand, 1 acre of timber may yield approximately 2,000 board feet of timber; a 2,000-square-foot house may use about 13,000 board feet of framing lumber.

botany—The study of plants and other similar organisms. One of the oldest branches of biology.

Business Continuity Plan (BCP)—This plan ensures that the essential business functions of the organization are able to continue (or restart) in the event of unforeseen circumstances; normally a disaster of some sort. The BCP will identify the critical people (by roles and functions), information, systems, and other infrastructures (e.g., telephones) that are required to enable the business to operate.

capital budget—The budget that includes the proposed expenditures and revenues for a given period of time. The capital budget includes the acquisition of major machinery, equipment, land, buildings, renovations, and construction. It does not include operating revenues or expenses. The board and the accountant determine the parameters of the capital items based on the life span, original cost, and other factors. See also *operating budget.*

capitalization—An accounting practice in which an asset is recorded on the balance sheet, rather than as an expense.

cartography—The art and science of making maps and charts. A cartographer is a person who makes maps.

chart of accounts—A list of account titles with an associated numbering system; used to monitor costs by category.

coliform—A commonly used bacterial indicator of the sanitary quality of foods and water. In most instances, coliforms themselves are not disease producers. Their absence from water is a good indicator that the water is bacteriologically safe for human consumption, or their presence is used to indicate that other pathogenic organisms of fecal origin may be present.

composting toilets—Toilets that use little or no water and treat toilet wastes on-site for reuse as compost.

computer-aided design (CAD)—Software used by architects, engineers, drafters, artists, and others to create precise two- or three-dimensional drawings or technical illustrations.

confidence rating—The level of confidence one has in the accuracy of data; an old map hand-drawn by a long-time volunteer, for instance, may be more accurate than a newer map drawn by a new staff person.

conflict of interest—A situation in which a person's objectivity may be compromised. An example: A board member's brother is a general contractor who is submitting a bid on an organization's project. The board member could be perceived as having mixed loyalties between his brother and the organization that he is serving.

conservation—The planned management, preservation, and protection of a natural resource to prevent exploitation, destruction, or neglect.

conservation easement—A legal agreement between a landowner and a nonprofit organization or government agency that requires the landowner to take specific actions to protect or preserve the environment in return for being paid a negotiated value for the property in its natural state. The payment may be a one-time lump sum amount or an annual amount for a particular period of time.

consumptive use—Water that has been evaporated, transpired, or incorporated into products, plant tissue, or animal tissue and, therefore, is not available for immediate reuse. Sometimes referred to as water consumption.

contractor—One who enters into a binding agreement to perform a certain service or provide a certain product in exchange for money, goods, or services. In the building trades, a contractor is one who is engaged in construction or building. The construction site is overseen by a prime, general, or specialty contractor who may perform the work with employees, subcontractors, or a combination of the two. Each state has unique license requirements for building contractors.

COPE—An acronym for property insurance underwriting criteria: construction, occupancy (type), protection and protective devices, and exposure.

cord—A measurement of cut wood. A cord contains 128 ft^3, or a stack of 2-foot lengths that is 8 feet long and 8 feet high.

corrective maintenance—Fixing items that do not work or have failed as a result of regular use, malfunction, defect, neglect, or vandalism by cleaning, adjusting, repairing, replacing, or restoring. Sometimes called emergency maintenance or breakdown maintenance.

covenant—A promise in a deed that affects or limits the use of the property.

CPM—An acronym for Critical Path Method. CPM originated in the 1950s by a joint venture between DuPont Corporation and Remington Rand Corporation for managing plant maintenance projects. Today, it is commonly used with all forms of projects, including construction, software development, research projects, and plant maintenance. CPM constructs a project model by listing all activities required, the time needed to complete each activity, and the dependencies between the activities. Using these values, CPM calculates the critical path.

CPTED—An acronym for Crime Prevention Through Environmental Design, which is pronounced "sep-ted." Techniques to increase security include facility design and location, lighting, maintaining fences, and trimming shrubs that obscure windows.

cubic foot/feet (cf)—The volume of a cube with each edge 1 foot in length.

cubic feet per minute (cfm)—A measurement of the amount of airflow (from a blower or fan) or water in a river past a stationary point in one minute.

dashboard—Similar to a car's dashboard, a technique for monitoring how the project, department, or organization is performing. It organizes and presents information in a way that is easy to read, usually with graphics.

deed—A signed legal document that transfers ownership of property from one party to another.

deferred maintenance—Delayed repairs, services, or scheduled work. Deferred maintenance may have higher subsequent repair costs.

demand meter—A device that measures the electricity used (in kWh), in addition to recording the highest demand created in a given time period, usually 15 minutes.

depreciation—An expense allowance, usually made for business tax purposes, to show wear and tear on an asset over its estimated useful life, based on its historical cost. Each year an amount is deducted to reflect the loss of value over time of property or equipment.

digitizing—The act of translating an image, a sound, or a video clip into a digital format for use on a computer. Also used to describe the process of converting coordinates on a map to computerized graphing coordinates.

divest—To reduce or dispose of; cease to hold an interest or transfer property.

Dominion Land Survey—The method used to divide most of western Canada into 1-square-mile sections. It is based on the layout of the Public Land Survey System used in the United States, but has several differences.

easement—A right or privilege a person or organization may have on another's land for specific purposes, such as power line access or utility work.

ecological integrity—The degree to which the physical, chemical, and biological components (including composition, structure, and process) of an ecosystem and their relationships are present, functioning, and capable of self-renewal. Ecological integrity implies the presence of appropriate species, populations, and communities and the occurrence of ecological processes at appropriate rates and scales as well as the environmental conditions that support these taxa and processes.

ecology—The study of the interrelationships of plants, animals, and their environment.

ecoregion—A physical region that is defined by its ecology, climate, landforms, soil, potential natural vegetation, hydrology, or other ecologically relevant variables, rather than geopolitical considerations.

ecosystem—A complex community of plants, animals, and microorganisms that interact with each other and the soil, water, and air.

effluent—Something that flows out, such as water or wastewater.

emergency warning system—Visual or audible alarms to notify people of an emergency.

erosion—The wearing away of soils by running water, glaciers, winds, overuse by humans, and waves.

facilities—Buildings and structures used for programs, maintenance, sleeping, and so on.

Facility Condition Index (FCI)—An objective way to measure the state of buildings. The FCI is the ratio of accumulated deferred maintenance divided by the current replacement value.

> Good 0 to 5 percent
>
> Fair 5.01 to 10 percent
>
> Poor >10 percent

fauna—A collective term for animal life.

Federal Township and Range System (FTRS)—A method to legally describe parcels of land. Used by 30 states (generally the midwest and west). Uses a surveyed rectangular system based on the prime meridian. See also *metes and bounds.*

floodplain—The areas of land that are subject to periodic flooding by a neighboring river, stream, or other body of water. Floodplains are classified according to the anticipated frequency of flooding.

flora—A collective term for plant life.

flow meter—A device to measure the flow of a stream or fluid in a pipe.

forest management plan—A written summary describing the activities for the current and future management of a forest area. Includes recommendations for proper care and control of wooded land to maintain or improve forest health, recreation, water quality, timber harvest, wildlife habitats, aesthetics, or soil condition—all based on the owner's objectives.

forester—A trained professional, usually with a degree in forest management, who consults with a landowner on various aspects of the forest. This includes forest growth, development, and regeneration; soils, geology, and hydrology; wildlife and fisheries biology; fire management; and timber harvesting operations.

fund accounting—A method of recording financial information that groups assets and liabilities into funds based on the purpose for which they are to be used. Generally used by government entities and nonprofits.

funding depreciation—Regularly setting aside dollars attributable to depreciation into a specially designated fund. This fund is used for future capital expenditures.

Gantt chart—A project management tool consisting of a graphic display of schedule-related information. Activities or other project elements are listed down the left side of the chart, dates are shown across the top, and activity duration is shown as horizontal bars.

generally accepted accounting principles (GAAP)—Uniform minimum standards of and guidelines to financial accounting and reporting. Currently, the Financial Accounting Standards Board (FASB), the Governmental Accounting Standards Board (GASB), and the Federal Accounting Standards Advisory Board are authorized to establish these principles.

geographic information system (GIS)—A "smart map." An interrelated collection of information technology, data, and procedures in the form of maps and descriptive information about spatially located features. The ability to collect, store, manipulate, analyze, and visualize information distinguishes GIS from other information systems and makes it valuable to a wide range of public and private enterprises looking to explain events, predict outcomes, and plan strategies.

geologic hazards—Naturally occurring or human-induced geologic conditions that present risks or are potential dangers to life and property, such as seismic areas, erosion areas, landslides, coal mines, and sinkholes.

geospatial data—Geographic and spatial information focusing on a specific area and the relationships among data.

gift in kind—Rather than making a financial contribution, the donor donates free services, materials, products, or supplies.

global positioning system (GPS)—A system using satellites, receivers, and software to allow users to determine their geographic position. Also refers to global positioning satellite.

governance—In the nonprofit sector, governance refers to the actions of the (volunteer) board of directors with respect to establishing and monitoring the long-term direction of the organization. See also *operations*.

grantee—The party in a deed who is the buyer.

grantor—The party in a deed who is the seller.

green buildings—Healthy, resource-efficient buildings that minimally affect ecosystems through sustainable site planning, safeguarding water and water efficiency, energy efficiency, and renewable energy.

grey water—Wastewater, such as sink drainage, washing machine discharge, and bath water. Does not contain human excrement. See also *black water*.

grounds—Landscaped areas, consisting of lawns, flowerbeds, trees, and bushes. It also encompasses manmade elements including sidewalks, fences, trails, roads, and so on.

groundwater—Underground water accessed by wells and springs.

habitat—The area in which an animal, plant, or microorganism lives and finds the nutrients, water, sunlight, shelter, living space, and other essentials it needs to survive.

hazardous tree—Any defective tree or tree part that creates a high risk to people or property. It usually has one or more defects that increase the potential for failure. The seven categories of defects are cracks; stem or branch decay; weak branch unions; cankers; poor tree architecture; root problems; and dead branches, tops, or trees.

hectare—A land and water area measurement commonly used in forestry and in many other countries, such as those in Central America and Europe. 1 hectare = 100 meters × 100 meters (or 10,000 square meters), or about 328 feet × 328 feet (107,637 square feet, or 2.471 acres).

herbicides—Chemicals used to kill undesirable vegetation; sometimes unintentionally kill desirable vegetation.

hour meter—A gauge on a piece of equipment that tells you the number of total operating hours the equipment has been in use. This gauge helps to maintain the equipment at proper service intervals.

hydrogeology—The branch of geology that deals with the occurrence, distribution, and effect of groundwater.

hydrology—The study of precipitation, runoff, evaporation, storage, and distribution of water above and underground.

incident report—The documentation of any unusual problem, accident, incident, or other situation that is likely to lead to undesirable effects or that varies from established policies and procedures or practices. Common categories include incident description (location, time, conditions), photographs, diagrams, witness accounts and contact information, and medical treatment. The document usually needs to be completed within 24 hours of the incident.

insecticides—Chemicals used to control undesirable insects.

invasive species—A plant or animal species that is nonnative (or alien) to the ecosystem under consideration and whose introduction causes or is likely to cause economic or environmental harm or harm to human health. Invasive plants include noxious weeds.

kilowatt—1,000 watts.

land patent—The transfer of land ownership from the federal government to the first private owner or titleholder of a piece of property.

land use plan—A proposal for how land should be used and where growth and renewal should occur. A land use plan, often one element of a comprehensive plan, is frequently developed concurrently with other closely related documents, such as transportation plans, environmental plans, and community facility plans. Land use plans often cover a 20- to 25-year time span.

landman—A professional who acquires gas and oil leases.

landscape architect—A professional who engages in the art and science of analysis, planning, design, management, preservation, and rehabilitation of the land. The scope of the profession includes site planning, garden design, environmental restoration, town or urban planning, park and recreation planning, regional planning, and historic preservation. Practitioners share a commitment of achieving a balance among preservation, use, and management of the country's resources. (American Society of Landscape Architects, www.asla.org)

leadership—The process of motivating, inspiring, and supporting people to strive willingly and enthusiastically toward the achievement of the organization's mission. See also *management*.

Leadership in Energy and Environmental Design (LEED)—The LEED Green Building Rating System is a voluntary, consensus-based national standard for developing high-performance, sustainable buildings.

license—The certification that states that a person has met the requirements for professional qualifications and assigns the right to practice in the state. Professionals that may need licenses include electricians, plumbers, heating and air conditioning specialists, architects, contractors, and foresters.

life expectancy—Also call useful life. The number of years depreciable business property is expected to be productive and in use. For depreciation purposes, the IRS has predetermined useful lives for most types of business properties.

lockout/tagout (LOTO)—A safety procedure to ensure that dangerous equipment and utility services are properly shut off and not started up again prior to the completion of maintenance or service work. It includes shutting down equipment, isolating it from its energy source(s), and preventing the release of potentially hazardous energy. This is accomplished by placement of a tagout device on an energy-isolating device, to indicate that the energy-isolating device and the equipment being controlled may not be operated until the tagout device is removed.

maintenance—The upkeep of property or equipment; includes replacement, improvements, and repairs or services that are corrective and preventive.

management—Actions that focus on planning, efficiency, consistency, forecasting, exercising control, timely accomplishment of specific tasks within the confines of existing resources, and solving problems to achieve results. See also *leadership*.

map scale—The relationship between a distance on a map and the corresponding distance on the ground. A larger scale is less accurate, because less information can be shown. Common scales for USGS maps are as follows:

> 1:24,000 scale: 1 inch represents 24,000 ground inches or 2,000 feet
>
> 1:100,000 scale: 1 inch represents about 1.6 miles
>
> 1:250,000 scale: 1 inch represents about 4 miles

master planning—A comprehensive planning process that integrates the program and operational goals with the land and facility opportunities. The master plan identifies all of the facilities required to meet the program requirements, locates them realistically on the property, identifies amenities and circulation, and projects preliminary costs.

Includes assessment of existing conditions related to the land and natural resources as well as of the facilities to determine the potential to serve new functions, be expanded, or retrofitted for future use.

Includes land use—matching the functional requirements of the site to land areas based on natural characteristics or the relationship of spaces to each other. (From Kaleidoscope, Inc. www.kaleidoscope-inc.com)

material safety data sheets (MSDS)—Sheets available from the product manufacturer that contain more information than is listed on the label of a product. They include chemical composition, hazards in using the product, proper handling and storage, disposal, regulatory requirements, and first aid and emergency procedures.

Per OSHA, "Employers must have an MSDS for each hazardous chemical which they use . . . . MSDSs must be readily accessible to employees when they are in their work areas during their work shifts. This may be accomplished in many different ways. You must decide what is appropriate for your particular workplace. Some employers keep the MSDSs in a binder in a central location" (U.S. Department of Labor, OSHA, n.d.).

metadata—Data about data. Describe the characteristics of the data: source, content, quality, condition, date, and so forth.

metes and bounds—A method for legally describing parcels of land. It is used by 20 states (the original 13 colonies, Hawaii, Kentucky, Maine, Tennessee, Texas, Vermont, and West Virginia). Describes the land in terms of the location of neighbors and natural features (stumps, rocks) with compass bearings. See also *Federal Township and Range System (FTRS)*.

mineral—A naturally occurring inorganic element or compound having an orderly internal structure and characteristic chemical composition, crystal form, and physical properties.

mineral lease—A legal document or contract between a landowner (lessor) and a company or individual (lessee) granting exploration and development rights of oil, gas, and mineral deposits.

mineral rights—The ownership of the minerals beneath the earth's surface with the right to remove them. Mineral rights may be conveyed separately from surface rights. Mineral rights constitute real property and can be leased, traded, divided, willed, sold, or given away.

mission statement—A succinct statement describing the purpose of an organization. The mission statement is broad enough to describe the range of activities or work, but narrow enough to imply boundaries. Describes "what we are about" and "why."

natural systems—The interaction of atmospheric, terrestrial, and aquatic forces and processes within the ecosystems of the natural environment.

Needs Index (NI)—An index that determines a holistic indicator of the facilities' needs. The Needs Index is the sum of outstanding capital renewal, deferred maintenance, and renovation and modernization divided by current replacement value.

noxious weed—A plant that is invasive and alien to the surrounding ecosystem, often forming monocultures. Noxious weeds are on a federal, state, or local list that recommends or mandates management of the plant.

Occupational Safety and Health Administration (OSHA)—A federal agency under the Department of Labor. OSHA's mission is "to assure the safety and health of America's workers by setting and enforcing standards; providing training, outreach, and education; establishing partnerships; and encouraging continual improvement in workplace safety and health" (U.S. Department of Labor, OSHA).

old growth forest—An area of forest that has attained great age and exhibits unique biological features. Old growth forests typically contain large live trees, large dead trees (sometimes called snags), and large logs. Old growth forests usually have multiple vertical layers of vegetation representing a variety of tree species and a variety of age classes. Sometimes called late-seral forest or ancient forest.

operating budget—The planning and controlling process for the daily operations with estimates of proposed expenditures and revenues for a given period of time. Expenditures include personnel, supplies, utilities, materials, travel, and fuel and the proposed means of financing them. It does not include capital expenditures. See also *capital budget*.

operations—The day-to-day management and activities carried out by staff, focusing on tactical planning and implementation. See also *governance.*

orthorectification—The process of removing the distortion in aerial photographs. When aerial photographs are taken, the most accurate place in the photograph is the center, and the most distortion occurs at the edges. With an orthorectified image, it does not matter where you look; you're looking straight down—just like looking at a map. Thus, orthorectified images are the most position-accurate aerial photographs.

parts per million (ppm)—A concentration equal to one part per one million parts. Roughly equal to one drop of food dye in 16 gallons of water.

percolation test (perc test)—A test of the soil to determine whether it will absorb and drain water adequately to use a septic system for sewage disposal.

personal property—Any property that is owned by the individual and not by the organization, such as money, savings accounts, appliances, cars, and boats.

PERT—An acronym for Program Evaluation and Review Technique. It is a method to analyze the tasks involved in completing a project, especially the time needed to complete each task and the time for the total project. Developed in the 1950s by Booz Allen Hamilton, Inc. to simplify the planning of complex projects, it uses nodes and lines to show events and activities, rather than start- and completion dates. PERT diagrams are used more in R&D projects where time, rather than cost, is a major factor.

pesticides—Chemical substances used to kill or control pests such as weeds, insects, fungi, mites, algae, and rodents.

pH—A measure of the acidity of soils, archival paper, water, and so on. On a scale of 0 to 14, 7 is neutral, <7 is acidic, and >7 is basic. Each number indicates a tenfold increase (e.g., a 3 is ten times more acidic than a 4). Acidic water may cause corrosion of pipes; basic water causes a corrosion buildup in water heaters and fixtures.

photovoltaic (PV)—*Photo* means "light"; *voltaic* means "electric." The production of electricity from sunlight. Commonly referred to as "solar electric."

planning—Prior to commencing work, setting objectives and determining methods to achieve the objectives necessary to complete it. See also *scheduling*.

policy—Broad statements intended to affect or control matters, based on values. The focus is on the ends, results, impacts, or outcomes, rather than specific problems.

preventive maintenance—Keeping land, equipment, and facilities in satisfactory operating condition through systematic inspections that result in the detection and correction of incipient failures either before they occur or before they develop into major defects. These services are intended to extend useful life and reduce the need for major repairs.

property—Site and facilities.

property management system—The people, processes, and data, along with appropriate tools, required to have a well-maintained and operating site and facility; considers the immediate, short-term, and long-term needs of participants and the organization.

property portfolio—Records that include various materials (inventory, planning, capital improvements, maintenance, regulations, maps, procurements, and divestments) that identify, categorize, and document pertinent site and facility information. Often used for insurance purposes.

property survey—A survey that describes, maps, and locates land ownership boundaries and corners, features, and improvements.

real property—All lands, buildings, fixtures, improvements, cabin trailers, and mobile homes used like buildings (not registered for highway use). Real property also includes mines, minerals, quarries, mineral springs and wells, oil and gas wells, overriding royalty interests, and production payments with respect to oil or gas leases.

reclamation—(1) The process of converting disturbed land or mined land to its former state or other productive uses or form, such as filling in open pits, grading the mined area, reducing high walls, replacing topsoil, planting, and revegetating. (2) The process of making a site habitable to organisms that were originally present or others like the original inhabitants. (3) Returning disturbed land to a form and productivity that will be ecologically balanced and in conformity with the predetermined land management plan.

relational database—A method of structuring (relating) data in tables that are logically associated to each other by shared attributes.

replacement amount—The cost of engineering, materials, supplies, and labor required to replace a facility or item of equipment at its existing size and functional capability, without deducting for depreciation. See also *actual cash value*.

request for information (RFI)—A process used by the organization to solicit information from vendors to aid in decision making; relies on the expertise of the vendor. The RFI will not result in a contract.

request for proposal (RFP)—A process used by organizations to solicit bids on specified products or services.

right of way—The right to pass over, travel through, or use another's land.

riparian—Ecosystems that border the banks of rivers and streams; include grasslands, savannas, woodlands, and forests.

riparian buffers—Areas of forested land adjacent to streams, rivers, marshes, or shorelines that form the transition between land and water environments. They reduce or control flooding, improve water quality, play an important role in the storage and filtering of groundwater, and provide shade and cover for animals.

riparian rights—The legal water rights to use water flowing on, through, or along the borders of the land, and sometimes groundwater underneath the land. Generally applies to the midwestern and eastern states. See also *appropriative rights*.

risk management—The goal of risk management is to improve performance by acknowledging and controlling risks. It puts the organization, not the risk, in charge. It's about protecting and conserving the organization's resources and providing goods and services sensibly.

rod—A unit of length equal to 16.5 feet. Also known as a pole or perch.

scheduling—A detail of the time allowed for a project and each activity, the people and skills required, and when activities are to be started and finished. See also *planning*.

site—The land, woodlands, forests, ecosystem, streams, and grounds.

soil survey—The process of determining the soil types or other properties of the soil cover over a landscape and mapping them for others to understand and use.

special-use permit—A requirement for any commercial activity on National Forest System (NFS) lands. Commercial use is defined as any use or activity on NFS lands (1) for which an entry or participation fee is charged and (2) the primary purpose of which is the sale of a good or service, and in either case, regardless of whether the use or activity is intended to produce a profit. May include water usage, land usage, and recreational activities.

spring—A place where groundwater naturally comes to the surface.

stewardship—An individual's or organization's responsibility to exercise short- and long-term care of resources, such as land, assets, and monies.

strategic planning—The process of providing overall, long-term direction to an organization to identify and move toward a desired future. It is usually the responsibility of a board of directors, who may work with an outside consultant. See also *tactical planning*.

surface rights—A right or easement granted with mineral rights, enabling the possessor to drill or mine through the surface.

surface water—All water open to the atmosphere, such as rivers, lakes, reservoirs, streams, impoundments, seas, and estuaries.

survey—The measurement and description of land by a registered surveyor.

sustainability—Using resources (economic, ecological, and social) to support the current mission without jeopardizing the future mission.

SWOT analysis—A tool used to evaluate the strengths, weaknesses, opportunities, and threats of a project or organization. It involves identifying the internal and external factors that are favorable and unfavorable.

systems thinking—A holistic approach to analysis that focuses on the way a system's constituent parts interrelate and how systems work over time and within the context of larger systems.

tactical planning—Short-term planning (usually one to three years) of specific activities and actions that make progress toward the strategic plan implementation. See also *strategic planning.*

Universal Transverse Mercator (UTM)—A grid system for mapping and GPS. Each "square" is 100,000 meters by 100,000 meters, or 6 degrees longitude by 8 degrees latitude. It came into use after World War II.

Unrelated Business Income Tax (UBIT)—A tax imposed on a nonprofit, exempt organization on income derived from an activity of a trade or business, regularly carried on, that is not substantially related to the organization's tax exempt purpose.

walk-through—An examination of various components (grounds, natural resources, utilities, equipment, buildings) by a qualified person to identify potential problems before they become more significant.

wildland–urban interface (WUI)—The area where human development comes into contact with undeveloped wildlands. This makes WUIs focal areas for human–environment conflicts such as wildland fires, habitat fragmentation, the introduction of invasive species, and biodiversity decline.

wildlife corridor—The artificial joining of fragmented habitats. Wildlife corridors are created to conserve habitat, improve the environment, or increase the gene flows between individual habitats. Wildlife corridors are susceptible to the edge effect; that is, certain species do not prosper near the edges of an ecosystem.

work order—An assignment to perform the work or task.

work request—A request for someone to do maintenance work, usually from a participant to a staff person. Upon receipt, the request is evaluated in terms of whether the request will be honored. Some requests are not in line with the mission or the work and are logged, but then discarded. Once it is determined that the request will be honored, it turns into a work order and is assigned a priority ranking.

workers' compensation—Laws designed to ensure that employees who are injured or disabled on the job are provided with treatment or fixed monetary awards.

REFERENCES

Agron, J. 2006a. A positive move: 12th annual college M&O cost study. *American School & University.* April. http://asumag.com/mag/university_positive_move/.

Agron, J. 2006b. Coming up short: 35th annual M&O cost study. *American School & University.* April. http://asumag.com/mag/university_coming_short/.

American Camp Association. 2006. Business operations profile survey: Residential camp summary. Page 14. Online whitepaper. www.acacamps.org/research/.

American Camping Association. 2003a. *Camp benchmarks: Program and operations, staffing, financial and demographic profiles.* Table 57: Year-round executive benefits: Maintenance director. CD-ROM. Published by American Camp Association.

American Camping Association. 2003b. *Camp benchmarks: Program and operations, staffing, financial and demographic profiles.* Table 16: Acreage by site. CD-ROM. Published by American Camp Association.

American Institute of Architects. www.aia.org/pub_yaya_identifyservice.

American Institute for Conservation of Historic and Artistic Works (AIC). http://aic.stanford.edu/library/online/brochures/objects.html.

APPA financial perspective: Needs Index. www.appa.org/Research/SAM/needsindex.cfm.

Association of Moving Image Archivists (AMIA). www.amianet.org/.

Aust, S. 2001. In search of . . . wayfinding: An overview of three wayfinding systems. *Signs of the Times, 222* (August): 94. www.signweb.com/ada/cont/wayfinding.html.

British Library. National Preservation Office. www.bl.uk/services/npo/npo.html.

Brooks, B. 2004. History of the Facility Condition Index. *Facilities Manager, 20* (March/April): 41-43. www.appa.org/facilitiesmanager/article.cfm?ItemNumber=1788&parentid=1762.

BuildingGreen, Inc. 2001. Checklist for environmentally responsible design and construction. *Environmental News 1*(2). www.buildinggreen.com/ebn/checklist.cfm.

Byers, F. 2003. Care and handling for the preservation of CDs and DVDs: A guide for librarians and archivists. National Institute of Standards and Technology (NIST). NIST Special Publication 500-252. www.itl.nist.gov/iad/894.05/docs/CDandDVDCareandHandlingGuide.pdf.

Cain, D., and M. Kinnaman. 2004. The Needs Index: A new and improved FCI. *Facilities Manager, 20* (March/April): 44-49. www.appa.org/facilitiesmanager/article.cfm?ItemNumber=1768&parentid=1762.

Christensen, N.L., et al. 1996. The report of the Ecological Society of America Committee on the Scientific Basis for Ecosystem Management. www.esa.org/pao/policyStatements/Papers/ReportOfSBEM.php.

Christian Camp and Conference Association. 2005. 2005 industry survey, 43. Christian Camp and Conference Association.

Christian Camp and Conference Association. 2005. 2005 industry survey, unpublished data. Christian Camp and Conference Association.

Colorado Archives. www.colorado.gov/dpa/doit/archives/bookbugs.html.

Commission on Engineering and Technical Systems (CETS). 1990. *Committing to the Cost of Ownership: Maintenance and Repair of Public Buildings* (Report 131). Washington, DC: National Academies Press. http://books.nap.edu/books/NI000264/html/R1.html.

Covey, S. 1989. *The 7 Habits of Highly Effective People.* New York, NY: Simon and Schuster.

Covey, S., A.R. Merrill, and R. Merrill. 1996. *First Things First.* New York, NY: Simon and Schuster.

Duncan, W. 1991. ITS chart. Workshop handout for International Association of Conference Center Administrators (IACCA).

Duncan, W. 1982. Temporary systems. *Camping Magazine, 54* (March/April): 7-10, 15.

Federal Facilities Council. 1996. *Determining Current Replacement Values.* Washington, DC: National Academies Press. www.nap.edu/openbook/NI000085/html/10.html#pagetop.

Forster, G. 1998. Organizing with story boards. *Camping Magazine, 71* (March/April): 31-33.

Forster, G. 2007. The right stuff . . . And getting it done before summer. *Camp Business, 7*(3): 30, 32-33.

Independent Sector. 2001. Giving and volunteering in the United States 2001. www.independentsector.org/programs/research/gv01main.html.

Library of Congress. n.d. Metadata Encoding & Transmission Standard (METS). www.loc.gov/standards/mets.

Library of Congress. Preservation. www.loc.gov/preserv/.

MAM-A Inc. 2003. Recommended handling and storage conditions for CD-R media. www.mam-a.com/.

MAM-A Inc. Storage facilities and procedures. www.mnhs.org/preserve/records/electronicrecords/erstorage.html.

Maslow, A. 1943. A theory of human motivation. *Psychological Review, 50*: 370-396.

Meyer, S., and S. Pegula. 2006. Injuries, illnesses, and fatalities in construction, 2004. Bureau of Labor Statistics. www.bls.gov/opub/cwc/sh20060519ar01p1.htm.

Minnesota Historical Society. Conservation. www.mnhs.org/preserve/conservation/index.html.

Muhlhausen, J. 2000. Wayfinding is not signage: Signage plays an important part of wayfinding—but there's more. *Signs of the Times, 192* (August): 90-91, 134. www.signweb.com/ada/cont/wayfinding0800.html.

National Library of New Zealand. Care of architectural material. www.natlib.govt.nz/en/services/2architecture.html.

National Survey of Giving, Volunteering and Participating (NSGVP). 2006. Statistics Canada, 12. www.givingandvolunteering.ca/pdf/CSGVP_Highlights_2004_en.pdf.

New York State Archives. www.archives.nysed.gov/a/nysaservices/ns_mhr_protect.shtml.

Oliver, B. 2003. *Managing Facility Risk: 10 Steps to Safety.* Washington, DC: Nonprofit Risk Management Center.

Pacific Gas and Electric Company. 1997. Food service equipment and applications: A Pacific Energy Center fact sheet. www.pge.com/003_save_energy/003c_edu_train/pec/info_resource/pdf/Food_Service_Equipment_And_Applications.pdf.

Pine, J., and J. Gilmore. 1999. *The Experience Economy: Work Is Theatre & Every Business a Stage.* Boston: Harvard Business School Press, 3, 12.

Print File, Inc. Archival storage. www.printfile.com/index.asp?PageAction=Custom&ID=1.

Ten-Elshof, P. 2000. Church budgets: You are what you spend. *Your Church, 46* (1): 70-75.

Thomas, E. 2002. Holy space: How our church buildings affect our worship life, fellowship and outreach. *The Mennonite, 5* (January 8): 9-11. www.themennonite.org/pdf/magazine_pdf_21.pdf.

Trotter, K. 2007. Kaleidoscope, Inc. www.kaleidoscope-inc.com/.

U.S. Census Bureau. 2002 Business expenses survey (BES). Data from three sectors. Sector 71, Arts, Entertainment and Recreation; Sector 72, Accommodation and Food Services; Sector 81, Other Services.

U.S. Department of Education, National Center for Education Statistics, National Forum on Education Statistics. 2003. Planning guide for maintaining school facilities. NCES 2003-347, prepared by T. Szuba, R. Young, and the School Facilities Maintenance Task Force. Washington, DC. Page 82. http://nces.ed.gov/pubs2003/2003347.pdf.

U.S. Department of Labor, OSHA. n.d. Guidelines for Employer Compliance (Advisory). Standard Number: 1910.1200 App E. http://www.osha.gov/pls/oshaweb/owadisp.show_document?p_table=STANDARDS&p_id=10104.

U.S. Department of Labor, OSHA. OSHA's Mission. http://www.osha.gov/oshinfo/mission.html.

Vogeler, I. 2006. Private property as a bundle of rights. www.uwec.edu/geography/Ivogeler/w270/bundleofrights.htm.

Wallace, C. 2004. ITS: Isolated Temporary System. Workshop handout for International Association of Conference Center Administrators (IACCA).

Wallace, C. 1994. The Environment We Create, Isolated Temporary Systems. Workshop handout for International Association of Conference Center Administrators (IACCA).

Whyman, W. 2004. Articulating the value of your site and facilities. *Camping Magazine, 77* (March/April): 56-58, 60-61.

Whyman, W. 2004. Site/facility archival management: How to avoid going on an archeological dig. *Camping Magazine, 77* (January/February): 60-65.

Whyman, W. 2004. Stretching your dollars: Preventive maintenance. *Camping Magazine, 77* (May/June.): 64-67.

Whyman, W. 2003. How do I start a property records system? *Camping Magazine, 76* (September/October): 25-27.

Whyman, W. 2003. Themes from a camp maintenance network: Camp maintenance and property personnel share their insights and challenges. *Camping Magazine, 76* (November/December): 54-56, 58-59.

Whyman, W., S. Mael, and M. Kunkel. 1999. Building assets with community effort: Computerized mapping aids long-term planning. *Camping Magazine, 72* (September/October): 24-27.

Wrenn Associates. Glossary of terms. www.wrenn.com/youparin/gloofter.html.

Wurman, R. 1989. *Information Anxiety.* New York: Doubleday, 58-63.

INDEX

Note: The italicized *f* and *t* following page numbers refer to figures and tables, respectively.

ABOUT THE AUTHOR

Wynne Whyman, MA, MSS, is currently president of Callippe Solutions LLC and a design faculty member at the Center for Creative Leadership (CCL) in Colorado. She has extensive experience working with camps and managing property. She earned a Master of Special Studies degree in computer education and applied communication from Denver University and a master of arts degree in information and learning technologies from the University of Colorado at Denver.

CD-ROM USER INSTRUCTIONS

System Requirements

You can use this CD-ROM on either a Windows®-based PC or a Macintosh computer.

Windows

- IBM PC compatible with Pentium® processor
- Windows® 98/2000/XP
- Adobe Reader® 8.0
- Microsoft® Word
- Microsoft® Excel (resource created using 2003 version)
- 4x CD-ROM drive

Macintosh

- Power Mac® recommended
- System 10.4 or higher
- Adobe Reader®
- Microsoft® Word
- Microsoft® Excel for Mac® (resource created using Windows® 2003 version)
- 4x CD-ROM drive

User Instructions

Windows

1. Insert the *Outdoor Site and Facility Management* CD-ROM. (Note: The CD-ROM must be present in the drive at all times.)
2. Select the "My Computer" icon from the desktop.
3. Select the CD-ROM drive.
4. Open the file you wish to view. See the "Start.pdf" file for a list of the contents.
5. To edit the file, choose File/SaveAs . . . and save the file on your desktop or in a folder on your computer prior to making your edits.

Macintosh

1. Insert the *Outdoor Site and Facility Management* CD-ROM. (Note: The CD-ROM must be present in the drive at all times.)
2. Double-click the CD icon located on the desktop.
3. Open the file you wish to view. See the "Start.pdf" file for a list of the contents.
4. To edit the file, choose File/SaveAs . . . and save the file on your desktop or in a folder on your computer prior to making your edits.

For customer support, contact Technical Support:

Phone: 217-351-5076 Monday through Friday (excluding holidays) between 7:00 a.m. and 7:00 p.m. (CST).

Fax: 217-351-2674

E-mail: support@hkusa.com